ADOLESCENT LITERACY, [FIELD TESTED]

Effective Solutions for Every Classroom

EDITORS Sheri R. Parris   Douglas Fisher   Kathy Headley

INTERNATIONAL
Reading Association
800 BARKSDALE ROAD, PO BOX 8139
NEWARK, DE 19714-8139, USA
www.reading.org

The International Reading Association attempts, through its publications, to provide a forum for a wide spectrum of opinions on reading. This policy permits divergent viewpoints without implying the endorsement of the Association.

Executive Editor, Books   Corinne M. Mooney
Developmental Editor   Charlene M. Nichols
Developmental Editor   Tori Mello Bachman
Developmental Editor   Stacey L. Reid
Editorial Production Manager   Shannon T. Fortner
Design and Composition Manager   Anette Schuetz

Project Editors   Tori Mello Bachman and Christina Lambert

Cover   Design, Monotype; Photograph, © 2009 Jupiterimages Corporation

Library of Congress Cataloging-in-Publication Data

Adolescent literacy, field tested : effective solutions for every classroom / edited by
Sheri R. Parris, Douglas Fisher, & Kathy Headley.
     p. cm.
  Includes bibliographical references and index.
  ISBN 978-0-87207-695-2
  1.   Reading (Secondary) 2.   Content area reading.   I. Parris, Sheri R.   II. Fisher,
Douglas, 1965– III. Headley, Kathy.
  LB1632.287 2009
  428.0071'2—dc22

                                                                      2009003376

CONTENTS

PART I
Literacy Instruction in the Secondary Classroom

PART II
Literacy Instruction With Special Populations

PART III
On the Front Line: Teachers, Classrooms, and Schools

ABOUT THE EDITORS

Sheri R. Parris currently teaches English language arts at South Hills High School in Fort Worth, Texas, USA. She is also completing her PhD in Reading Education at the University of North Texas where she has taught courses in reading education to preservice teachers. She is coeditor of the book *Comprehension Instruction: Research-Based Best Practices* (2008, 2nd ed.) and has contributed chapters to *Literacy Processes: Cognitive Flexibility in Learning and Teaching* (2008), and *Building Collaborative Literacy: Engaging Strategies for Gifted Readers* (2006).

Sheri has also published articles in the *Journal of Adolescent & Adult Literacy*, *The Reading Teacher*, and *Journal of Educational Psychology*, and she has been a conference presenter for the International Reading Association (IRA) and the National Reading Conference. She has served on the IRA's Adolescent Literacy Committee and currently serves as both secretary and treasurer of the IRA's special interest group for gifted and creative students.

Sheri is the mother of a daughter, India, who is currently a third grader, and a son, Alexander, a sixth grader. Her husband, Ed, is a Texas real estate broker who also designs and builds small-scale wooden buildings for children and collectors. Sheri's website is www.sheriparris.com, and she can be contacted by e-mail at sheri.parris@gmail.com.

Douglas Fisher is a professor of language and literacy education in the Department of Teacher Education at San Diego State University (SDSU), San Diego, California, USA, and a classroom teacher at Health Sciences High & Middle College (HSHMC), San Diego, California. He is the recipient of an International Reading Association (IRA) Celebrate Literacy Award, the Farmer Award for excellence in writing from the National Council of Teachers of English, as well as a Christa McAuliffe Award for excellence in teacher education from the American Association of State Colleges and Universities. He was the chair of the Adolescent Literacy Committee for the IRA.

Doug has published numerous articles on reading and literacy, differentiated instruction, and curriculum design as well as books such as *Better Learning*

Through Structured Teaching: A Framework for the Gradual Release of Responsibility (with Nancy Frey, 2008), and *Teaching English Language Learners: A Differentiated Approach* (with Carol Rothenberg, 2006), and *Creating Literacy-Rich Schools for Adolescents* (with Gay Ivey, 2006). He has taught a variety of courses in SDSU's teacher-credentialing program as well as graduate-level courses on English-language development and literacy. An early intervention specialist and language development specialist, he has taught high school English, writing, and literacy development to public school students. Doug can be reached at dfisher@mail.sdsu.edu.

 **Kathy Headley,** Associate Dean for Research and Graduate Studies in the College of Health, Education, and Human Development at Clemson University, Clemson, South Carolina, USA, is also a professor of reading education and a faculty member at Clemson since 1987. She began her career as an elementary classroom teacher and reading specialist in Georgia before completing her doctorate in reading from Auburn University where she taught undergraduate courses in reading instruction and learning strategies.

Kathy's areas of expertise include adolescent literacy and writing. She has published articles on young adult and children's literature in journals such as *The Reading Teacher* and *The ALAN Review* along with research on adolescent motivation in the *Journal of Adolescent & Adult Literacy*. Publications also include a chapter on writing in *Comprehension Instruction: Research-Based Best Practices* (Block & Parris, 2008, 2nd ed.), a coauthored chapter with Linda Gambrell in *The Vocabulary-Enriched Classroom: Practices for Improving the Reading Performance of All Students in Grades 3 and Up* (Block & Mangieri, 2006), and a teacher-partnered chapter in *Improving Comprehension Instruction: Rethinking Research, Theory, and Classroom Practice* (Block, Gambrell, & Pressley, 2002). Kathy served as coeditor of *Literacy Teaching and Learning* and as a review board member for *The Reading Teacher* and *The ALAN Review.*

Kathy works extensively with schools throughout South Carolina and has contributed to systemic curricular changes in standards and assessment. Her travels have included professional development presentations in Scotland, Costa Rica, Estonia, Washington, D.C., and towns large and small across the southeastern United States.

Committed to literacy within our schools and communities, Kathy was elected as the South Carolina State Council of the International Reading Association's (IRA) 1993–1994 President and as the IRA State Coordinator for South Carolina,

1997–2006. She has chaired several committees for the IRA such as Bylaws and Special Service Award, and she is currently a committee member for IRA's Outstanding Dissertation of the Year Award.

Kathy is the mother of one daughter, Casey Hulsey, who resides near Gainesville, Georgia, with her husband, Corey, and attends a nearby university. Kathy's husband, Carl Headley, works for Houghton Mifflin Harcourt. They enjoy living on Lake Keowee in upstate South Carolina. You can reach her by sending e-mail to ksn1177@clemson.edu.

CONTRIBUTORS

Aida Allen
Health Sciences High & Middle College
San Diego, California, USA

Irma F. Brasseur-Hock
The University of Kansas
School of Education
Lawrence, Kansas, USA

Karen Bromley
State University of New York,
   Binghamton
Binghamton, New York, USA

Faye Brownlie
Consultant
Vancouver, British Columbia, Canada

Doug Buehl
Consultant
Madison, Wisconsin, USA

Pamela Sissi Carroll
Florida State University
College of Education
Tallahassee, Florida, USA

Kelly Chandler-Olcott
Syracuse University
Syracuse, New York, USA

Rachel De Luise
Florida State University
Tallahassee, Florida, USA

Roni Jo Draper
Brigham Young University
Provo, Utah, USA

Douglas Fisher
San Diego State University
San Diego, California, USA

Nancy Frey
San Diego State University
San Diego, California, USA

Victoria Gillis
Clemson University
Clemson, South Carolina, USA

Maria Grant
California State University, Fullerton
Fullerton, California, USA

Sally Hampton
America's Choice
Fort Worth, Texas, USA

Kathy Headley
Clemson University
Clemson, South Carolina, USA

Michael F. Hock
The University of Kansas
School of Education
Lawrence, Kansas, USA

Tiffany Howard
Florida State University
Tallahassee, Florida, USA

Vicki A. Jacobs
Harvard University
Cambridge, Massachusetts, USA

Joan F. Kaywell
University of South Florida
Tampa, Florida, USA

Eileen Kintsch
University of Colorado
Boulder, Colorado, USA

Donna Ogle
National-Louis University
Chicago, Illinois, USA

Sheri R. Parris
University of North Texas
Denton, Texas, USA

Carol Rothenberg
San Diego Unified School District
San Diego, California, USA

Daniel Siebert
Brigham Young University
Provo, Utah, USA

Jay Simmons
University of Massachusetts, Lowell
Lowell, Massachusetts, USA

Cheryl Taliaferro
University of North Texas
Denton, Texas, USA

Gail L. Thompson
The Claremont Graduate University
Claremont, California, USA

INTRODUCTION

Sheri R. Parris, Douglas Fisher, Kathy Headley

As editors, we are fortunate to have had this opportunity to tap into the knowledge and experience of the exceptional chapter authors who contributed to this book, which provides a substantial yet practical examination of the important topics in the field of adolescent literacy. These chapters give us an overview of research-based instructional practices and extend this discussion to the front lines by providing specific lessons for classroom application. Additionally, this book describes effective teaching methods for both the general secondary student population and special populations that provide challenges for teachers today.

The first section of this book includes an opening chapter that provides an overview and historical perspective of the field of adolescent literacy as well as a look at the types of literacy instruction that are needed in content area classrooms today. This is followed by chapters that discuss best practices in the major areas of interest in the field of adolescent literacy: writing, comprehension, vocabulary, cooperative learning, new literacies, assessment, and the content areas of English language arts, math, and science. There is not a specific chapter to address the history/social studies classroom, but instructional applications for this content area are found throughout the book.

The second section contains five chapters that discuss the adaptation of instructional practices to the needs of specific populations where achievement gaps continue to occur (struggling and reluctant readers, English-language learners, and African American learners). Although achievement gaps have narrowed for Hispanic and African American students over the years, data from the Nation's Report Card in 2005 and 2007 (National Assessment of Educational Progress, 2006, 2008) show that a significant gap still exists for these students in reading and math.

The final section, containing four chapters, takes the reader into the classroom to observe adolescent literacy practices in the context of actual school environments and from the viewpoints of frontline educators themselves. In these chapters, we look at a model high school environment, a forward-thinking professional development program for secondary educators, effective practices of award-winning teachers, and recommendations for progressive inservice professional development programs.

Adolescent Literacy, Field Tested: Effective Solutions for Every Classroom, edited by Sheri R. Parris, Douglas Fisher, and Kathy Headley. © 2009 by the International Reading Association.

This book brings together, in one place, teaching practices that have been shown to create significant literacy gains for secondary students and highlights the qualities of highly effective secondary teaching behaviors. By compiling instructional practices that most effectively address the questions of secondary teachers, this volume holds the potential to help us make the most of our instructional time. This is especially relevant because secondary teachers (unlike elementary teachers) often instruct multiple groups of students daily, and in many cases this includes more than one grade level. Thus, it is imperative that we make the most of the limited amount of time that we have with each of our students.

Additionally, secondary content courses, even English language arts courses, are built upon the assumption that students already know how to read well. Thus, the proportion of time spent learning how to promote literacy growth in adolescents must be increased for all secondary educators, regardless of the content area they teach. This book provides an essential foundation of knowledge to help teachers reach a more thorough understanding of the components of highly effective adolescent literacy teaching practices.

Even teachers who must use school- or district-mandated curricula will find helpful ideas for their classrooms. Secondary teachers are now feeling pressure to produce high student performance on state tests and need to know what highly effective teachers are doing to achieve results. Each chapter provides this important information. We suggest that to attain, and maintain, the ability to teach effectively, teachers must be aware of and actively implement practices that are proven to work with adolescent students. The many exceptional authors in this book have provided secondary teachers with the tools they need to more effectively use their instructional time and to significantly increase the literacy achievement, as well as the content learning, of their middle and high school students.

REFERENCES

National Assessment of Educational Progress. (2006). *The nation's report card: Reading 2005.* Retrieved February 11, 2009, from nces.ed.gov/nationsreportcard/pdf/main2005/2006451.pdf
National Assessment of Educational Progress. (2008). *The nation's report card: Reading 2007.* Retrieved February 11, 2009, from nces.ed.gov/nationsreportcard/pdf/main2007/2007496.pdf

PART I

Literacy Instruction in the Secondary Classroom

CHAPTER 1

The Landscape of Adolescent Literacy

Vicki A. Jacobs

KEY POINTS AND STRATEGIES

Defining Adolescent Literacy

Current Issues

Adolescent Literacy and Content Learning

The Role of Content Teachers

"Some day I hope to pick up a program of a mathematics or a science teachers' conference and see that a section has been devoted to the improvement of reading on the high-school level. When the teaching of reading is taken out of the cradle of the English classroom and permitted to romp about and to gain attention in the classrooms of other subjects, I think that we shall have a sturdier, healthier reading situation."

—*Marie Corrigan (1942)*

This chapter provides a survey of issues related to adolescent literacy. First it examines reasons for the recently intensified attention to adolescent literacy in the United States. It then offers a definition of adolescent literacy that demonstrates the interrelationship of reading, writing, and content learning processes. Next, this chapter investigates the question of who is responsible for the teaching of adolescent literacy. Finally, it considers the challenges that institutions face in supporting the development of adolescent literacy and the professional development of those they would have teach it.

Adolescent Literacy, Field Tested: Effective Solutions for Every Classroom, edited by Sheri R. Parris, Douglas Fisher, and Kathy Headley. © 2009 by the International Reading Association.

Why Is Adolescent Literacy Important Now?

Attention to the challenges of adolescent reading is far from new. Histories of reading instruction in the United States (e.g., Anders & Guzzetti, 1996; Fresch, 2008; Robinson, 1977; Ruddell, 2005; Smith, 2002) note distinctions that have been made for centuries between the skills and instruction required for beginning and later reading. The current debate about who should be responsible for older students' reading-skill development is also at least a century old (e.g., Huey, 1908/1968; Thorndike, 1917/1958). However, adolescent literacy has only recently received the focused attention it has long deserved.

The roots of this attention are found in *A Nation at Risk* (National Commission on Excellence in Education, 1983), which reported alarming statistics about the reading achievement of U.S. high school students. For example, the report noted that almost 15% of all 17-year-olds and as much as 40% of minority youth could be considered functionally illiterate, almost 40% of all 17-year-olds could not draw inferences from written material, and only one-fifth could write a successful persuasive essay (National Commission on Excellence in Education, 1983, p. 11). The National Assessment of Educational Progress's (NAEP) 1984 *Report Card* (1985) reinforced the National Commission's findings, and, 20 years later, NAEP's 2002 and 2007 Report Cards would convey little to assuage national concern (Alliance for Excellent Education, 2005; Lee, Grigg, & Donahue, 2007). Such results and those of a recent study indicating that U.S. fourth graders' reading achievement was only in the middle of international rankings (Mullis, Martin, Kennedy, & Foy, 2007) have given policymakers little confidence that adolescents can contribute successfully to an increasingly global workforce that requires high levels of multiple literacies (Jacobs, 2008; Levy & Murnane, 2004; Murnane & Levy, 1996; National Governors Association Center for Best Practices, 2005).

Response to the apparent crisis in adolescent literacy was slow in coming, perhaps because of the concentrated attention the country had been giving to the definition and instruction of primary-grade reading (National Institute of Child Health and Human Development [NICHD] 2000; Snow, Burns, & Griffin, 1998; U.S. Department of Education, 2001). One of the first responses was a position paper from the International Reading Association (IRA) that outlined principles for promoting adolescent literacy growth (Moore, Bean, Birdyshaw, & Rycik, 1999). IRA followed this position paper with recommendations and guidelines for the preparation of reading practitioners (IRA, 2000a, 2000b, 2004, 2006). Similarly, the National Council of Teachers of English (NCTE) Commission on Reading (2004) issued its own call for action and outlined its principles for literacy reform policy (NCTE, 2006, 2007). National reports and papers have outlined state and national literacy goals (McCombs, Kirby, Barney, Darilek, & Magee, 2005), the imperative for research (RAND Reading Study Group, 2002), and guidelines for and criteria of effective adolescent literacy programs (Alliance for Excellent Education, 2004;

Biancarosa & Snow, 2004; National Association of Secondary School Principals, 2005; National Governors Association Center for Best Practices, 2005). More recently, the federal government has authorized *Striving Readers* (U.S. Department of Education, Office of Communications and Outreach, 2007), a program designed to provide additional support to struggling middle and high school students attending low-income schools. (For a more detailed discussion of the history of the definition of reading and reading instruction, see Jacobs, 2008.)

Although intensified attention to adolescent literacy is relatively recent in the United States, the issues related to adolescent literacy are long standing. These include questions about the very definition of adolescent literacy, the responsibility for adolescent literacy instruction, and institutional support. The remainder of this chapter examines each of these issues.

What *Is* Adolescent Literacy?

Adolescence, in the United States, is typically associated with the "tween" and teenage years—the middle school and high school grades. However, although it is convenient to think of "later" reading as adolescent, theories on the stages of reading development (Chall, 1983) suggest that the requirements of middle school and high school reading actually begin much earlier than grade 6 or 7—at about grade 4 (Heller & Greenleaf, 2007; McCombs et al., 2005; National Governors Association Center for Best Practices, 2005). Therefore, when we speak of adolescent literacy, we must have in mind students from about grade 4 on.

The earliest stage of reading development spans the time before children enter kindergarten and lays many of the foundations of both primary-grade and later reading. During these preparatory years, children learn about the role that literacy can play in everyday life, the intrinsic enjoyment that reading can provide, and the basic differences between the syntax and vocabulary of print and that of everyday oral language. Children often play at reading and writing and, through rhyming, learn about syllabification and hone their phonemic skills. By going on a variety of outings outside their everyday environments and by listening to and discussing printed texts of varying challenge levels, children have the opportunity to expand their vocabulary, conceptual bases, and understanding of language (Chall, 1983; Chall & Jacobs, 2003).

When children enter kindergarten—and continuing through about grade 3— they require direct instruction to hone phonemic awareness, acquire alphabetic principles, and understand how to blend sounds. Children also require structured means to practice these skills to become fluent in their decoding of words and of larger meaning-bearing groups of words, or chunks. Because the materials children use to acquire and practice these skills are necessarily contrived to focus their attention on practicing particular skills, teachers need to continue to challenge students' language development by reading a variety of genres to students and then discussing those genres. Such language enrichment is especially critical for those children who come to school without the advantage of having had access to literacy-rich environments (Chall, Jacobs, & Baldwin, 1990; Delpit, 1988; Snow, Barnes, Chandler, Goodman, & Hemphill, 1991).

The importance of being able to decode print fluently by grade 4 cannot be underestimated. Around grade 4, text becomes increasingly technical, conceptual, and specialized by content. Unable to access information and concepts that are incrementally introduced through print, nonfluent readers fall increasingly behind their fluent peers in academic achievement—experiencing what educators have long recognized as the fourth-grade slump (Chall, 1983; Chall & Jacobs, 2003).

Those who are ready to make the transition from beginning to later reading must develop an additional cadre of skills to meet the increasing challenges of content-based reading and to become independent readers in a variety of academic disciplines. Just as students in primary grades need direct instruction in beginning reading skills, so do older readers deserve direct instruction in the myriad skills *and* processes required of later reading as they

> use their background knowledge and experience (the "given") to develop a context for their reading and [develop] the ability to organize and use that background knowledge to learn most efficiently from text (the "new"). They develop the metacognitive ability to monitor and adjust their reading as needed. They learn how to apply vocabulary, comprehension, and study skills to determine purposes for reading; make predictions; locate main ideas; question, analyze, and synthesize text; navigate varied text structures; identify and clarify multiple points of view; acknowledge the effect of context on meaning; and draw on background knowledge and previous academic and life experience to construct meaning (Armbruster, Lehr, & Osborne, 2001; Chall et al., 1990; Curtis, 2002; NICHD, 2000). (Jacobs, 2008, p. 14)

Who Is Responsible for Adolescent Literacy?

The first national alarm related to adolescent reading arose around the time of World War II over concern about soldiers' abilities to read even the simplest directions (Smith, 1965). To address the situation, schools assigned reading specialists to provide struggling readers with remedial instruction in particular skills such as decoding, fluency, reading speed, comprehension, and vocabulary (Ruddell, 1997, p. 8). Generally, such instruction was separate from and supplemental to content instruction and was delivered in pull-out programs, using materials that were generally independent from those found in content classrooms (Dole, 2004, pp. 462–463). In 1965, Title I, a U.S. government–funded program to support compensatory reading instruction for students living in poverty (Dole, 2004), served to reinforce reading instruction as skill based and separate from content.

It was no wonder, then, that content teachers' responses to the national Right to Read campaign of the 1970s—whose slogan was "Every teacher a teacher of reading"—ranged from, at best, suspicion, to, at worst, antagonism (Early, 1977;

Ruddell, 1997). Although content teachers understood that reading was critical to their students' learning of content, they rightfully complained that they didn't have the training or the time to stop and teach reading (Jacobs & Wade, 1981). Their job, they argued, was to teach their content; reading, based on their experience, was a separate subject for which the reading specialist, elementary teacher, or English language arts teacher was responsible.

The earliest textbooks on how to teach reading within the content areas (e.g., Herber, 1970) did little to help teachers understand the connection between the teaching of discrete reading skills (such as comprehension, vocabulary, and studying) and the teaching of content-specific goals (Jacobs, 2008). Further, because of economic policies in the 1980s, funding for professional development as well as for reading specialists decreased, leaving content teachers with few resources to support students who struggled with the demands of content reading.

As cognitive science turned its attention from learning as discrete skill acquisition to the cognitive processes required of learning (Anderson & Pearson, 1984; Rumelhart, 1980, 1984), interest in the reasoning processes required of learning particular content grew as well. In the 1990s, the term *literacy* emerged, making a distinction between the demands of being literate in an academic context and in other contexts in which students participated outside of school. Literacy drew attention to the multiple factors that influence learning (including language, socio-economics, race, ethnicity, gender, culture, motivation, and special needs) and to the importance of collaborative reasoning and problem solving in learning (Bean, Bean, & Bean, 1999; Vygotsky, 1986/1934). What better place, educators wondered, to engage students in the development of becoming academically literate than in the content classroom, where understanding something significant about a discipline and mastering the reasoning processes required of a particular discipline took precedence?

The Relationship Between Adolescent Literacy and Content Learning

To clarify the relationship between literacy and content learning, we need to examine the relationship between the general term *literacy* and what it means to be literate in a particular content area. Traditionally, literacy has been defined simply as reading and writing, and being literate meant having the skills required of basic reading and writing (Urdang, 1968, p. 782). However, content literacy requires more than basic reading and writing skills. It requires the ability to use particular skills to extract information and understand concepts given the demands of reading and writing in a particular discipline—to be an ongoing and independent student of an academic discipline.

Content-Based Learning Goals

The learning goals that content teachers establish and the strategies that they use to accomplish those goals reflect how they define what it means to become literate in their disciplines. One common goal for content learning is knowing. Knowing typically involves the memory and recall of facts, dates, names, details, definitions, and processes. Another goal for content learning is understanding. Understanding is conceptual and involves understanding something about what we know. To understand, students must engage in the construction of meaning through problem solving and inquiry.

Teaching for Understanding

Teaching for understanding has four fundamental steps, which are illustrated in an outline of a sample social studies unit, presented in Figure 1.1. The first step is to select a generative topic for a unit of study, one that is central to a field of inquiry as well as connected to other topics within and without a particular discipline (Perkins & Blythe, 1994, p. 6; Perrone, 2000, p. 107). The generative topic for the sample unit in Figure 1.1 is "U.S.–Russian Relations." Generative topics for units in other content areas might include photosynthesis, dramatic tragedy, or prime numbers. Such topics allow room for teachers to activate and use students' diverse background knowledge and experiences as personal points of entry into their study.

FIGURE 1.1
Teaching for Understanding: A Unit on Russia

Step 1: Choose a generative topic for the unit.	U.S.–Russian Relations
Step 2: Determine the unit's understanding goals in relation to the generative topic.	Students will understand • How and why the United States and Russia are similar and different from each other concerning geography, government, and trade. • How similarities and differences concerning one of these aspects has influenced the outcome of one U.S.–Russian historical event.
Step 3: Determine how students will demonstrate their achievement of understanding goals.	Students will present an analysis of how similarities and/or differences in U.S. and Russian geography, government, or trade have influenced the outcome of one U.S.–Russian historical event (chosen from a list of possibilities).
Step 4: Ensure ongoing, formative assessment.	

Second, teaching for understanding asks that teachers establish and be explicit about their goals for students' understanding for a unit as well as for individual lessons (in relation to the generative topic). Understanding goals, expressed either in the form of a statement or an essential question (Wiggins & McTighe, 1998), require students to explore the reasoning behind or the application of a concept or fact (e.g., how a poet uses imagery to develop theme; how photosynthesis is relevant to global warming; whether the U.S. Civil War was inevitable; how the Pythagorean theorem was developed; or why the calculation of pi cannot be finite). The understanding goals for the sample unit in Figure 1.1 are for students to explore how and why similarities and differences between Russia and the United States have influenced relations between the two countries.

Third, and necessarily the next step in teaching for understanding, is the determination of how students will demonstrate their understanding (of both unit and lesson goals). Demonstrations of understanding are more than explaining (because we can memorize explanations). They involve application—the ability to teach a concept; express personal value; extrapolate; assume varied critical points of view; compare and contrast something known with something new; explain the how and why of a process, event, or topic; or translate a theory into practice (Perkins, 2004; Perrone, 2000; Wiggins & McTighe, 1998). The assessment in the sample unit asks students to apply what they have learned by analyzing how similarities and differences in U.S. and Russian geography, government, or trade have influenced the outcome of a particular U.S.–Russian historical event.

Finally, teaching for understanding requires ongoing, formative assessment of how well instruction is supporting students through the understanding process—the journey from goals to the demonstration of learning. Formative assessment strategies often double as instructional strategies. For example, during the preparatory stage of learning, teachers can ask students to complete a survey or a brainstorm related to the generative topic—to activate students' background knowledge and experience as well as to assess its adequacy. Exit tickets help students become self-aware of what they have learned, and at the same time they provide teachers with a sense of how well the entire class and individuals have met lesson goals—information that teachers can then use in designing the next lesson.

Instruction That Supports Learning as Understanding

Inquiry-based instruction provides students with means by which they can proceed through three stages of the learning process: prelearning, guided learning, and postlearning. Figure 1.2 outlines a lesson that scaffolds students' learning through these three stages.

The first stage of inquiry—prelearning—introduces the text of a lesson as a problem, puzzle, or dilemma to be solved as a means to study a larger question (and not just a fact to be memorized). During this preparatory stage, teachers

Lesson Focus	Geography

Lesson Goals	• Students will know
	  1. The size, geographic location, population, and demographics of Russia
	  2. The major mountains and rivers of Russia
	  3. Similarities and differences between U.S. and Russian geography
	• Students will understand
	  1. Why the geography and demographics of Russia have an impact on U.S.–Russian trade relations.

Lesson Assessments	Of knowing goals: • Students will complete a graphic organizer comparing the geography of the United States with that of Russia. Of understanding goals: • Students will answer the following question for homework: "At one point in history, the United States restricted one of its exports to Russia to put political pressure on Russia. What do you think that export was, and why would the United States choose it given what you have learned today about U.S. and Russian geography?"
Stage I: Prelearning/Reading	Activating background knowledge and experience—the "given" • Each student brainstorms words they associate with "Washington, DC" Organizing the "given" to anticipate the "new" and "leveling the playing field" • Teachers ask for each student to share one item from his or her brainstorm and write these items on the chalkboard. (List) • While collecting ideas, teachers question, emphasize, and clarify information and concepts about the United States that they know will be relevant to later discussion of Russia. • Teachers then put students in preassigned groups to divide the brainstorm list into categories and to label the categories (e.g., monuments, government, tourist attractions, social protest). (Group/label) Promote engagement and motivation by developing a need-to-know • Each small group then selects one category and lists facts about Moscow that parallel those they listed for Washington, DC and/or questions that need to be answered to complete their list for Moscow. • As small groups report out, teachers pose "how" and "why" questions about the students' responses that will be most relevant to learning goals.
Stage II: Guided Learning/Reading	Providing students with means by which they can investigate the text of a lesson with progressively deeper understanding • Cloze exercise 1. Students, individually, complete a cloze exercise involving a passage from a textbook on Russia in which the word *Russia* has been replaced with *U.S.* Each blank in the text focuses the students' attention on a concept that is relevant to understanding similarities and differences between the U.S. and Russia's geography. For example, the following text on Russia would be changed as follows.

(*continued*)

FIGURE 1.2
Sample Introductory Lesson Plan (continued)

Stage II: Guided Learning/Reading	Original: "Almost three fourths of Russia's people live in large cities." "More than 80 percent of Russia's residents consider themselves to be Russians, descendants of the Slavic peoples...." (Baerwald & Fraser, 2005, p. 427). Modified: "Almost (what fraction?) of people in the United States live in large cities. More than 80% of U.S. residents consider themselves to be (what ethnicity)?" 2. Students return to their small groups and come to a consensus about an answer for each blank. 3. Students report back to the large group, and teachers emphasize and question the facts and concepts most relevant to the lesson's learning goals. • Questioning 1. Instead of asking such a factual question as "What are the major rivers in Western Russia?" teachers rephrase the question as a problem that students need to solve to reach the learning goals of the lesson. For example, "How would the United States have been settled differently if the Mississippi River didn't exist? What would be the impact on Russia if the Volga River didn't exist? Use what you have learned today about the relation between geography and cities as evidence for your argument."
Stage III: Postlearning/Reading	Consolidating and reflecting on learning • Students complete an exit ticket that asks, "What facts and ideas did you learn today that you think are most important to understanding the trade relations between the United States and Russia?" and "Name at least one learning strategy that we used in class today as a means to learn those facts or ideas—a strategy that you could use in the future in your learning."
Homework	At one point in history, the United States restricted one of its exports to Russia to put political pressure on Russia. What do you think that export was and why would the United States choose it given what you have learned today about U.S. and Russian geography?

provide students with means by which they can activate and organize their personal points of entry—the "given" that teachers know will be relevant to achieving lesson goals. Teachers also introduce vocabulary, central concepts, and knowledge in such a way that students develop questions about them as well as the motivation to investigate the questions. In the sample lesson, teachers prepare students for learning about Moscow by activating and organizing what they know about Washington, DC, a city that is more familiar to them. Teachers promote students' curiosity and engagement by having them investigate what a similar list might include for Moscow and by posing how and why questions about the similarities and differences between the cultures that each city represents.

During the second stage of the inquiry process—guided learning—teachers provide students with means to actively engage in problem solving the text of the lesson (integrating the given with the new), practicing new skills, revising preliminary questions, and making tentative generalizations and assertions about what they are learning. In the sample lesson, students inquire more deeply into the similarities and differences between the United States and Russia through a cloze exercise. This exercise asks students to debate answers to questions that capitalize on their background knowledge and experience while focusing their attention on issues that are particularly pertinent to understanding the dilemma of Russian geography. Discussion questions focus on the significance of facts rather than the memorization of facts.

During the third stage—postlearning—students consolidate their learning by articulating what they think they have learned and how they think they have learned it. They test the validity of their tentative generalizations and assertions and refine them, preparing for evaluation or the demonstration of their understanding. In the model lesson, students complete an exit ticket that requires them to state what they think they have learned (i.e., what knowledge and understanding they have gained) as a result of the lesson and to explain how they think they learned it. The homework assignment asks students to name an export the United States might have restricted to put political pressure on Russia and to explain why the United States would choose to restrict that particular export given what the students learned in class about U.S. and Russian geography. The following day's lesson might begin with students collaboratively sharing and testing their assertions and evidence.

The Role of Reading and Writing in Developing Students' Content Literacy

Comprehension is, above all, a meaning-making process through which readers acquire information and seek to understand concepts presented in printed text. As such, comprehension is, in effect, a kind of problem-solving process typical of inquiry. It is thus not surprising that the comprehension process very much resembles the inquiry process required of understanding content, more generally. To be successful readers of content, students need to have the skills necessary to engage in each stage of the reading process (prereading, guided reading, and postreading) and an explicit understanding of how to use those skills to navigate each stage of comprehension. In fact, one of the most critical differences between better and poorer adolescent readers is the degree to which they are metacognizant of the why and how of reading in general and of reading the specific kinds of texts that are characteristic of any one content area.

Similarly, the literature on writing to learn has long recognized the contributions that writing can make to learning, such as engaging students with content and providing them with a record of their thinking (Knoblauch & Brannon, 1983). In addition, preparing to draft an essay involves a process called inquiry (Hillocks, 1986) through which students compose and organize their thoughts before they write about them. This inquiry process has three stages that are similar to the three stages of learning and comprehension in that they support students' understanding of something significant about content so that they are ready to demonstrate their learning by writing about it. During the initial stage, students find and state specific relevant details from personal experience—similar to activating the given during prelearning/prereading. Next, students analyze data sets (e.g., texts) to pose generalizations, argumentative points of view, or assertions about text—similar to the process of integrating the given and the new during guided-learning/guided reading. Finally, students test the validity of their generalizations and arguments by predicting and countering potential opposing arguments—similar to the process of articulating and testing learning during postlearning/postreading (Hillocks, 1986, p. 249).

Addressing Content Teachers' Concerns About Their Role in Literacy Development

Because of the similarities among learning, comprehension, and composition processes, it is not surprising that many of the strategies that teachers use to guide students through the process of achieving content lesson goals are the same that they might use to support students' reading and composing. For example, in the sample lesson in Figure 1.2, the prelearning activities accomplish the goals of the K (what do I know?) and W (what would I like to know?) of the commonly used reading strategy K–W–L (Ogle, 1986). The prelearning brainstorm asks students to practice the comprehension skill of list-group-label. The comparison between Moscow and Washington, DC, previews vocabulary and concepts and organizes students' background knowledge and experience in anticipation of reading the new. The guided-learning, cloze exercise engages students in active reading, and the discussion question provides means by which students must return to the text to interpret facts. The postlearning strategy accomplishes the goals of the L (what have I learned?) in K–W–L. Through the exit ticket, students hone their metacognitive ability to reflect not just on what they have learned but on how they have learned it as well.

Content teachers' concern about taking time from their content instruction to teach reading is well founded as long as we persist in defining reading and writing as discrete skill development. Until we treat strategies as the means toward ends that they are, instead of simply ends in themselves, teachers and students will continue to miss the vital connection between the skills required to learn content and the skills required for successful comprehension and composition. Similarly, although it is true that content teachers are not teachers of the content of reading and writing as separate disciplines, they are responsible for ensuring that how they use reading and writing supports their students' achievement of content goals most effectively. By providing students with scaffolds through learning and by being explicit with students about how and why those strategies support learning in a particular content area and at a particular stage of learning, we are providing students with means by which they can develop the habits of mind that are necessary for being independent learners, the ultimate goal of any disciplinary instruction.

Looking Ahead

The challenges that schools and teachers face in implementing curriculum that promotes adolescent content literacy are numerous and large. Questions that must be answered include the following:

- What is the role of the reading specialist (e.g., that of reading teacher, reading coach, or literacy coach) in supporting the development of adolescents' content literacy and in supporting the literacy development of struggling readers and writers?
- What kind of services will schools provide for older struggling readers (such as those who struggle with fluency, English-language learners (ELL), and those who have language disabilities), and who will provide these services? What can we borrow from the literature on the effectiveness of whole-school programs (e.g., Fisher, 2001; Schoenbach, Greenleaf, Cziko, & Hurwitz, 1999), the reading development of adolescent ELLs in the content classroom (e.g., Ariza, 2006; Chamot & O'Malley, 1994; Echevarria, Vogt, & Short, 2000), after-school programs (e.g., Hartry, Fitzgerald, & Porter, 2008), and the use of technology-aided literacy instruction in literacy development (e.g., Hall, Hughes, & Filbert, 2000)?
- What are the implications of teaching for both depth and breadth in an era of standardized testing, which often requires broad rather than deep coverage of content?
- What supports can a school provide for content teachers so that they can examine the relationship among the goals of their discipline, comprehension, and composition?

The Alliance for Excellent Education (Heller & Greenleaf, 2007) provides guidelines for how we might proceed to answer these questions and support content teachers' examination of the relevance of literacy to their instruction.

1. The roles and responsibilities of content area teachers [in literacy instruction] must be clear and consistent.
2. Every academic discipline should define its own essential literacy skills.

3. All secondary school teachers should receive initial and ongoing professional development in the literacy of their own content areas.

4. Content-area teachers need positive incentives and appropriate tools to provide reading and writing instruction. (pp. 25–29)

These principles encourage schools to approach the question of adolescent literacy itself as a matter of inquiry, one that requires the same collaborative problem-solving processes in which our students need to be engaged to learn. The disciplinary content of such professional development is teaching and learning, and the focus of such work is to articulate our beliefs about the goals of content learning and to understand the allegiance of our instruction to those goals.

The notion of using reading and writing to learn is far from new, just as content teachers' discomfort about teaching reading and writing has historical roots. This chapter suggests that the content teacher's job is not to teach the disciplines of reading and writing as much as it is to use reading and writing in service of their disciplinary goals. Providing students with means by which they can achieve understanding of content as well as an understanding of the processes of learning a particular content is, essentially, providing students with the tools they need to be the independent learners we all want them to be.

EXTEND YOUR THINKING

■ Examine state or schoolwide curriculum frameworks for different content disciplines. How is reading defined in relation to learning in particular content areas?

■ Think of a lesson you have taught. What were your goals for the lesson? Which were knowing goals and which were understanding goals? How did you make these goals explicit to students? What strategies did you use to help achieve these goals? How did these strategies also serve the purposes of prelearning, guided learning, and postlearning? Which of these strategies could also be considered comprehension or composition strategies and why?

REFERENCES

Alliance for Excellent Education. (2004, May). *How to know a good adolescent literacy program when you see one: Quality criteria to consider* (Issue Brief). Retrieved December 10, 2008, from www .all4ed.org/files/archive/publications/Criteria%20for%20Adolescent%20Literacy%20Programs.pdf

Alliance for Excellent Education. (2005, January). *Adolescent literacy: Opening the doors to success* (Issue Brief). Retrieved December 10, 2008, from www.all4ed.org/files/archive/publications/ AdolescentLiteracyOpeningDoors.pdf

Anders, P.L., & Guzzetti, B.J. (1996). *Literacy instruction in the content areas.* New York: Harcourt.

Anderson, R.C., & Pearson, P.D. (1984). A schema-theoretic view of basic processes in reading comprehension. In P.D. Pearson, R. Barr, M.L. Kamil, & P.B. Mosenthal (Eds.), *Handbook of reading research* (pp. 255–291). New York: Longman.

Ariza, E.N.W. (2006). *Not for ESOL teachers: What every classroom teacher needs to know about the linguistically, culturally, and ethnically diverse student*. Boston: Pearson Education.

Armbruster, B.B., Lehr, F., & Osborne, J. (2001). *Put reading first: The research building blocks for teaching children to read (kindergarten through grade 3)*. Washington, DC: The Partnership for Reading.

Baerwald, T.J., & Fraser, C. (2005). *World Geography: Building a global perspective*. Boston: Prentice Hall.

Bean, T.W., Bean, S.K., & Bean, K.F. (1999). Intergenerational conversations and two adolescents' multiple literacies: Implications for redefining content area literacy. *Journal of Adolescent & Adult Literacy, 42*(6), 438–448.

Biancarosa, G., & Snow, C.E. (2004). *Reading next: A vision for action and research in middle and high school literacy: A report from Carnegie Corporation of New York*. Washington, DC: Alliance for Excellent Education. Retrieved December 10, 2008, from www.all4ed.org/files/ReadingNext.pdf

Chall, J.S. (1983). *Stages of reading development*. New York: McGraw-Hill.

Chall, J.S., & Jacobs, V.A. (2003). Poor children's fourth-grade slump. *American Educator, 27*(1), 14–15, 44.

Chall, J.S., Jacobs, V.A., & Baldwin, L.E. (1990). *The reading crisis: Why poor children fall behind*. Cambridge, MA: Harvard University Press.

Chamot, A.U., & O'Malley, J.M. (1994). *The CALLA handbook: Implementing the cognitive academic language learning approach*. Reading, MA: Addison-Wesley Higher Education.

Curtis, M.E. (2002, May). *Adolescent reading: Trends in recent research and implications for instruction*. Paper presented at Practice Models for Adolescent Literacy Success: The Second Workshop on Adolescent Literacy, Baltimore, MD.

Delpit, L. (1988). The silenced dialogue: Power and pedagogy in educating other people's children. *Harvard Educational Review, 58*(3), 280–298.

Dole, J.A. (2004). The changing role of the reading specialist in school reform. *The Reading Teacher, 57*(5), 462–471. doi:10.1598/RT.57.5.6

Early, M. (1977). Reading in the secondary school. In J.R. Squire (Ed.), *The teaching of English: The seventy-sixth yearbook of the National Society for the Study of Education, Part I* (pp. 189–196). Chicago: University of Chicago Press.

Echevarria, J., Vogt, M.E., & Short, D. (2000). *Making content comprehensible for English language learners: The SIOP model*. Boston: Allyn & Bacon.

Fisher, D. (2001). "We're moving on up": Creating a schoolwide literacy effort in an urban high school. *Journal of Adolescent & Adult Literacy, 45*(2), 92–101.

Fresch, M.J. (Ed.). (2008). *An essential history of current reading practices*. Newark, DE: International Reading Association.

Hall, T.E., Hughes, C.A., & Filbert, M. (2000). Computer-assisted instruction in reading for students with learning disabilities: A research synthesis. *Education & Treatment of Children, 23*(2), 173–193.

Hartry, A., Fitzgerald, R., & Porter, K. (2008). Implementing a structured reading program in an after-school setting: Problems and potential solutions. *Harvard Educational Review, 78*(1), 181–210.

Heller, R., & Greenleaf, C.L. (2007). *Literacy instruction in the content areas: Getting to the core of middle and high school improvement*. Washington, DC: Alliance for Excellent Education. Retrieved January 11, 2008, from www.all4ed.org/files/LitCon.pdf

Herber, H.L. (1970). *Teaching reading in content areas*. Englewood Cliffs, NJ: Prentice Hall.

Hillocks, G., Jr. (1986). *Research on written composition: New directions for teaching*. Urbana, IL: ERIC Clearinghouse on Reading and Communication Skills and the National Conference on Research in English.

Huey, E.B. (1968). *The psychology and pedagogy of reading*. Cambridge, MA: MIT Press. (Original work published 1908)

International Reading Association. (2000a). *Excellent reading teachers* (Position statement). Newark, DE: Author. Retrieved February 19, 2009, from www.reading.org/downloads/positions/ps1041_excellent.pdf

International Reading Association. (2000b). *Teaching all children to read: The roles of the reading specialist* (Position statement). Retrieved May 5, 2006, from www.reading.org/downloads/positions/ps1040_specialist.pdf

International Reading Association. (2004). *The role and qualifications of the reading coach in the United States.* Newark, DE: Author.

International Reading Association. (2006). *Standards for middle and high school literacy coaches.* Newark, DE: Author. Retrieved January 11, 2008, from www.reading.org/downloads/resources/597coaching_standards.pdf

Jacobs, V.A. (2008). Adolescent literacy: Putting the crisis in context. *Harvard Educational Review, 78*(1), 7–39.

Jacobs, V.A., & Wade, S.E. (1981). Teaching reading in secondary content areas. *Momentum, 12*(4), 8–10.

Knoblauch, C.H., & Brannon, L. (1983). Writing as learning through the curriculum. *College English, 45*(5), 465–474.

Lee, J., Grigg, W., & Donahue, P. (2007). *The Nation's Report Card: Reading 2007.* (NCES 2007-496). Washington, DC: National Center for Education Statistics; Institute of Education Sciences, U.S. Department of Education.

Levy, F., & Murnane, R. (2004). *The new division of labor: How computers are creating the next job market.* Princeton, NJ: Princeton University Press.

McCombs, J.S., Kirby, S.N., Barney, H., Darilek, H., & Magee, S. (2005). *Achieving state and national literacy goals, a long uphill road.* Report to the Carnegie Corporation of New York, RAND Corporation Technical Report Series. Santa Monica, CA: RAND. Retrieved January 11, 2008, from www.rand.org/pubs/technical_reports/TR180–1/

Moore, D.W., Bean, T.W., Birdyshaw, D., & Rycik, J.A. (1999). *Adolescent literacy: A position statement for the Commission on Adolescent Literacy of the International Reading Association.* Newark, DE: International Reading Association.

Mullis, I.V.S., Martin, M.O., Kennedy, A.M., & Foy, P. (2007). *Progress in international reading literacy study in primary schools in 40 countries.* Chestnut Hill, MA: TIMSS & PIRLS International Study Center, Boston College.

Murnane, R., & Levy, F. (1996). *Teaching the new basic skills: Principles for educating children to thrive in a changing economy.* New York: Free Press.

National Assessment of Educational Progress. (1985). *The reading report card: Progress toward excellence in our schools: Trends in reading over four national assessments, 1971–1984.* Princeton, NJ: Educational Testing Service.

National Association of Secondary School Principals. (2005). *Creating a culture of literacy: A guide for middle and high school principals.* Reston, VA: Author.

National Commission on Excellence in Education. (1983). *America at risk: An imperative for educational reform.* Washington, DC: Author. Retrieved from www.ed.gov/pubs/NatAtRisk/index.html

National Council of Teachers of English. (2006). *NCTE principles of adolescent literacy reform: A policy brief.* Urbana, IL: Author.

National Council of Teachers of English. (2007). *Adolescent literacy: A policy research brief.* Urbana, IL: Author.

National Council of Teachers of English Commission on Reading. (2004). *A call to action: What we know about adolescent literacy and ways to support teachers in meeting students' needs.* Urbana, IL: Author. Retrieved from www.ncte.org/positions/statements/adolescentliteracy?source=gs

National Governors Association Center for Best Practices. (2005). *Reading to achieve: A governor's guide to adolescent literacy.* Washington, DC: Author. Retrieved from www.nga.org/files/pdf/0510govguideliteracy.pdf

National Institute of Child Health and Human Development. (2000). *Report of the National Reading Panel. Teaching children to read: An evidence-based assessment of the scientific research literature on reading and its implications for reading instruction* (NIH Publication No. 00-4769). Washington, DC: U.S. Government Printing Office.

Ogle, D.M. (1986). K-W-L: A teaching model that develops active reading of informational text. *The Reading Teacher, 39*(6), 564–570. doi:10.1598/RT.39.6.11

Perkins, D. (2004). Knowledge alive. *Educational Leadership, 62*(1), 14–18.

Perkins, D., & Blythe, T. (1994). Putting understanding up front. *Educational Leadership, 51*(5), 4–7.

Perrone, V. (2000). *Lessons for new teachers.* Boston: McGraw-Hill.

RAND Reading Study Group. (2002). *Reading for understanding: Toward an R&D program in reading comprehension*. Santa Monica, CA: RAND. Retrieved January 11, 2008, from www.rand.org/publications/MR/MR1465/

Robinson, H.A. (1977). Reading instruction and research: In historical perspective. In H.A. Robinson (Ed.), *Reading & writing instruction in the United States: Historical trends* (pp. 44–58). Newark, DE: International Reading Association.

Ruddell, M.R. (1997). *Teaching content reading and writing* (2nd ed.). Boston: Allyn & Bacon.

Ruddell, M.R. (2005). *Teaching content reading and writing* (4th ed.). Hoboken, NJ: John Wiley & Sons.

Rumelhart, D.E. (1980). Schemata: The building blocks of cognition. In R.J. Spiro, B.C. Bruce, & W.F. Brewer (Eds.), *Theoretical issues in reading comprehension* (pp. 33–58). Hillsdale, NJ: Erlbaum.

Rumelhart, D.E. (1984). Schemata and the cognitive system. In R.S. Wyer & T.K. Srull (Eds.), *Handbook of social cognition* (pp. 161–188). Hillsdale, NJ: Erlbaum.

Schoenbach, R., Greenleaf, C.L., Cziko, C., & Hurwitz, L. (1999). *Reading for understanding: A guide to improving reading in middle and high school classrooms*. Urbana, IL: National Council of Teachers of English.

Smith, N.B. (1965). *American reading instruction* (Rev. ed.). Newark, DE: International Reading Association.

Smith, N.B. (2002). *American reading instruction* (Special ed.). Newark, DE: International Reading Association.

Snow, C.E., Barnes, W.S., Chandler, J., Goodman, I.F., & Hemphill, L. (1991). *Unfulfilled expectations: Home and school influences on literacy*. Cambridge, MA: Harvard University Press.

Snow, C.E., Burns, M.S., & Griffin, P. (Eds.). (1998). *Preventing reading difficulties in young children*. Washington, DC: National Academy Press. Retrieved from www.ed.gov/inits/americareads/ReadDiff/read-sum.html

Thorndike, E.L. (1958). Reading as reasoning. In C.W. Hunnicutt & W.J. Iverson (Eds.), *Research in the three R's* (pp. 139–141). New York: Harper & Row. (Original work published 1917)

Urdang, L. (1968). *The Random House dictionary of the English language: College edition*. New York: Random House.

U.S. Department of Education. (2001). *No child left behind*. Retrieved from www.ed.gov/policy/elsec/leg/esea02/index.html

U.S. Department of Education, Office of Communications and Outreach. (2007). *Guide to U.S. Department of Education Programs*. Washington, DC: Author. Retrieved from www.ed.gov/programs/gtep/gtep.pdf

Vygotsky, L.S. (1986). *Thought and language* (A. Kozulin, Trans.). Cambridge, MA: MIT Press. (Original work published 1934)

Wiggins, G.P., & McTighe, J. (1998). *Understanding by design*. Alexandria, VA: Association for Supervision and Curriculum Development.

CHAPTER 2

Writing Instruction in the Secondary Classroom: Surviving School Reform

Jay Simmons

> KEY POINTS
> AND
> STRATEGIES
>
> Strategies That
> Writers Use
>   Brainstorming
>   Persuasive Essay
>   Writing
> Specific Product Goals
> The Study of Models
> Collaborative Writing
> Inquiry Activities in
> Writing for Content
> Learning

"That writing workshop stuff sounds like pie in the sky. I have to teach my students the five-paragraph essay for MCAS."

—Massachusetts middle school teacher

The beginning middle school teacher quoted above was describing how her colleagues had told her to teach writing—present a prompt and a five-paragraph graphic organizer for each week's day or two of writing—all in the name of better performance on the state test. When I asked who had issued the order, she checked and found it had been the principal. I was working on a state standards committee at the time and asked a person writing the test items if such a mandate were state policy. She winced. "No, Jay," she explained. "In fact, we wish we didn't get so many five-paragraph essays. It's all they turn in now."

The bad news here is that our schools are shooting themselves in the foot. The good news is that the state will be happy if we stop. Ravitch (2008) writes, "All of this test prep ... leads to higher scores but worse education" (p. 5). As teachers of English we must, and can, change this condition. Graham and Perin (2007) in *Writing Next: Effective Strategies to Improve Writing of Adolescents in Middle and High Schools* have conducted an analysis of selected research on teaching writing. They spell out principles of instruction found to be "effective for helping adolescent students learn to write well" (Graham & Perin, 2007, p. 4). Unfortunately, they also describe unduly prescriptive methods for teaching to those principles. We can adopt their principles, but do so in a less narrow way than the report's authors, and the principal mentioned above, suggest. Specifically, we can teach students writing strategies, incorporate specific product goals, incorporate the study of models, use collaborative writing, use inquiry activities in writing for content learning, and follow a process writing approach (Graham & Perin, 2007).

Instructional Practices That Work

Perhaps because Graham and Perin (2007) specialize in educating students with learning difficulties, their meta-analysis of research about writing and their suggestions follow a scripted, clinical model. In many settings over the years, good teachers of writing have taught using the principles on which the *Writing Next* suggestions rest. Therefore, this chapter will demonstrate ways to incorporate these principles, not scripted models, into their daily work.

Writing Strategies

The *Writing Next* report calls for direct instruction in strategies that writers use. In the report, Graham and Perin (2007) note success for teaching brainstorming, collaboration for peer reviewing, and writing persuasive essays. The following paragraphs describe brainstorming strategies and persuasive writing strategies that I've used successfully in my classroom. I discuss collaboration at length later in the chapter. The *Writing Next* report cites Graham's own 2002 study of self-regulated strategy development (De La Paz & Graham, 2002) with six stages: (1) develop background knowledge, (2) describe the strategy, (3) model it, (4) memorize it, (5) support it, and (6) use it independently. Of course, these are the steps of direct instruction used by many of us in the gradual release of responsibility model (Pearson & Gallagher, 1983; Routman, 2003), with the exception of drilling the steps into memory.

The following teaching ideas meet some of the suggestions from *Writing Next*, but they are techniques that teachers have used successfully in classrooms intended for all learners, not simply those thought to learn only through rigid drill.

Brainstorming. I suggest a procedure I call Write with Me (Simmons, 2000) for brainstorming. It is based on Murray's (1985) First Hour of the First Day and mimics what he did with a teacher workshop I attended in 1976. I have done this lesson as an assessment with students who have never received useful writing instruction; that is, students who have never been taught what writers do.

1. Explain that you will be asking the students to write with you to begin a piece of writing, but probably not to finish it. The whole process won't take more than 20 minutes.

2. Ask the students to list as quickly as possible the people, places, or things they care about and know about. Say you will be doing this, too. (Allow 3 minutes.)

3. Stop the students and share your list. Ask if anyone else would like to share. If no one volunteers, discuss at least how you would group your list into a set of items that go together. Ask students to group their lists. (Allow 3 minutes.)

4. Ask the students if they would like to share their groups. If they would not, share yours and pick one group to write about. Ask students to choose one of their groups to write about. Think of one or two titles that might work for a piece that includes the ideas in your group and share the title ideas with the students. Allow the students about 3 minutes to write as many titles as possible for their group. You write, too.

5. Share your titles with the class and ask them to share as well. Pick one title you might write about and share reasons. Ask the students to select one and think of why they selected it.

6. Take 3 minutes to write a sprint draft on that title.

7. Share yours and talk about what you might write next, if you continue it. Ask students to share and talk about what they might do next.

Notice what we have done here: We have given students the background knowledge that writers often start a piece but don't always finish it. It's the starting that counts! We have described each step of the process and then modeled it by doing it with students. Because writing is an internal process, we have talked about what we were thinking so that students can observe the invisible part of writing, too. This is the first of 10 strategies I normally teach students to use to begin writing. The complete list is shown in Figure 2.1.

It is important to support students in their first attempts to use each strategy with an in-class minilesson. Students can then keep the lists, notes, and sprint drafts in their writing notebooks or folders for reference in those dry spells when they are stuck. Students can also use the strategies independently, at first to finish the initial piece and thereafter to begin others.

Persuasive Essay Writing. Most of us have struggled getting students to write the dreaded persuasive essay. We have assigned topics, provided sample readings, given them outlines, or asked to have the outlines submitted in advance, all with more or less deadening results (at least in terms of our Sunday evening reading time). I have observed colleagues brainstorming evidence with class members writing on the same given thesis statement in addition to providing a list of transition words and a graphic organizer with space for each sentence in the five paragraphs.

FIGURE 2.1
10 Ways to Get Started Writing

1. List/Group/Title/Write (Write With Me)
   a. Brainstorm a list of things you know about and care about.
   b. Group the items that go together in some way.
   c. Pick one group.
   d. Write as many titles as possible for pieces about items in that group.
   e. Choose one title.
   f. Write a sprint draft under that title, using as many of the items as possible.

2. Sprint/Circle/Write
   a. Write a sprint draft, not stopping or letting your pencil come off the page.
   b. Reread the draft, circling any words or phrases that interest you.
   c. Choose one circled part or group of circled parts and write a new, focused draft about those.

3. Read the World/Question/Choose/Write
   a. Think back over the last 24 hours of your life. On the left half of the page only, write down what has happened and occurred to you.
   b. Reread your draft and, on the right side of the page, write questions that occur to you. Think about which experiences or thoughts might be of interest to other people.
   c. Choose one question or set of questions and write a sprint draft in answer to it.

4. Daybook/Reread/Highlight/Write
   a. Keep a daybook, a collection of journal entries, reading clippings, or reading responses collected by you as a writer.
   b. Reread your daybook (or a manageable section of it) and highlight any parts that interest or surprise you.
   c. Choose one highlighted part or group of parts that might interest someone else.
   d. Write a sprint draft about that section.

5. Read/Write Back
   a. Choose a book, magazine, pamphlet, handout, commercial package, or newspaper to read.
   b. As you read, write your reactions, thoughts, or questions in the margins or on a separate paper.
   c. Write back to the author, telling what you thought or felt about the piece.

6. Read/Write an Extension
   a, b. Follow steps for #5.
   c. Continue the piece after the point at which the author chose to stop. This might be, for instance, a sequel to a story, the other side of an argument, or a new story or argument using some part of the original reading.

7. Read/Write in the Manner of
   a, b. Follow steps for #5.
   c. Write a new piece imitating the style and tone of the original.
   d. As an alternative, you may "down write," or exaggerate, the original writer's style to poke fun at it by doing it badly.

8. List/Group/Concept Map/Write
   a. Brainstorm a list of things you know about and care about.
   b. Group the items that go together in some way.
   c. Pick one group.
   d. Create a concept map from the items in the group.
   e. Write a sprint draft, using the concept map as a guide.

(continued)

FIGURE 2.1
10 Ways to Get Started Writing (continued)

9. Sprint/Summarize/Topic Sentence/Write
   a. Write a sprint draft on one topic, not letting your pencil come off the page.
   b. Read over your draft.
   c. Draw a line across the page at the end of the draft.
   d. Below the line, write one sentence that summarizes the main idea of the piece.
   e. Use that sentence as the topic sentence of the first paragraph of a new piece.

10. Object/List/Write
   a. Select an object that means something to you.
   b. Place it on the desk in front of you and write down as many impressions describing it or memories associated with it as you can.
   c. Write a sprint draft about the list.

Note. Modeled after Graves, 1994; Hall & Birkerts, 1998; Murray, 1985.

Guided writing (Meeks & Austin, 2003) serves as an alternative to these scripted measures. My version has four parts:

1. Concept Introduction

   • Give a definition of the type of writing. Example: A persuasive essay attempts to convince a reader to adopt a particular opinion or course of action.

   • Run a discussion in which students briefly define this type of writing in their own words. Example: "It means get them to agree with you or do what you want."

   • Present an example from literature. Read aloud, or have the class read silently, an example to find out how the piece attempts to move the reader to believe something or take a particular action. Example: An editorial opposing off-shore drilling.

   • Run a discussion in which students say briefly why the example fits the definition. Example: "The paper wants people to see that drilling will harm local beaches but not produce much oil. They want people to conserve oil and contact their reps in Congress to vote against it."

2. Teacher Demonstration

   • Draft an example of the type of writing introduced.
   • Think aloud to show how you make decisions.
   • Write on the chalkboard or an overhead.
   • Invite questions about process.

3. Shared Writing

- Lead a brainstorm session about characteristics of, techniques for, and examples of that type of writing.
- Write on the chalkboard or an overhead projection sheet.
- Ask why students make their brainstorm suggestions.
- Display examples of the type of writing or reproduce examples for writing folders.
- Include strategic steps in examples.

4. Independent Writing

- Students write their own piece of the same type.

Given a brief sample piece (for instance, an editorial from the local paper or *The New York Times*), the first two steps might occur in one class period. The next day, you might do the shared writing on a topic brainstormed by the class at the end of the first day. This gives students a chance to think about the topic under discussion overnight as well as think about issues they might like to address for the independent assignment. I gave this assignment to an eighth-grade class, producing with class members a letter of protest to the manufacturer of my car after the engine seized up. Customer service had assured me I was not covered, but our letter (sent via registered mail to the CEO of the company) produced reimbursement for my loss! A science class testing crackers for the presence of starch or sugar before and after partial digestion via immersion in saliva found that the crackers contained sugar, although the listed ingredients did not. A letter to the company received an apology and an assortment of classroom snacks!

Specific Product Goals

In 1966 educators from all levels in American and British schools and colleges attended a conference at Dartmouth College sponsored by the Modern Language Association and the National Council of Teachers of English. One conservative website calls the Dartmouth conference "the Woodstock of the composition professions" (MacDonald, 1995) because the educators gathered there allegedly favored openness and expression over rigor and accurate use of the language. Certainly, Murray's (1985) First Hour of the First Day asks students to write about what they know about and care about, unlike a more traditional assignment that asks for a carefully constructed essay giving three reasons why Emily Dickinson's work was daring in her lifetime. Still, Murray warns us that if we have expectations for the final piece, we need to share them with the writers in advance.

We can follow Murray's advice without telling students what to think (about Emily Dickinson, for instance) or how many reasons there are for believing it. The

2011 National Assessment of Educational Progress (ACT, Inc., 2007) will include prompts such as the following:

1. Write a response for the newspaper in which you define a good community and explain what elements make a good community. Be sure to use specific examples and details to explain your ideas. (p. 31)

2. Write a response for the contest on "Achieving Goals," telling about the experience of achieving a goal and the importance of that experience in your life. Be sure to include details in your response that help readers understand your experience and its importance. (p. 32)

The first prompt is for grade 12, and the second for grade 8. The NAEP planners avoid the constraining suggestions of studies in *Writing Next* (Graham & Perin, 2007). They do not dictate how many details, what sorts of paragraphs, or which common elements of persuasion or exposition to include.

Spandel (2008) provides open student checklists for narrative, informational, persuasive, and literary analysis writing. The simple persuasive checklist includes the following goals: helps reader think through issues; makes writer's position clear; shows why others might not agree; gives facts, quotations, and examples; and saves the best argument for last (p. 399). Our rubrics and assignments can, like Spandel's, tell students what good writers do in argument or exposition while not dictating what the correct opinion must be, or the number or order of specific pieces of proof.

The Study of Models

As in the guided writing model mentioned earlier (Meeks & Austin, 2003), writers study the work of published authors to see how others have tackled similar tasks. Historically, students copied ancient texts because printed versions either did not exist or were prohibitively expensive even after the invention of fixed-type printing. This is no longer the case, but strict imitation of models is also inappropriate because it is based on an associative model inappropriate for language learning. Rather, in the style of Portalupi and Fletcher (2001), writers can be shown, for example, how to examine the use of personal experience by Peter Lourie in his non-fiction writing or how writers of *Time* use transitions. Portalupi and Fletcher also show student writers how to use what professionals have done to solve problems in their own writing. Therefore, models of writing have moved from being associative practice and repetition to being literature-based lessons in the procedural knowledge writers must have to put what they read to work in their own writing.

Collaboration

Graham and Perin (2007) found sizeable student gains using collaborative enterprises in writing, including collaborative peer response. My research (Simmons, 2003) has shown that merely having students share their work with one another does not ensure that they will learn to respond helpfully to their peers. However, those who do respond well and know how to use response, write better. Clearly, we need to teach students how to talk about writing and how to use feedback they receive.

Tim McLaughlin of Bunker Hill Community College (Simmons, 2003) teaches his students using the following steps:

1. Students read one another's work in class and respond.
2. Students share the responses generated in pairs with the whole class.
3. Tim and the class members comment on the helpfulness of the response.
4. The whole class comments on the same piece, first those written by persons in class and then those by their outside partners.
5. Tim reviews the comments being given by peers.
6. Tim confers with those students still needing to improve their responses.

What were improved responses, though? Students with more experience in reading workshops offered less global praise ("Good paper!"), fewer personal comments ("You sound like a sincere person."), and fewer text edits ("Run-on sentence"). Instead, they were more likely to comment on what they were affected or confused by as readers ("I couldn't tell on the first page what confused you about your new school."). They also offered suggestions as fellow writers ("Perhaps you might start your paper on what is now page four where the action really begins.").

Rief (2003) scripts her middle-school peer conferences by having students who share consider the following points. The writer fills in line 1, and the audience or partner responds to lines 2–4:

1. You can help me by _____.
2. Tell me what phrases you hear, are surprised by, or stick with you (that I wrote).
3. What questions come to mind (as I read to you)?
4. What's one suggestion you could give me (based on what I asked for as help)?

I use the following format, which is based on Murray (1985) and Graves (1994), for sharing a new or extensively revised piece of writing:

The Writer must do the following:

1. Tell the one thing the piece is about
2. Tell what works in the piece
3. Tell the audience what to read or listen for

The Writer may do the following:

1. Tell where the idea came from and what has been done so far
2. Tell where the piece is going and what needs to be done next
3. Identify problems with the writing process or the paper and ask for suggestions

The Responder must do the following:

1. Tell what you remember from the piece
2. Answer the writer's questions

The Responder may do the following:

1. Tell what you liked
2. Ask for clarification or more information
3. Make suggestions, if requested

I find that middle school, high school, undergraduate, and graduate students all have trouble with the second thing the writer must do: Tell what works. Most of us are used to people (teachers) finding fault with our writing, so we apologize in advance. University of New Hampshire poet Mekeel McBride uses an "apology pig" in some of her classes. Students who apologize before reading a piece are fined 25 cents, which they must deposit in the piggy bank. At the end of the course, she says, there is always enough for pizza! Ralph Fletcher (Fletcher & Portalupi, 2007) says that a writer needs to be able to find the good parts of his or her writing and make the rest live up to those parts. In my peer response form, the writer needs to know what he or she is working on (the one thing it's about) and both Rief (2003) and I ask writers to know where they need help.

Inquiry Activities in Writing for Content Learning

Graham and Perin (2007) in *Writing Next* and the National Writing Project (NWP, 2006) list many of the same activities for content area learning: logs or journals, essay questions, and summaries. Graham and Perin also mention studies that showed positive effects for student note-taking, while the NWP cited work by Robert Tierney in which students wrote for audiences other than the teacher. With the increased test preparation in schools today, we probably don't need to worry about students writing test-like essays in all content areas. Specific ideas for teaching inquiry, however, are another issue. Graham and Perin (2007) note that when last studied in 1986, inquiry activities generally asked students to analyze data before writing.

As a high school teacher, I taught a course called Exploring Contemporary Issues. Students selected it because they could choose the issues to study. I wanted to teach the research process to students who might not always be planning to attend a four-year college.

We spent the first week brainstorming issues to be covered. The Middle East, witchcraft, the John F. Kennedy assassination, and rape were among the first set. Groups then divided the topics among themselves, and each group further divided the individual topic into sections, assigning one person to cover each part. In the group covering rape, there were people investigating rape on college campuses, services for victims, and the history of rape.

All students kept two journals. In one journal, students reported findings they had made during each week in one-page research summaries. Students read one another's findings in group meetings, and the team members decided how to extend the work or reshape their questions. Early on, one young woman was shocked to encounter statistics about the number of male victims of rape. She and the group decided to focus one part of their report on that phenomenon.

The second journal kept track of the research process, noting both successes and frustrations in attempting to find information. Again, the groups shared these experiences through the journals, and I sat in to provide solutions as needed. We had access to both the high school and university library databases, stacks, and interlibrary loan, so the ability to search online sources, e-journals, and digital card catalogues provided a steep learning curve for most of the students.

To teach note-taking, I provided students with a version of the I-Chart (Tierney & Readence, 2005) shown in Figure 2.2. Presented electronically, the columns and rows can expand to fit the information collected. In the numbered boxes at the top of the columns, students write their questions. In the boxes to the left, students write the sources in which they expect to find answers to the questions. Summary

FIGURE 2.2
I-Chart

TOPIC		Guiding Questions				Interesting Facts and Figures	New Questions
		1.	2.	3.	4.		
S O U R C E S	WHAT WE KNOW						
	1.						
	2						
	3.						
	SUMMARY						

writing, included in both Graham and Perin (2007) and NWP (2006), is captured in the I-Chart and the weekly journals.

One young woman had been a victim of rape and convinced her group to present their findings, in part, through a structured viewing of *The Accused*, a film about a rape set in a neighboring state. Working with the principal, we wrote permission slips to go home and developed a viewing guide, and we spent three days viewing and discussing the film.

Other groups presented more traditional research reports, written and distributed in advance of in-class presentations of their findings. Their classmates, informed by the reading the night before and the ongoing discussions during the course, made much better audiences than typical book report "victims"!

Process Writing Approach

Finally, the *Writing Next* authors (Graham & Perin, 2007) say that research supports following a process writing approach. This is good news in an era of mindless reform that has produced the quotation at the beginning of this chapter. More disheartening is the testimony of a third-grade teacher who told a researcher (Sullivan, 2007) that before reform

> you would have seen more of a writing workshop model.... I can remember my kids having folders with different topics, you know, and they got to choose what they wanted to write about that week or that week and a half. They constantly had different items, and I would say, "Oh, that is a great idea! Why don't you write that down in your folder, and we will use that later." (p. 80)

Today, unfortunately, these same teachers are drilling students in five-paragraph essays, despite the fact that they feel it is developmentally inappropriate to do so (Sullivan, 2007). The good news is that all of the procedures outlined in this chapter constitute a process approach to writing, and they are supported by the most accepted research currently in print.

Overcoming Challenges

Where Will I Find the Time?

We know students need to write more to write better, but secondary teachers in this country regularly face five sections a day of as many as 35 students. Reading even 500 words a week from each of them requires 87,500 words per assignment. At an average of 250 words per minute, that activity alone occupies nearly 6 hours, or a full day of reading. No commenting, no editing, not much time for thinking. Just good-bye Sunday.

Until communities support smaller class sizes, we can at least read the papers in front of students, as Don Murray did with me in the workshop I attended. I bring a piece of my writing to class and begin each conference by handing it to my student to read while I read his or hers. Then we trade responses. A number of birds with one stone: conferring, modeling response, spreading six hours over all the periods devoted to writing that week, treating students like contributors to your writing process.

How Can I Prepare All Those Minilessons?

Luckily, we as a profession have been at this process since Woodstock. Atwell's *Lessons That Change Writers* (2002), Fletcher and Portalupi's *Craft Lessons* (2007), and Portalupi and Fletcher's *Nonfiction Craft Lessons: Teaching Information Writing K–8* (2001) all provide middle school teachers with literature and process-based, classroom-proven lesson plans for a reasonable price. *Come to Class: Lessons for High School Writers* (Jago, 2008) does the same thing for high school teachers.

In the long run, you'll want to save good records of your own lessons, including handouts and student work samples. Also, trade lessons and handouts with colleagues!

Looking Ahead

Clearly, governments both local and national must commit to funding schools so that the smaller class sizes promised by No Child Left Behind actually come to pass. School leaders need to heed the words of Ravitch (2008) and others who have called for an end to education as test preparation. As is clear in Massachusetts, the state officials who mandated the tests and created the prompts never intended that students from the earliest grades onward would write nothing but responses to test prompts scripted with graphic organizers that codify outdated pedagogy from two centuries past.

In this chapter we have seen that it is possible to follow the dictates of current research and still allow students to choose their topics, craft their own arguments, apply the lessons of their reading to writing, and help themselves and others by commenting frequently and in-depth on one another's writing (and ours!). We can engage students in long-term investigations into topics that concern them, and they will amaze us with reports and presentations crafted for living audiences of their peers and their community. We call on our leaders to end reductive test preparation and help our schools live up to these challenges, but we're not waiting around. We can start today!

EXTEND YOUR THINKING

■ How might I package the conclusions of the *Writing Next* report to convince my principal, school board, or community to support the conditions necessary to teach writing well, including smaller class size?

■ What is one change that I can make in my classroom immediately that will move me closer to a process writing approach or improve the process I already have?

■ Think about the best piece of writing you have ever produced. It doesn't matter what it is or whether it happened in school or whether anyone has ever read it. How did it come to be, step by step? What conditions allowed you to take those steps? How can you create those conditions for your students?

REFERENCES

ACT, Inc. (2007). *Writing framework for the 2011 National Assessment of Educational Progress.* Iowa City, IA: Author.

Atwell, N. (2002). *Lessons that change writers.* Portsmouth, NH: Heinemann.

De La Paz, S., & Graham, S. (2002). Explicitly teaching strategies, skills, and knowledge: Writing instruction in middle school classrooms. *Journal of Educational Psychology, 94*(4), 687–698. doi:10.1037/0022-0663.94.4.687

Fletcher, R., & Portalupi, J. (2007). *Craft lessons: Teaching writing K–8* (2nd ed.). Portland, ME: Stenhouse.

Graham, S., & Perin, D. (2007). *Writing next: Effective strategies to improve writing of adolescents in middle and high schools.* Washington, DC: Alliance for Excellent Education.

Graves, D.H. (1994). *A fresh look at writing.* Portsmouth, NH: Heinemann.

Hall, D., & Birkerts, S. (1998). *Writing well* (9th ed.). New York: HarperCollins.

Jago, C. (2008). *Come to class: Lessons for high school writers.* Portsmouth, NH: Heinemann.

MacDonald, H. (1995). *Why Johnny can't write—teaching grammar and logic to college students.* Retrieved August 25, 2008, from findarticles.com/p/articles/mi_m0377/is_n120/ai_17379682

Meeks, L., & Austin, C. (2003). *Literacy in the secondary English classroom: Strategies for teaching the way kids learn.* Boston: Allyn & Bacon.

Murray, D.M. (1985). *A writer teaches writing* (2nd ed.). Boston: Houghton Mifflin.

National Writing Project, & Nagin, C. (2006). *Because writing matters: Improving student writing in our schools* (Rev. ed.). San Francisco: John Wiley & Sons.

Pearson, P.D., & Gallagher, M.C. (1983). The instruction of reading comprehension. *Contemporary Educational Psychology, 8*(3), 317–344. doi:10.1016/0361-476X(83)90019-X

Portalupi, J., & Fletcher, R. (2001). *Nonfiction craft lessons: Teaching information writing K–8.* Portland, ME: Stenhouse.

Ravitch, D. (2008). How school testing got corrupted. *The Huffington Post.* Retrieved July 20, 2008, from www.huffingtonpost.com/diane-ravitch/how-school-testing-got-co_b_47497.html

Rief, L. (2003). *100 quickwrites: Fast and effective freewriting exercises that build students' confidence, develop their fluency, and bring out the writer in every student.* New York: Scholastic.

Routman, R. (2003). *Reading essentials: The specifics you need to teach reading well.* Portsmouth, NH: Heinemann.

Simmons, J. (2000). *You never asked me to read: Useful assessment of reading and writing problems.* Boston: Allyn & Bacon.

Simmons, J. (2003). Responders are taught, not born. *Journal of Adolescent & Adult Literacy, 46*(8), 684–693.

Spandel, V. (2008). *Creating writers through 6-trait writing: Assessment and instruction* (5th ed.). Boston: Pearson.

Sullivan, A. (2007). *The effects of topic choice and prompts on student writing and student attitudes about writing.* Unpublished doctoral dissertation, University of Massachusetts, Lowell.

Tierney, R.J., & Readence, J.E. (2005). *Reading strategies and practices: A compendium* (6th ed.). Boston: Allyn & Bacon.

CHAPTER 3

Reading Comprehension Across the Disciplines: Commonalities and Content Challenges

Donna Ogle

KEY POINTS AND STRATEGIES

Matching Reader to Text

Navigating Texts

Making Thinking Visible: INSERT Notes

Checking Multiple Perspectives

Susan Fumo:	As you work in your table groups, should I hear you talking?
Students:	Yes.
Susan:	Why?
Student:	So we make sure we understand what we are reading and learning.
Susan:	You are so right! This is the time for you to share your ideas from the articles you read using what you wrote on your sticky notes.

Comprehension is the key to learning. Much of what we learn is from printed texts—from textbooks and novels to magazines, articles, and short Internet bites. Despite the development of powerful strategies and studies that highlight what good teachers and students do, we are challenged to make this knowledge work for all our students. As the RAND study (2002) explained and the Reading Next report (Biancarosa & Snow, 2004) underscored,

> Some 70 percent of older readers require some form of remediation. Very few of these older struggling readers need help to read the words on a page; their most common problem is that they are not able to comprehend what they read. (p. 3)

This chapter begins with a visit to a language arts classroom where rich comprehension instruction takes place. Important features of the instruction are highlighted in hopes that this example will help readers think about their own ways of developing students' abilities to engage meaningfully with authors of varied texts. It is used, too, because the teacher employs a mix of fiction and informational text in the same unit.

Adolescent Literacy, Field Tested: Effective Solutions for Every Classroom, edited by Sheri R. Parris, Douglas Fisher, and Kathy Headley. © 2009 by the International Reading Association.

The Classroom Visit

Susan Fumo is an eighth-grade language arts teacher at Hanson Park, an urban school serving an 89.7% Hispanic and 94.4% low-income student population. Reflecting her commitment to her students' success, her instruction weaves together her understanding of her students with her content goals and her team's commitment to empowering their students as strategic learners.

As part of a grant (Transitional Adolescent Literacy Leadership [TALL], funded by the McDougal Family Foundation) to help build Latino students' academic confidence and support their graduation from high school, Susan has been videotaped working with her classes. As the TALL Project Director, I encourage teachers to make their work public; these videotapes enable teachers in the project to see how others implement strategy instruction through their content lessons. Central to the project goals is that teachers build students' knowledge of strategies they can use to be successful, independent learners. Teachers explain to students that they need to approach their reading with clear purposes and strategies. Before reading, students assess the materials and decide how to read and respond. As students read, they learn to take notes and monitor their comprehension. They continue consolidating and reflecting on their engagement and learning when they complete the reading (Blachowicz & Ogle, 2008; Buehl, 2009; Ogle, Klemp, & McBride, 2007). In preparation for writing this chapter, I watched a videotape of Susan's lessons while her students were reading the novel *Homeless Bird* (Whelan, 2008). This novel is about a 13-year-old Asian Indian girl, Koly, who is given in marriage by her family to a sickly young boy. Susan selected the novel as a way to help her students stretch their cultural understanding and address issues of growing up and learning to solve problems.

The videotaped lesson came after the students had read two chapters of the book. Susan was aware that her students knew little about Asian Indian culture but chose to let the students dip into the book before helping them deepen their knowledge. She wanted the students to have their own questions and personal reasons for reading more about Asian Indian culture. She also wanted them to realize that many times we as readers need to build additional background knowledge when reading and learning about new topics.

Susan structured this lesson by using a familiar strategy, the K–W–L (What I *K*now, What I *W*ant to Learn; What I Have *L*earned), which students do individually and in small groups, with a note-taking strategy called Interactive Notation System for Effective Reading and Thinking (INSERT; Vaughan & Estes, 1986). She had collected four articles for the students to read so they would gain deeper understanding of India. The articles were about Indian grandparents, respecting elders, teaching children virtues and values, and women's freedom and equality. The lesson began with Susan noting that the novel was set in a foreign culture and that some students had commented on the setting being different from their own. She explained that she wanted the students to think about what they knew now about Asian Indian culture and write their ideas in the K column on their individual K–W–L organizers. Then they would share in small groups, and, finally with the whole class.

Students' comments in the whole-class sharing gave Susan diagnostic information about the depth of their understanding. The sharing included these ideas:

- India is a country in South Asia.

- Women are treated as second-class citizens and not given rights.

- Religion is a very important part of their lives. (When Susan asked which religions, there was no elaboration. She mused, "There might be many religions—what do you think?")

- Women wear red dots on their foreheads. (When Susan asked students if they knew why the dots are worn, no one contributed ideas. She suggested that might be a topic they'd like to pursue.)

- Women don't have as much education as men do.

- They eat bugs. (Susan responds, "They might; in many cultures people eat what they can find locally.")

- They don't have the same technology we have. (Susan probes, "Do you think their technology is higher or lower than ours?" A student replies, "I think lower." And Susan responds, "That might be.")

As students responded, Susan realized that several of them wouldn't have made any verbal contributions earlier in the year. Yet creating settings where students could talk together with partners and small groups before sharing with the whole class had made a real change. Susan was careful to provide time for students to think and write down their ideas first, then share them at their tables and test out others' responses, with the result that many were willing to contribute to the whole class.

Susan also realized that her hunch was right: The students had very little knowledge of the Indian setting of the novel, and her plan to have them read some informational pieces was on target with their needs. She wanted students to be able to appreciate the emotional issues, visualize the setting, and compare the protagonist, Koly, with their own experiences.

Susan's next step was to ask students to write questions they wanted answered about India. Working at their tables they constructed the W column on their K–W–L graphic organizer. During the whole-group sharing that followed the brief discussions, students' questions were recorded by a student on large chart paper. The following important questions were asked:

- How can women put up with the lack of education?

- Do they pray to one god or many?

- What kinds of manual work do Indian women have to do to cook?

- Why are marriages arranged at such young ages and why are they arranged?

- What are schools like in India?

- How many languages are spoken?

- Why do they think education for women isn't so important?

Susan was pleased that her students seemed to be asking good questions and would gain from reading the articles she had prepared for them.

Her next step was to explain the new strategy they would use as they read their articles. She had the description of INSERT on the dry-erase board and went over the four markings (A = Agree; + = New information or idea; − = Disagree; ? = Unclear) that she wanted students to use with their sticky notes. For each marking she gave an example and checked for students' understanding. This is particularly important for her English-language learners (ELLs) for whom procedural terms can be confusing.

Susan:	When you read something that contradicts something you already know, make a mark of [−] beside it. What does *contradict* mean?
Student:	Disagree.
Susan:	Yes. Suppose that you read in an article that religion isn't important.
Student:	That would contradict what we've just read in our book.
Susan:	Yes, so you would mark that with a [−]. Do you see how to use this marking?

When Susan completed the explanation of the marking system, she drew students' attention to the large charts on the board. There were four charts with four columns on each. The column headings were the four symbols for student responses. Susan pointed out to the students that they would post their comments about the articles on the large charts so other students could read them later. This would give added weight to the notations students would make because there would be group accountability for the work. (See Figure 3.1 for an example of an INSERT chart). Susan continued, explaining to her students:

> So, what we're going to do is use the four articles. Each group has four copies of the same article. Examine and discuss the article together. Use sticky notes to write the symbols you have chosen and add any comments you want. Discuss the article with your group. At the end of 5 minutes, share your ideas and post your notes on the wall chart. Is this clear? Will someone retell the steps we will use? [A student repeats the steps.]

Susan then asked, "Should I hear conversations?" Students respond affirmatively, to which she replies: "Yes, that's right. If I don't, that means you're not working together as a group. OK, get started."

FIGURE 3.1
INSERT Chart

Group members _____ _____
          _____ _____

A	+	−	?

Susan did a lot to support her students' comprehension development. She was clearly aware that students need to have purposes for their reading if they are to engage fully. She sensitively waited to build background knowledge about India until students were aware of why it was needed and were able to frame questions to guide their reading of the informational articles. She may go back later, as students finish the novel and other readings, to have the students self-assess this approach to learning. It is common that when good readers begin something new, they need to build more knowledge than a single text provides. Whether in language arts or in other content areas, it is good practice to seek added resources to fill in missing pieces and build students' schemata.

As this unit progresses, Susan may want to put out a box or basket into which students can add articles, pictures, and artifacts related to India. Once their awareness is raised, they can make new connections that otherwise might have gone unnoted (Ogle et al., 2007). Even music, DVDs, and television programs can help students build the texture for Indian life and culture. With Bollywood being in the press frequently, students might find more interest in these stories. This study also provides a great time to connect literature and social studies. Reading maps; looking at the political, social, and sports issues in the news; and reviewing the world cultures textbook that students studied the previous year can help them become more knowledgeable.

Instructional Practices That Work

This visit to Susan Fumo's classroom illustrates the kind of instruction that helps students build their own understanding of and control over their reading and learning. In this section of the chapter, I identify some of the aspects of instruction that teachers can provide to ensure students can confidently engage with a variety of text types and learning contexts. These include helping students identify purposes for their reading, matching readers' purposes and background with appropriate texts, navigating texts, making thinking visible, and checking multiple perspectives.

Beginning With Clear Purposes

One of the most important practices for teachers to model and students to adopt is having a clear purpose for engagement with a text. Students need a more personal purpose than just completing assigned readings. Readers begin with purpose and plans—we select texts for particular reasons. For example, I may want to read a short article to find out why my favorite sports team lost the last game. I may want to learn about ways to cut my calorie intake and lose weight. I may want to escape in a story by a favorite author. In some way I have a purpose for my reading, regardless of whether I articulate it fully. I know why I am reading and if I don't feel satisfied, I stop. I also calculate at some point if my knowledge and background help me engage with the author in a meaningful way. If I feel frustration, I may change texts and find one that's more comprehensible. I also determine how I should approach the text—can I skim through it, do I want to preview the article and look at the headings and visual features, or do I want to read the last paragraph and see how it feels to me? There are many ways we engage with texts, and students need to be given opportunities to articulate their own purposes. They need to be able to think about the ways they will read and monitor their comprehension so they can be successful, and they need to learn to adjust their approach when it is not working.

Matching Reader to Text

Another strategy for readers' success is checking for the match between the author's assumptions of what readers know and the particular knowledge of readers. We like the strategy Beck and her colleagues have developed called Questioning the Author (Beck, McKeown, Hamilton, & Kucan, 1997). With this strategy, students learn to query the author, and one of the questions that might be asked is, How could the author have made this clearer? Many secondary-level teachers overlook the difficulty readers have when they are assigned material that requires knowledge of cultures, content, time periods, and values different from those of their own experience.

Comprehending new material often requires looking for connections to prior experiences and finding ways to buttress one's own knowledge. With the Internet, magazines, and videos readily accessible, it is important that students learn to use these resources. This means helping them assess their own level of knowledge and needs as learners and then helping them find the right resources so they can participate in the curricular experiences and be successful at the level demanded. Passivity when confronted with meager knowledge poses a real threat to successful comprehension, but it can be overcome with good guidance and support.

Navigating Texts

Critical to students' comprehension is developing an active stance during reading. Teachers who model thinking aloud as they read texts help students gain a window on the active, constructive nature of reading. Content areas with dense texts call for more teacher guidance through teacher-constructed reading guides and graphic organizing tools (Buehl, 2009). These guides help students identify key concepts, the organization of information, and vocabulary terms. Students also need to learn ways to find the precise meanings of terms in a particular content domain. Students can assess their levels of knowledge of the vocabulary and develop note cards or notebook entries to help them build more elaborated understanding of the terms (Blachowicz & Fisher, 2008).

Texts in each content area have a particular organization and way of displaying visual information. Therefore, teachers can guide students in how to use them. Textbook scavenger hunts and other previews help students navigate textbooks (Daniels & Zemelman, 2004; Ogle et al., 2007). Following an introduction to the text, teacher-developed reading guides help students identify the organization and key features of their texts (Ogle, 2007; Wood, Lapp, Flood, & Taylor, 2008). The time spent orienting students to text features can be very important. Think of the differences between using a mathematics textbook and reading novels or short stories in English (Ogle & Blachowicz, 2002). Reading and understanding math requires a reader to attend to visual information (sample problems, mathematic sentences, etc.), while fiction depends on the reader's ability to turn words into visual images. In mathematics, descriptions are provided visually and the content is even presented in reverse order from most science and history materials (Fogelberg et al., 2008). In social studies, students are often asked to read texts showing maps, timelines, photographs, and political cartoons. Students need to learn to integrate these varied forms with the narrative content. If primary-source documents are being used in high school history with document-based questions, providing guides for using these materials is important.

Making Thinking Visible

A basic yet often overlooked way to monitor one's comprehension is to check to see if one can visualize what is being read. Students may do this regularly when reading fiction but may not have transferred this skill to informational reading. Teachers can help by establishing ways students can make their own thinking visible as they read. This helps students track their thinking and deal with challenges as they build understanding along with the authors' presentation of ideas. Using journals or logs while reading, asking students to construct T-charts with author ideas and quotations on one side and student responses on the other, creating visual images, and using the INSERT note-taking system are all ways teachers can help students stay actively connected. The practice of having students read and respond to short sections of text with a partner is also valuable for many striving readers. Informational texts are often very dense, and sharing responses to short segments can help students build meaning more effectively than trying to read long sections without reflection.

Several strong instructional frameworks exist that help students monitor their comprehension in both fiction and informational materials. These frameworks vary by the kind of texts students read and the purposes for their engagement, yet there are enough ways to help students monitor their own comprehension that every content area can provide support. In addition to those suggested earlier, having students create visual maps of the sections of texts they read and then sharing those maps with others enhances their deep engagement with ideas. Most recently, the practice in mathematics of having students describe how they solve problems is an important metacognitive monitoring tool.

As students complete sections of texts or complete works, it is valuable to reflect immediately on what they think they have understood. Again, making notes and illustrations of the reading is valuable. Some teachers who have students work in literature circles or book clubs incorporate this as a regular practice. One teacher with striving readers makes this activity more palatable by having students ask 3–5 questions from their reading that they want to bring to their group the next day. This can be a very positive entry point for reluctant readers.

Checking Multiple Perspectives

The practice of asking questions of the text is valuable in all content areas. It can lead nicely into extended inquiry and checking other sources for added ideas and information. Making a policy of always trying to read from more than one author for additional points of view helps develop a critical perspective. Asking questions such as How would someone else explain this scientific process? or Is this the interpretation that international experts give this event? can interest adolescents, who love to challenge authority. The reality of the 21st century is that students regularly have access to multiple perspectives—using this rich array of points of view in the classroom and helping students develop their critical inquiry can deepen their interest in subjects being studied.

Overcoming Challenges

A few key challenges come to mind when I visualize the good teachers I observe regularly and think of our conversations. First among these is the impact of years of passive educational experiences on students' motivation and engagement. Students' questions and curiosity seem stifled. Their sense of self-efficacy is deflated. Teachers who want to share ideas and challenge students often are exhausted by resistant students. All students deserve to have teachers who listen to them, respond to and extend their interests, and create engaging contexts for learning. Many times the primary-grade teachers are the ones who nurture students. By the time students are in middle and high school, they move so quickly from one teacher to another that the personalization of education is missing for the students who most need it: those who are shy, lack confidence in themselves, or have missed some key components of education.

The tools to reengage students are in our hands already. Discussion groups, debate, dialogue journal writing, active note-making, computer chat rooms, exit cards, and all student response tools are ways teachers can listen to students. Students respond to teachers who listen to and care about them. We may need to rethink ways to connect more over extended periods of time with our students by, for example, keeping the same students for 2–3 years as the middle school model suggests. Adolescents deserve teachers who know them well and can support them in their transitions.

A Team Approach

The more that teachers work together, the more successful they and their students are (Irvin, Meltzer, & Dulan, 2007; Ogle, 2007). The tension for secondary educators is always real; there just isn't enough time to do everything. They often ask, How can teachers sacrifice content for reading and learning strategies? The solution comes when content area teachers work together and create a literacy team for the school. By working together, a small set of reading and learning strategies can be taught and reinforced across the content areas. When students hear the same language and see the same instructional tools being used by different teachers, they begin to build the habits needed in strong learners. In the TALL project, each school has defined a few key strategies that include an approach to note-taking, connecting students with text, and learning academic vocabulary. One teacher can introduce the strategy (K–W–L or INSERT notes, for example), and the other content team members reinforce it by using it where appropriate. Soon students learn even to anticipate which strategy will work. We heard one student ask his teacher, "Mr. Payne, why didn't you start out with a K–W–L? It would have helped us figure out what we needed to learn." By working together across grade levels, students gain more confidence in their strategies. Note-taking approaches are developed from sixth grade through ninth grade, so by the time the students go to high school, they know how to take INSERT notes, create graphic organizers, and then construct Cornell notes, required by some teachers. With a common orientation to instruction, ninth-grade teachers can expect students to use these tools with little review.

Appropriate Reading Materials

As a reading educator, I am distressed when I observe classrooms in which struggling readers aren't given accessible reading materials but are assumed to be able to handle complex texts. I also chafe when teachers don't find students' interests and use them as an entry point to creating engaged readers. Even when programs are implemented to support struggling readers, the regular education faculty is often disengaged from these efforts. Students need teachers who model the benefits of reading both personally and academically and who help them develop their own habit of reading. Recent attention to boys as readers by male educators and authors such as Alfred Tatum, Marc Aronson, and Jon Scieszka may help us recognize the importance of reaching this important group in our classrooms.

A potential ally in increasing reading is the Internet. There is so much available that all students can gain from using, yet our poorest students often lack access to this resource in their homes and have limited access in school. Finding ways to help all students learn to use the Internet effectively is a real challenge. The resources are amazing; we need to get them to our students. Teachers also need to help students adjust to the unedited nature of the Internet, too. We hear too many stories of middle and high school students who have developed erroneous ideas about history and world cultures by accessing materials that are available online. Some instruction in how to check for site sponsors, how to use the categories and organization of information on sites, and how to read across sites is important. These skills can build critical thinking and motivate students.

Regular Reading

In many schools, teachers seem to have little commitment to the importance of students' engaging in reading on a daily basis. There is almost an attitude that it is not possible that students might engage in any reading, and clearly not in self-selected reading. And, in many schools, the students who are the least able readers are put in courses where no reading materials are being used; the books are above the students' levels, so teachers work around print by lecturing, having students engage in practical assignments, and showing video presentations. For ELLs, this is particularly detrimental because they need to have a clear presentation of the English and opportunities to read and reread the same information so they can match the oral and written forms of the content. Students won't become better readers unless they read regularly from materials at their instructional and interest levels.

Looking Ahead

Comprehension takes effort. A major concern of many in our field is how to attract students and motivate them so they will engage fully in and develop thoughtful habits for reading. Watching adolescents multitask and move quickly from one activity to another can raise concerns. Some reading needs to be slow and thoughtful. Two positive attributes of students can be used to develop more reflection: First, they challenge authority and points of view, and second, adolescents are very interested in their peers. These preferences can be a useful force in developing their critical thinking. Students can learn to use what they read to develop arguments and debate different points of view in class (see McBride, 2008). A basic version of debate has been developed in the discussion web (Alvermann, 1991). A key to using a discussion web is that all students must do their homework and bring in the web already filled out before they can take part in the group discussion. On the web students must provide arguments both for and against the basic statement for debate.

With Internet technology, this curiosity and challenge can also be directed by connecting students with their counterparts in other parts of the world. Interesting dialogues can be developed as students from Bulgaria and Asia, for example, communicate with students in the United States (see *Literacy in the Digital Age* [Burniske, 2008] for ideas). Students can discuss their responses to a piece of literature, find their perspectives on current events, and share explorations in science and mathematics. U.S. students can learn about the expectations of secondary education elsewhere. These activities might be a good reminder that soon they will be competing with these international counterparts in a global economy. Debate, both in class and through blogs and chat rooms, can enhance students' desire to learn and master information. As McBride (2008) puts it in his book title, "If they can argue well, they can write well."

The increased availability of the Internet and mass media can be a great support to teachers and students. Having enough background knowledge and ability to visualize ideas and contexts in written text can be almost ensured when multiple sources are used. Students who have had no idea what Egypt and life along the Nile River might be like can watch short video clips and be much more prepared for the unit on Ancient Egypt. High school students who are interested in the latest microchip technology can be connected online to scientists who are working on the latest ground-breaking advances and live the process with them. Building knowledge and comparing ideas are so much easier with the technological tools that are and will be available.

Visual literacy is becoming more a partner with traditional literacy using the resources of technology. Students can read displays and images that make ideas clearer than written text alone. They can watch both still and moving images and create their own. Learning how to be critical viewers and careful creators of images is part of the future. Already high schools are teaching visual literacy courses, and students are mastering ways of communicating that were not possible even a few years ago. Technology can open many doors for students as they explore their own thinking and find ways to make their own contribution.

While looking ahead to new technological resources, it is also important to celebrate the wide world of print materials available to us. Graphic novels and Japanese manga are just two examples of engaging materials that teens love. So are their own original zines and the wealth of magazines targeted to particular interests. When we asked our striving readers to bring in samples of what they read at home, we were amazed. Several subscribed to wrestling magazines, and one brought in a favorite set of collectors issues. Others had soccer magazines and baseball cards. Yet these texts had never been included in the school libraries. The way one author, J.K. Rowling, has reenergized readers means we don't dare overlook the power of print magazines and books in our students' futures.

Developing students' abilities to comprehend an increasingly diverse range of texts is the responsibility of all teachers who use written and visual texts in their teaching. Comprehension, therefore, is most effectively taught when teachers work together across content areas to ensure that students learn, use, and gain control over a variety of approaches to their own reading and learning. Students need to learn to preview texts and identify the ways authors have organized them. They need to use provided guides to important concepts and then find ways to match their own purposes and needs with the available texts. The more densely presented the ideas are, the more effort it takes readers to engage fully and learn. That's why having a set of approaches or strategies is important; students need to know when to make marginal notes, when to sketch ideas, and when to create more elaborate journals, graphic organizers, or formal notes. The range of ways information can be accessed now makes it important to critically assess the authority and veracity of information. This also helps students understand that they have a voice and need to develop and share their understanding and interpretation as they learn. Reflecting, talking, writing, and creating visual displays are all parts of the communication process essential in learning.

EXTEND YOUR THINKING

■ What kinds of reading materials pose the biggest challenge for you? Why?

■ What tools do you use with students to help them access challenging texts? How can teachers help students develop their own repertoire of strategies to use independently?

■ What strategies do you most frequently use when reading challenging texts, and how can you share these strategies with students to help them become aware of what mature readers do? (i.e., Do you start with an easier text, draw visual diagrams and pictures, make marginal notes, underline, or use other tools?)

■ What are the biggest challenges you think teachers face in developing students' comprehension?

REFERENCES

Alvermann, D.E. (1991). The discussion web: A graphic aid for learning across the curriculum. *The Reading Teacher*, 45(2), 92–99.

Beck, I.L., McKeown, M.G., Hamilton, R.L., & Kucan, L. (1997). *Questioning the author: An approach for enhancing student engagement with text.* Newark, DE: International Reading Association.

Biancarosa, G., & Snow, C. (2004). *Reading next—A vision for action and research in middle and high school literacy: A report to Carnegie Corporation of New York* (2nd ed.). Washington, DC: Alliance for Excellent Education.

Blachowicz, C.L.Z., & Fisher, P.J. (2008). *Teaching vocabulary in all classrooms* (4th ed.). Upper Saddle River, NJ: Pearson Education.

Blachowicz, C.L.Z., & Ogle, D. (2008). *Reading comprehension: Strategies for independent learners* (2nd ed.). New York: Guilford.

Buehl, D. (2009). *Classroom strategies for interactive learning* (3rd ed.). Newark, DE: International Reading Association.

Burniske, R.W. (2008). *Literacy in the digital age* (2nd ed.). Thousand Oaks, CA: Corwin.

Daniels, H., & Zemelman, S. (2004). *Subjects matter: Every teacher's guide to content-area reading.* Portsmouth, NH: Heinemann.

Fogelberg, E., Skalinder, C., Staz, P., Hiller, B., Bernstein, I., & Vitantonio, I. (2008). *Integrating literacy and mathematics: Strategies for K–6 teachers.* New York: Guilford.

Irvin, J., Meltzer, J., & Dulan, M. (2007). *Taking action on adolescent literacy.* Alexandria, VA: Association for Supervision and Curriculum Development.

McBride, W. (2008). *If they can argue well, they can write well.* Nashville, TN: Incentive Publications.

Ogle, D. (2007). Best practices in adolescent literacy instruction. In L.B. Gambrell, L.M. Morrow, & M. Pressley (Eds.), *Best practices in literacy instruction* (3rd ed., pp. 127–156). New York: Guilford.

Ogle, D., & Blachowicz, C.L.Z. (2002). Beyond literature circles: Helping students comprehend informational texts. In C.C. Block & M. Pressley (Eds.), *Comprehension instruction: Research-based best practices* (pp. 259–274). New York: Guilford.

Ogle, D., Klemp, R., & McBride, W. (2007). *Building literacy in social studies.* Alexandria, VA: Association for Supervision and Curriculum Development.

RAND Reading Study Group. (2002). *Reading for understanding: Toward an R&D program in reading comprehension.* Santa Monica, CA: RAND.

Vaughn, J.L., & Estes, T.H. (1986). *Reading and reasoning beyond the primary grades.* Boston: Allyn & Bacon.

Wood, K.D., Lapp, D., Flood, J., & Taylor, D.B. (2008). *Guiding readers through text: Strategy guides for new times* (2nd ed.). Newark, DE: International Reading Association.

LITERATURE CITED

Whelan, G. (2008). *Homeless bird.* New York: Hedgehog Books/HarperCollins.

CHAPTER 4

Supporting Cumulative Knowledge Building Through Reading

Eileen Kintsch, Sally Hampton

The boys had numerous misconceptions about what was involved in reading and about how they were to handle the language encountered in text. Among the most serious misconceptions were the following:

- Decoding is reading—that is, when the words in a text have been pronounced, especially aloud, the text has been read.

- Missing a line or a sentence in a text doesn't matter much since each is independent of the others—in fact, missing a line while reading a text hardly gets noticed.

- Texts are made up of bunches of sentences. Each sentence has the same weight as the others. Meaning, to the extent that a text is supposed to be meaningful, comes from dealing with each sentence in turn.

- Verbatim recall of what you have read is evidence that you have understood it. (Fillmore, 2008, p. 15)

In her unpublished manuscript "Expectations and Diversity," Fillmore (2008) writes about three high school boys who struggle to learn. She worked with these students for several years to help them overcome their struggles. During this time, Fillmore learned that some students approach reading as if being able to pronounce the words on the page is sufficient. These students read from sentence to sentence without trying to link the ideas. To them, paragraphs are simply a series of unrelated sentences and whole texts a collection of paragraphs! For these students, each text is distinct; it's not related in any way to text they've read previously nor has it any bearing on text they will read in the future. Once they've read the information, they are through with it. No storage in long-term memory. No wonder such students struggle to learn!

How, you may wonder, can this be? As with other problems in education, there's no single right answer, but there is an obvious factor that just might explain

Adolescent Literacy, Field Tested: Effective Solutions for Every Classroom, edited by Sheri R. Parris, Douglas Fisher, and Kathy Headley. © 2009 by the International Reading Association.

the problem these students share: They have learned what we have taught them. We have taught them to decode—they decode. We have asked them to repeat back information from the text—they can provide verbatim recall. We have worked on fluency—they are fluent. If they get lost in the text, they know to reread. All of these are good things, but what we've taken for granted—and never adequately addressed directly—is that in reading, it's the meaning—what the text says—that's important.

Our examination reveals that the typical reading materials used in classrooms today are basal series and the like, which focus on decoding skills and comprehension repair strategies. There is no attention given to how to link ideas to form a network—no attention to connectors or syntax. Typical reading materials include a variety of genres, or forms, but are heavily narrative. This emphasis on narrative develops students' capacity to understand narration—especially story structure—but does not prepare students to understand informational text. The reading selections address a variety of topics. There is no grouping of reading selections to develop in-depth understanding of any particular concept. There is not enough emphasis on learning content and using that content knowledge to understand related and more complex text. Comprehension is monitored through interrogation, response, and evaluation (IRE). Students are asked questions that can be answered by recall rather than application. Thus, students have only a cursory understanding of what they have read. And, finally, the reading selections require no background knowledge. In the event that background knowledge would be useful, teachers provide it, so students never learn to search their own memory banks to determine if they have any relevant knowledge or to determine what is and is not relevant. All of these features undermine reading comprehension.

The crucial role of comprehension in reading instruction has been recognized only rather recently. Yet according to National Assessment of Educational Progress (NAEP) results, more than two thirds of U.S. 8th and 12th graders do not read at grade level proficiency, and only 3% of 8th graders and 5% of 12th graders achieve advanced proficiency (Heller & Greenleaf, 2007). Despite growing awareness of the number of struggling readers, programs that offer explicit instruction in comprehension together with extensive opportunities for guided practice in reading informational texts have not caught on very broadly in most school settings. Instead, struggling readers typically receive even heavier doses of decoding instruction while falling further and further behind in their academic courses because of their inability to deal with challenging academic texts.

Powerful theoretical models of text comprehension supported by empirical research have contributed to a better understanding of reading processes (e.g., Kintsch, 1998). Many tools developed for studying comprehension and learning have made it out of the research lab and have been translated into workable programs and interventions with impressive success, but for the most part these programs have been implemented only in isolated classrooms and schools. The reasons for this sporadic pattern of implementation are many and varied (see, for example, Torgesen et al., 2007). Among them is the reluctance of many educational policymakers and administrators to support an instructional model that appears different from that imposed by the requirements of accountability testing. Specifically, depth of understanding has been sacrificed to broad (and superficial) coverage of topics because of the fear of leaving something out that might be targeted by standardized assessments. Students who do not read on grade level are vulnerable on state tests, so they are given increased doses of decoding and practice passages.

Without substantial changes to our assessment procedures and the resulting instructional delivery system, widespread implementation of a more progressive instructional model—one that emphasizes deep comprehension—is difficult to achieve. To help readers who struggle with text, classroom practice must address the specific cognitive processes that underlie successful reading. The adoption of new instructional programs and technology should be based on how well they incorporate current, research-based principles of comprehension and learning.

Attention to Language Structures: Building a Textbase

Carol Lee (cited in Torgesen et al., 2007) warns that although a small percentage of struggling adolescent readers have difficulties with basic decoding, most of these students struggle instead with vocabulary, insufficient or incorrect prior knowledge, and lack of knowledge of syntax at the level of sentences. They are frustrated by a lack of understanding about syntactic markers of logical relations and coherence. Although teaching vocabulary today has received increased attention, there is still an instructional void in the teaching of syntactic structures, cohesion, and coherence. No text (except for a legal document) is fully explicit. Therefore, skilled readers automatically form bridging inferences as they read to fill in missing links: They infer the referents for pronouns or synonymous terms, and they specify the implied causal, temporal, or other relationship between elements of the text (e.g., so, because, then, next, but). Without attention to these elements, readers cannot develop the ongoing understanding of the relationships between the words, phrases, clauses, sentences, and paragraphs in a text. Linking these structures appropriately forms an interconnected mental structure called the textbase, which is fundamental to comprehension (Kintsch, 1998).

Attention to Content: Constructing a Mental Model

A reader's valid textbase is evidence that the reader has built a coherent understanding of the text as written. With a coherent textbase, the reader can easily provide the gist of what he or she has read. However, for deep comprehension to take place, the reader must connect the information from the printed page with relevant background knowledge he or she has stored in long-term memory. The result of this process is the reader's mental model. For example, in reading about how some bird species defend their young against predators, a reader might recall suddenly being startled by a ptarmigan flying up before her on a mountain path. She may then recall a host of other details about ptarmigans, such as their seasonal change in plumage from summer brown to winter white, and use this personal knowledge to enrich her understanding of the idea that camouflage is an adaptive mechanism for survival. True learning depends on deeply understanding a given subject matter. This kind of learning goes beyond the mere ability to repeat back received information, whether it is obtained from reading text or from listening to presented information. Deep learning involves the creation of knowledge structures in one's memory that are long lasting and that can be accessed in varied situations.

In this chapter we will consider in more detail some instructional implications underlying reading comprehension processes. Specifically, we will describe three comprehension programs that demonstrate quite different approaches to instruction, all of which seek to maximize opportunities for meaning construction among students at different grade levels. Our goal in this chapter is to encourage practitioners to think about how a given program might be adapted to their own instructional context and purposes.

The instructional programs described in the following section are directed primarily at two levels of comprehension: making the text's meaning coherent (linking ideas appropriately) and integrating the content with one's existing knowledge. The three approaches employ somewhat different instructional activities toward this goal, but in each case the instruction and practicing of literacy skills, reading comprehension, and writing strategies are embedded in subject matter learning rather than taught through reading unrelated texts, as in traditional language arts classes. Meaningful learning and comprehension proficiency go hand in hand with these programs, which focus on the growth and use of prior knowledge: New content is added to and integrated with existing knowledge in a cumulative, spiraling fashion, forming a foundation for ever deepening understanding.

Instructional Practices That Work

The IDEAS Model

Vitale and Romance (2001, 2007) have developed and tested a knowledge-based instructional program, called IDEAS, for elementary students. Replacing the traditional language arts class, comprehension proficiency develops with science knowledge in a two-hour IDEAS class that combines science instruction with language arts skills. The science content follows the logical organization of concepts and relationships outlined in curricular guidelines. A variety of activities that are typical of inquiry-based approaches are used, including reading science materials from printed and Internet sources, hands-on experimentation, concept mapping, journaling, and report writing. Teachers model the strategies and guide students through the mostly pencil-and-paper activities in interactive dialogues.

Vitale and Romance (2001) established the effectiveness of the IDEAS model in a multiyear study. Students in grades 2 to 5 who were taught in a year-long IDEAS implementation were compared with students from the same grade in traditionally taught science and language arts classes. Students in the IDEAS classrooms consistently demonstrated greater progress than traditionally taught students, performing significantly higher (up to an entire grade equivalent) on national standardized tests of both science and reading proficiency. Moreover, students in IDEAS classes displayed significantly more positive attitudes about science as well as about reading, according to teachers' ratings of student performance and detailed observations of their classroom participation. The large number of classrooms across the 5-year study interval encompassed student ability levels ranging from at-risk to above average. Implementation of the program required a 30-hour week of teacher training during the summer plus 30 hours of follow-up training during the academic term, with occasional mentor support and discussion groups. (Guidelines on implementing the IDEAS model are presented in the appendix of the 2001 article by Vitale and Romance.) A main reason why this instruction is so successful, according to Vitale and Romance, is the time devoted to in-depth conceptual understanding of structured content: The combined science and language arts curriculum allowed enough time for the students to build and elaborate their knowledge about important scientific topics and to apply this knowledge in meaningful ways. Within the IDEAS framework, comprehension and learning strategies become effective tools that are refined and extensively practiced in the pursuit of knowledge.

The Adolescent Literacy Support Project

The Adolescent Literacy Support Project (ALSP), designed by Herman and Gomez (2009; Gomez, Herman, & Gomez, 2007), targets urban Chicago students in grades 9 and 10 whose low reading skills make it difficult to impossible for them to comprehend the grade-level science texts they are supposed to learn from in content area classes. Instead of using watered-down, remedial texts, ALSP embeds instruction in effective comprehension in science learning, using complex grade-level texts. Comprehension and scientific inquiry are supported by computer-based reading support tools as well as by some pencil-and-paper tools. Instruction (with teacher modeling and guidance) takes place during task-focused routines. There are three main computer-based tools: First, an annotation system facilitates understanding the argument structure of the text by helping students differentiate between the roles played by parts of the text in developing a scientific argument. Students use the annotator to label text segments as claims or evidence, definitions or examples, counterclaims, opinions, and so on. Second, the double-entry journal (DEJ) technique provides a graphic display (like a T-chart) to organize students' comments, questions, and areas of confusion about specific sentences or text segments. The third tool, Summary Street, provides individualized, online feedback to help students synthesize their understanding of the content at the gist level. Several publications describe classroom trials with Summary Street (e.g., Caccamise, Franzke, Eckhoff, Kintsch, & Kintsch, 2007; Wade-Stein & Kintsch, 2004). Feedback from Summary Street consists of a graphic display showing how adequately students have covered the content within prescribed length constraints. Additional tools help students locate redundant, irrelevant, or plagiarized sentences in their summaries.

Comprehension activities and scientific argumentation in ALSP classrooms are additionally supported by specific, clearly defined routines that scaffold the instructional flow for both students and teachers. For example, set routines focus explicitly on text comprehension problems, on relating reading to the students' personal science learning goals, on integrating multiple readings and related activities, on scientific reasoning and communication, and on assessing the products of learning (e.g., graphic organizers, concept maps, summaries, reports, and the like). This kind of organizing structure with concrete, doable tasks is probably an important reason why the program appears to work with multiply challenged inner-city students and seems to encourage teachers to rethink and redesign their instruction, although it also requires extensive and ongoing teacher development to implement the program.

Literacy Navigator

Hampton's (2007) Literacy Navigator is a research-based intervention program designed to help students in grades 4 through 10 who struggle with reading and comprehending informational text. This course augments and enhances—but does not replace—a school's reading curriculum and English language arts program. As a supplemental program, it helps students master the key comprehension concepts they need to succeed as they move up grade levels.

The course design reflects the most current theory and research in reading comprehension (Hirsch, 2006; Kintsch, 1998). Accordingly, lessons are embedded in content that students are to comprehend and apply as relevant background knowledge when they move through the lesson sequence. All of the selections in the lessons are authentic texts, and they are all clustered around an overarching concept. For example, at grades 7 and 8 the readings deal with the concept of adaptation; at grade 4 the concept is endangered species. The difficulty levels of the reading selections cover a broad spectrum from highly engaging and relatively simple (lessons 1 and 2), to more complicated (lessons 7 and 8), to very complex in the last series of lessons (lessons 26 and 27). The texts are purposely arranged to become increasingly difficult, conceptually and structurally, because each text the students read contributes to an expanded mental model, a growing elaboration of topic knowledge that aids their comprehension of future texts. Simply put, the structured materials are designed to help students become increasingly expert on the topic, so that even at advanced levels, new text related to the same topic becomes relatively easy to read.

Emphasis is placed on the following strategies:

- Recasting the text in the reader's own words: Students work in pairs to recast the text in their own words. The teacher monitors this activity to ensure that students comprehend appropriately.

- Explaining how ideas and sections of text cohere: As student pairs recast the text, they also track the network of ideas to understand how the text builds. The teacher monitors this activity.

- Developing Level III vocabulary as it relates to the overarching concept.

- Answering open-ended questions that require using text to justify answers: Level III vocabulary words are content specific. Because the texts are all clustered around an important topic from science or social studies, students must use the domain vocabulary.

- Developing an awareness of text structures: As students trace the network of ideas, the teacher guides them to recognize how the text is organized. This recognition allows a reader to anticipate how the text will develop.

- Creating graphic organizers to display the organization of ideas/concepts in text(s): Constructing a graphic organizer requires the reader to display visually the ideas put forth in the text. The teacher can check for appropriate comprehension by seeing if the graphic the students create represents the organization of the text.

- Discussing related ideas across texts.

- Writing to display understanding: Discussion and writing both require a reader to develop an expanded understanding of a text being read. These activities also encourage the students to make connections between texts.

Comparison of the Programs

The three programs described earlier—the IDEAS Model, ALSP, and Literacy Navigator—share many common features, though instructional tasks and routines vary in each case. First, all three programs incorporate current theories and research on comprehension processes and strategies of proven effectiveness. All of the programs are based on the premise that comprehension instruction should go hand in hand with building knowledge in a particular content area. Successful comprehension does not occur in isolation, but rather builds on and extends existing knowledge, for, as they say, "the more you know, the more you're gonna learn."

A coherent, well-structured progression of textual materials centered on an over-arching concept serves this goal and is especially well described in the Literacy Navigator program. All three programs similarly emphasize building a coherent textbase as a starting point for comprehending new text. As Fillmore's (2008) students, who are discussed at the start of the chapter, demonstrate so poignantly, students need to go beyond deciphering the meaning of individual sentences and consider the relationships between and among sentences, ideas, and larger segments of text. Understanding how texts are structured helps this process and supports the ability to follow the logic of a developing argument. A coherent textbase lays the foundation for deeper comprehension and often culminates in a written summary of the overall meaning, or gist, of a text. But true learning also depends on finding links beyond what is explicitly stated in the text: links to pieces of personal knowledge and links between different parts of the text or to outside reading or follow-up activities. Activities like essay writing, discussing, analyzing and critiquing other viewpoints, and defending one's own viewpoint all serve to embed the new material firmly in one's memory, thereby creating long-lasting and useful knowledge.

Overcoming Challenges

Teacher development is a key requirement for implementing knowledge-based literacy programs such as the three described above. Teacher manuals that accompany these programs provide guidelines for instruction. However, even when routines are spelled out in detail, as with Literacy Navigator, teachers who are not used to a more interactive, inquiry-based classroom need practice and coaching themselves to model effective strategy use and to guide the communal knowledge building. Teacher training should emphasize detailed understanding of the mental processes involved in comprehending written text and should provide sufficient opportunity for teachers to build a personal repertoire of routines, tasks, and instructional techniques that target different levels of processing.

In addition, we cannot stress enough the value of thorough and deep mastery of the content area of instruction. The educational model employed by many of our public schools fosters an underclass of marginally literate, average, and low average students with low rates of academic success that affect their ability to pursue more highly skilled occupations. Adopting literacy instruction throughout the curriculum, including all content area classes, from social sciences and history to the hard sciences (earth, biological, and physical sciences) and mathematics would go a long way toward helping more students become successful learners. This approach has been strongly recommended by studies such as those conducted by Bransford, Brown, and Cocking (2000), Biancarosa and Snow (2006), and Heller and Greenleaf (2007). As Heller and Greenleaf have noted, content classes provide a context for learning and practicing effective comprehension and writing skills, which in turn support better knowledge building, enabling struggling and average readers to be competent and confident learners.

Looking Ahead

We now know a lot about how to improve education for students at all grade levels and for struggling adolescent learners in particular. Psychological research has elucidated the processes underlying skilled reading. Educational research has translated theory into effective instructional practice in many instances, beyond the three examples discussed in this chapter. Observational evidence and some empirical findings strongly suggest that a coherent, knowledge-based approach to comprehension can be highly effective. Rather than teaching reading as a hierarchy of separate skills by using simplified basal readers, reading complex text should be treated as a problem-solving activity: Struggling readers are taught the strategies that skilled readers use to comprehend difficult text. They are provided with explicit tools and routines to help them get the meaning of a grade-level text and to integrate it fully with their own growing knowledge base. Instruction takes place in interactive, dialogue-based, "inquiry" settings. Making the transition from a traditional, didactic teaching model requires some time for professional development to help teachers or even entire schools redesign their instruction. However, the variety of tools and instructional supports described in these programs are easy to implement and pose few technological requirements. They function as scaffolds for teachers and learners alike and are fairly easy to adapt to other grade levels and texts.

Still missing is the broad-scale commitment to genuine, deep educational reform, despite the alarming statistics on our students' performance at the middle and upper grades. Commitment to reforming the educational delivery system must come at every level—politicians and policymakers, school administrators and curriculum specialists, parents, taxpayers, and especially classroom teachers must unite in the effort to replace a complacent business-as-usual approach with one that focuses on in-depth content instruction.

Until this broad-scale commitment to reform takes place, teachers must struggle to provide the best learning experiences possible for their students. One way to do this is to reconstruct the instructional materials they have at hand. First, however, we must accept the idea that there is no single program that in itself effectively teaches all students to comprehend (and surely we all know this to be true, because if such a program existed, we'd all be using it and there would be no struggling readers!). Given, then, that all programs have some inadequacies, classroom teachers should delete exercises that are ineffective and supplement the remaining materials with those that provide the kinds of instruction their students need. This is a kind of pruning and grafting process that teachers do all the time. Here, however, we are suggesting that teachers adapt their core reading program by grafting in a sequence of passages of increasing difficulty that share an overarching concept. These materials should be both engaging and challenging. And they should be informational rather than narrative.

Working with these materials, students should be taught how to form a text-base and construct a mental model. Conceptual information in the series of materials should provide the necessary background knowledge for students to be able to build an extended mental model. Creating graphic organizers, discussing the ideas in the materials they read, and writing about their new knowledge will make reading pleasurable and worthwhile for students, especially those like the students Fillmore (2008) describes, for whom reading is simply a functional activity that they have always struggled with.

EXTEND YOUR THINKING

■ Each program tackles the problem of deficient comprehension by first emphasizing text-based strategies—activities that help students construct a coherent and accurate understanding of the content of a text. Give examples of some of these text-based activities. Then use your own knowledge as well as examples from the programs discussed in this chapter to describe some activities that would serve to extend and enrich the text content and to embed it in a student's memory.

■ Which of the three instructional programs described in this chapter would best suit the grade level and needs of your particular students? Choose one of the programs and explain how it could be adapted to your own school and curriculum. What would be the main obstacles to implementation? Are they surmountable? How could they be addressed?

■ Design a topic unit to serve as a model for how to reconfigure your available text and other resources. Instruction, taking place over several weeks, should focus on a single overarching concept, with readings organized along a pathway of increasing difficulty.

REFERENCES

Biancarosa, G., & Snow, C.E. (2006). *Reading next—A vision for action and research in middle and high school literacy. A report to Carnegie Corporation of New York* (2nd ed.). Washington, DC: Alliance for Excellent Education.

Bransford, J.D., Brown, A.L., & Cocking R.R. (Eds.). (2000). *How people learn: Brain, mind, experience, and school.* Washington, DC: National Academy Press.

Caccamise, D., Franzke, M., Eckhoff, A., Kintsch, E., & Kintsch, W. (2007). Guided practice in technology-based summary writing. In D.S. McNamara (Ed.), *Reading comprehension strategies: Theories, interventions, and technologies* (pp. 375–396). Mahwah, NJ: Erlbaum.

Fillmore, L.W. (2008). *Expectations and diversity.* Unpublished manuscript.

Gomez, L.M., Herman, P., & Gomez, K. (2007, Winter). Integrating text in content-area classes: Better supports for teachers and students. *Voices in Urban Education, 14,* 22–29.

Hampton, S. (2007). *Literacy navigator.* Washington, DC: America's Choice, National Center on Education and the Economy.

CHAPTER 5

Vocabulary Instruction in the Secondary Classroom

Karen Bromley

KEY POINTS AND STRATEGIES
Visual Representations and Symbols
K-W-L Charts
Zooming In and Zooming Out
Interview a Word

> *"I'm always looking for ways to teach vocabulary without using the traditional method of students looking up words in the dictionary, the teacher going over the words, and then students forgetting them until a quiz is given."*
>
> —*Greg, social studies teacher, grades 9–12*

For many content area teachers, vocabulary instruction means assign, define, and test. Likewise, many teachers do not view vocabulary knowledge as a foundation for comprehension and learning. However, all students, especially struggling adolescent learners, need vocabulary instruction before, during, and after reading narrative, nonfiction, and electronic texts to comprehend and learn content material. This instruction needs to include the use of students' prior knowledge, the construction of new meaning, and active involvement of students with one another and the text. Without effective vocabulary instruction, struggling students may learn little, become disinterested, do poorly on tests, and ultimately disengage from school.

Rather than what typically occurs, there are sound instructional practices supported by theory and research that Greg, the teacher in the opening quote, and other content area teachers of adolescents can adopt to involve students actively in semantically focused, multidimensional, and socially interactive encounters with words. This chapter includes current theory and research on vocabulary teaching and identifies sound instructional practices for academic vocabulary instruction.

Adolescent Literacy, Field Tested: Effective Solutions for Every Classroom, edited by Sheri R. Parris, Douglas Fisher, and Kathy Headley. © 2009 by the International Reading Association.

Heller, R., & Greenleaf, C.L. (2007). *Literacy instruction in the content areas: Getting to the core o middle and high school improvement*. Washington, DC: Alliance for Excellent Education.

Herman, P., & Gomez, L.M. (2009). Taking guided learning theory to school: Reconciling the cogn tive, motivational, and social context of instruction. In S. Tobias & T.M. Duffy (Eds.), *Constructiv theory applied to instruction: Success or failure?* New York: Taylor & Francis.

Hirsch, E.D. (2006). *The knowledge deficit: Closing the shocking education gap for American childre* Boston: Houghton Mifflin.

Kintsch, W. (1998). *Comprehension: A paradigm for cognition*. New York: Cambridge University Pres

Torgesen, J.K., Houston, D.D., Rissman, L.M., Decker, S.M., Roberts, G., Vaughn, S., et al. (200° *Academic literacy instruction for adolescents: A guidance document from the Center on Instructic* Portsmouth, NH: RMC Research Corporation, Center on Instruction.

Vitale, M.R., & Romance, N.R. (2001). Implementing an in-depth expanded science model in elem tary schools: Multi-year findings, research issues, and policy implications. *International Journa Science Education, 23*(4), 373–404.

Vitale, M.R., & Romance, N.R. (2007). A knowledge-based framework for unifying content-area re ing comprehension and reading comprehension strategies. In D.S. McNamara (Ed.), *Read comprehension strategies: Theories, interventions, and technologies* (pp. 73–104). Mahwah, Erlbaum.

Wade-Stein, D., & Kintsch, E. (2004). Summary Street: Interactive computer support for w it *Cognition and Instruction, 22*(3), 333–362. doi:10.1207/s1532690xci2203_3

Rationale for Direct Instruction

The link between vocabulary and comprehension is strong. Vocabulary knowledge predicts comprehension consistently with positive correlations (Nagy & Scott, 2000; Pearson, Hiebert, & Kamil, 2007). Of course, a correlation means only that two things share components, not that one causes the other or vice versa. Little research exists to show that vocabulary knowledge enhances learning beyond the topic to which the vocabulary relates, thus, better global measures of comprehension than we now have may show this (Pearson et al., 2007). However, we know that without adequate vocabulary knowledge, students comprehend very little of what they read. Thus, direct instruction in best-practice strategies is critical for comprehension and learning.

Both theory and research conclude that the purpose of vocabulary instruction is to help students develop independence in word learning (Blachowicz & Fisher, 2002; Graves, 2006; Stahl & Fairbanks, 1986). It is critical that students make connections between what they know and what they are about to learn in order to become independent word learners. Thus, learning new words needs to be semantically focused (Graves, 2006; Greenwood, 2004). Repetition alone does not work as a word-learning strategy. When the focus is on semantics, or meaning, however, repetition is effective. Semantically focused vocabulary instruction links students' prior knowledge to new words, so new words stick and are personally relevant. When students make meaningful connections, the likelihood that they will remember the word and the concept for which it stands increases, thereby improving comprehension.

Evidence also supports the notion that word learning should be multidimensional. To acquire in-depth knowledge of a word, students need introductions to the different dimensions or characteristics of a word (Bromley, 2002; Juel & Deffes, 2004). For example, to know the word *retrospect* well, it helps to know its spoken dimension or pronunciation. In addition, knowing that the word has two parts and that each has a different meaning, *retro* (backward) and *spect* (to look or see), adds a semantic, or meaning, dimension. Recognizing the visual letters, or graphic dimension, increases the likelihood that students will spell the word correctly in writing. Seeing or hearing the word in a sentence that begins with "In retrospect, ..." lets students infer its grammatical dimension and realize it is a noun. In addition to teaching the linguistic dimensions of a word, using nonlinguistic dimensions, such as a visual, auditory, or other sensory images, improves learning (Paivio, 1990). Knowing the multiple dimensions of a word enhances the probability of learning the word and building independent word learning strategies (Baumann, Kame'enui, & Ash, 2003; Nagy & Scott, 2000).

Both theory and research conclude that learning is a social enterprise and interaction with others enhances learning (Vygotsky, 1986). Evidence also suggests that students who engage in socially interactive encounters with new words learn them better and have improved comprehension. When students participate in peer teaching, both the teacher and the learner experience learning gains (Harmon, 2002), and the classroom community becomes a place where students share in the learning process (Greenwood, Delquadri, & Hall, 1989). As you model for students a word learning strategy, such as using context clues, you show them how to develop their own ways to figure out unknown words they encounter as they read (Fisher, Frey, & Lapp, 2008). Additionally, when students share with others the ways they use context clues, they promote the metacognitive modeling and social interactions that build independent strategies. When students explain how they use context and understand the multiple dimensions of a word, this process can be as rich as or richer than some teacher explanations.

Instructional Practices That Work

Studies of teachers' beliefs about vocabulary, how it is taught, how students learn, and reviews of vocabulary theory and research suggest several challenges for content area teachers. Discussions of three of these challenges—flexibility, creativity, and engagement—follow, along with some best-practice instructional strategies that work with adolescent readers to develop semantically focused, multidimensional, and socially interactive encounters with new words.

Flexibility

Some teachers teach vocabulary before reading because they see vocabulary as helping students understand what they will read, not as contributing to better speaking or writing (Robb, 2000). These teachers limit vocabulary instruction to using new words in context and paraphrasing sentences that hold new words. However, important for students' successful word learning is a flexible teacher who knows which words are worth teaching, when to teach them, and how to involve students in learning them. Strategies to use include the following:

- Assess student knowledge and a word's importance before teaching it. Students may already know a new word, and you may not need to teach it. On the other hand, the new word may be unique and it may not appear again soon in anything students read (Nagy & Scott, 2000). Teach only words that represent critical concepts, are important to comprehension, and will likely appear repeatedly in students' reading, writing, and speaking.

- Vary *when* you teach new words. Sometimes it makes sense to teach a few keywords *before* reading that are critical to comprehension. However, sometimes it makes sense to meet new words *during* reading so students can practice word learning strategies independently. Then you can assess whether students' strategies work and, if necessary, teach new vocabulary *after* reading. In fact, it is often a good idea to spend time after reading to develop the multiple dimensions of a word.

- Let students identify the words they do not know and need to learn. You can do this by occasionally waiting to teach new words until after students have read the material. In this way, you let students use their own independent strategies for unlocking new words, and you may discover they know more and can do more than you or they suspected.

- Remember that "a picture is worth a thousand words." When you teach new vocabulary, attach a visual or sensory image to a word, because this greatly enhances remembering (Bromley, 2007). In a vocabulary notebook or dictionary, have students draw pictures to represent new words and include text with definitions or sentences (see Figure 5.1). When students keep a notebook like this, they can review entries to support correct spelling on reports and homework. Reinforcement and review is especially important for English-language learners (ELLs; August, Carlo, Dressler, & Snow, 2005).

- Model for students the metacognitive strategies you use to unlock new words. Think aloud about the way you understand a word's meaning and pronunciation. This provides a window into thought processes that students can imitate. For example, "I connect *neutron* to the word *nucleus*, which is at the center of the atom. Because it begins like '*new*,' I think of it as being small and having no charge." Ask students to share the vivid personal connections they make to understand new words. A student might say, "I know what *neutron* means because it's the same as *neutral* on the gear shift of my car."

Creativity

Many content manuals include instruction focused on definitions, with matching terms and fill-in-the-blank activities found in review sections (Harmon, Hedrick, & Fox, 2000). Often there are few suggestions for helping students work interactively to manipulate word meanings. However, teachers who vary their methods of teaching new vocabulary build student motivation for word learning that will help students learn content. Strategies to use include the following:

- Teach fewer words well rather than teach many words poorly. Tell students you are intentionally leaving some new words for them to figure out on their own. Challenge students to report to the class about how they unlock these words.

- Limit your teaching to 4–8 new words in one lesson that are critical for comprehension and teach the words in depth. Help students understand the multiple dimensions of words, both linguistic and nonlinguistic. Otherwise, too many new words can overwhelm struggling students and ELLs.

FIGURE 5.1
A Vocabulary Notebook With Pictures and Text

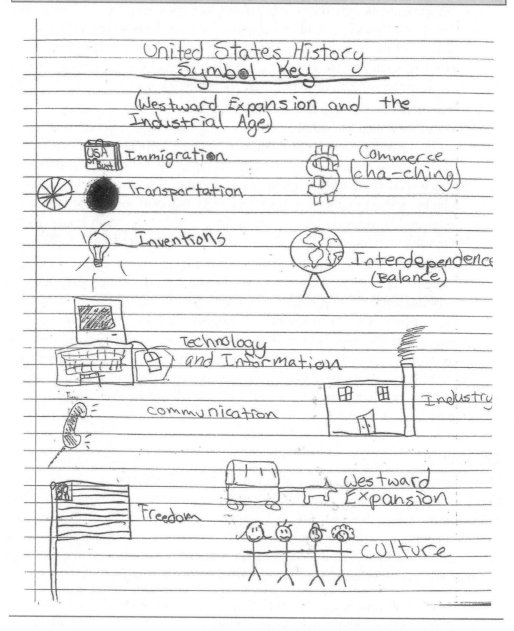

- Ask, rather than tell, students what you want them to learn. Activate prior knowledge with questions like "What do you already know about this word?" Stimulate metacognitive understanding of how students learn with questions like "What do you want to know to remember this word?" and "How did you learn that word?" Initially, use Ogle's (1989) K–W–L chart (know, want to know, learned) to transcribe responses until students can ask questions independently (see Figure 5.2).

- Start a "Word Wealth" program in your classroom. Each day have a student teach the class a new word. Let students choose the word they will teach, because choice builds interest and ownership. Have students choose a "spelling demon" that troubles them when they write or a content word from an upcoming chapter. Make it a 90-second teachable moment and add each word to a word wall you review at the end of class with students.

- Use strategies like Zooming In and Zooming Out to encourage in-depth word learning and build conceptual knowledge (Bromley, 2002; Harmon & Hedrick, 2000). "Zooming in" provides a microscopic look and "zooming out" gives a panoramic view of the word. Use zooming at different times to support comprehension of content material—before reading to activate prior knowledge, during reading to help students rely on context for meaning, or after reading to summarize and review information about a word, term, or person (see Figure 5.3 for directions and Figure 5.4 for a completed student example).

FIGURE 5.2
A Completed K–W–L Chart for the Vocabulary Word *Philanthropy*

K- Know	W- Want to Know	L- Learned
• Starts like "Phillip" • Also like "Philadelphia" (city of brotherly love) • Has "an" and "ant" • Has "thr" • Is a noun (person, place, or thing) • Maybe a thing because of the "y" that is like "photography"	• Does "phil" mean love? • How to say it? • Meaning? • Is "anthro" like "anthropology"? • Does "anthro" mean people?	• Means "love of people" • Like Bill Gates and the Gates Foundation that gives money to schools • Has 4 syllables

---

FIGURE 5.3
Directions for Creating a Zooming In and Zooming Out Organizer

1. Explain the purpose of the Zooming strategy and the *microscope* (close up) and *panoramic* (big picture) views of a word.
2. Show students a completed Zooming organizer for a word they know.
3. Choose a content area word or concept students already know.
4. Model the creation of the two parts of "Zooming Out" ("Similar to" and "Related to").
5. Encourage students to share ideas and help you decide on the "Zooming In" parts of the organizer.
6. Discuss the word with students and have them create the "Zooming Out" summary statement.
7. Have students work in small groups or pairs to create Zooming organizers for another content term with which they are familiar.
8. Encourage the use of texts and notebooks to help students.
9. Post completed organizers on a bulletin board for students to use as a reference in their writing.

Name _____ Date _____

Zooming In and Zooming Out

❖ ❖ ❖ ❖ ❖

Zooming Out...

6. Summary

Barack Obama is an inspiring speaker who will be the Democratic presidential candidate. He has gained enough support from Blacks & whites to unite the US & make changes!

3. Similar to:
- Jesse Jackson
- Jack Kennedy
- Martin Luther King

4. Related to:
- Michelle Obama
- George Bush
- Dick Cheney

1. Concept

Barack Obama

Zooming In...

2. Most important information:	**Least important information:**	**5. What** _Barack_ **might not tell us:**
• IL Senate - 4 yrs. • US Senate - 2 yrs • Democratic Presidential Candidate • Promises change • Inspiring speaker • He is mixed-race "brown" • He is calm, positive & a good listener	• Grew up in Hawaii • Raised by mother + grandmother • Moved to Chicago • Harvard Law School • Basketball player • Has 2 daughters • He's going to get a dog.	• Royalties he has made on his books • That he bowled a 37 on a campaign stop • He once thought Cher was "hot" • He admires Hillary C. • What goes on when the "O Team" meets • Likes Rev. Wright

Note. From Bromley, K. (2002). *Stretching students' vocabulary.* New York: Scholastic. Reprinted with permission.

Engagement

To gain complex, multifaceted knowledge of a word, students need meaningful and active experiences with the word. Providing multiple and varied opportunities to process words and construct meanings both alone and in interactions with others is critical to learning new words (Blachowicz & Fisher, 2002; Fisher & Frey, 2008). Active participation and linking the new to the known helps reinforce word meanings. Then students can personalize what they learn about a new word and begin to adopt strategies for independence. Strategies to use include the following:

- Have students work in pairs and take turns reading new material together. In addition to reading, have students take turns telling each other how they use prior knowledge, context clues, and word structure to unlock difficult words. This engages students actively in processing meanings, practicing pronunciation, and relating new words to other words they know. Pair a struggling student with a capable student but change pairings often so everyone works with a variety of learners.

- Help students develop the complex concepts that some words represent. When students participate in strategies like Interview a Word (Bromley, 2002), they take another perspective, think deeply about words, and work together to understand the multiple dimensions of a word. In this strategy, students "become" a word as they consider various aspects of a word's meaning, function, and relationship to other words. Then students answer questions asked by an interviewer, and the class guesses the word that is "interviewed." Use this strategy to review and summarize concepts after reading a chapter, unit, or book (see Figure 5.5 for directions and Figure 5.6 for a completed student example).

- Use the Divide and Conquer strategy with students (Rasinski, Padak, Newton, & Newton, 2008). Although this strategy is used with words having two prefixes, such as *reconstruction* (*re-* and *con-*), it is a novel way for students to think about all multisyllabic words. Because science is heavy with these words, knowing how to divide and conquer can improve comprehension and science learning. Often overlooked by teachers is the fact that students can infer as many as 60% of new words they meet by analyzing meanings of word parts (Nagy & Scott, 2000). So, help students analyze new words by looking at the meanings and derivations of word parts, and relate new words to similar words. It is especially important for struggling students and ELLs to know how to dissect words and learn the meanings of prefixes, roots, and suffixes. For example, in the word *transformer*, *trans-* means "to change," *form-* means "shape," and *-er* means "one who does something." Knowing these meanings, students can then connect this knowledge to meanings of other words, such as *transportation* and *transmission*.

FIGURE 5.5
Directions for Using the Interview a Word Strategy

1. Explain the purpose of the strategy, which involves taking the perspective of someone or something else.
2. Show students a completed interview sheet for a word they know and explain how the answers were chosen.
3. Choose several keywords from a chapter or unit students have read.
4. Create teams of 3–5 students depending on the number of key vocabulary words and class size.
5. Give each team a word and the interview questions, without revealing the words to the class. (Or put words on slips of paper and let teams choose a word.)
6. Have each team "become" their assigned word by taking its perspective as team members write answers to the questions.
7. Assemble the class and ask one team the interview questions. To involve everyone in the group, have team members take turns giving answers.
8. Ask the other teams to guess the word being interviewed. (The team that guesses correctly can go next or choose another team to go next.)
9. To broaden vocabulary and reinforce close but incorrect guesses, list all guessed words on the chalkboard and discuss differences in meanings from the target word. (Encourage students to add humor to the answers and use a dramatic interviewer's voice to make the strategy authentic).

- Be engaged and passionate about learning new words and share those feelings. Your curiosity and interest in words and language will be contagious (Bromley, 2007). Tell students that English grows and changes daily, and that each year the dictionaries drop unused words and add new ones, such as *sudoku*, *DVR*, *ginormous*, and *Bollywood* (Merriam-Webster, 2007). Adding new words depends on analyses of both print and nonprint media to determine which new terms or slang words appear often enough to warrant adding them to a dictionary. Have students find new words they feel might become part of a dictionary and post the words on a bulletin board.

Looking Ahead

Creating word-rich environments in every classroom can help all students become word wealthy. However, a schoolwide, focused commitment to vocabulary growth is also a powerful way to build students' lexicons and enrich content area learning. Students need repeated exposures to semantically focused, multidimensional, and socially interactive encounters with words to learn words well. Both teachers and administrators need to appreciate the role vocabulary plays in listening, speaking, reading comprehension, writing, thinking, and learning. Professional development is an important way to implement a thoughtful, schoolwide focus on best-practice vocabulary instruction. This professional development can include course work, membership in professional organizations, conferences,

Name _____ Date _____

Interview a Word

harlem Renaissance

1. Who are your relatives?

Black migration

2. Would you ever hurt anyone? Who? Why?

NO, because I am an African American cultural movement.

3. Are you useful? What is your purpose?

Yes, because I helped African-Americans to blend with other races as well as feel at home in the country.

4. What don't you like? Why?

The KKK because they wanted to eradicate African Americans in America.

5. What do you love? Why?

Art and artistic expression because I am an artistic movement.

6. What are your dreams?

To extend African-American culture throughout the country and be accepted.

Stretching Students' Vocabulary • Scholastic Professional Books • An explanation of how to use this reproducible appears on page 47.

122

Note. From Bromley, K. (2002). *Stretching students' vocabulary.* New York: Scholastic. Reprinted with permission.

workshops, seminars, action research groups, and study groups. Study groups that read relevant materials can improve classroom instruction and schoolwide practices when everyone in the school community works together. When teachers gain knowledge and experience using sound strategies such as those described in this chapter, they will be able to support students' word learning.

EXTEND YOUR THINKING

▓ What best-practice vocabulary strategies have you seen or used to promote social interaction among students? Is the interaction worth the time involved? Why or why not?

▓ What best-practice vocabulary strategies have you seen or used for independent word learning? Are they appropriate for every content area? What are the advantages and disadvantages of each? How might you adapt one for a specific content area?

▓ How would you set up a study group on best-practice vocabulary instruction and encourage all teachers and administrators to attend? What journal article(s) or professional book(s) would you suggest the group read? Why?

REFERENCES

August, D., Carlo, M., Dressler, C., & Snow, C. (2005). The critical role of vocabulary development for English language learners. *Learning Disabilities Research & Practice, 20*(1), 50–57. doi:10.1111/j.1540-5826.2005.00120.x

Baumann, J.F., Kame'enui, E.J., & Ash, G.E. (2003). Research on vocabulary instruction: Voltaire redux. In J. Flood, D. Lapp, J.R. Squire, & J.M. Jensen (Eds.), *Handbook of research on teaching the language arts* (pp. 752–785). Mahwah, NJ: Erlbaum.

Blachowicz, C.L.Z., & Fisher, P.J. (2002). *Teaching vocabulary in all classrooms* (2nd ed.). Upper Saddle River, NJ: Pearson.

Bromley, K. (2002). *Stretching students' vocabulary.* New York: Scholastic.

Bromley, K. (2007). Nine things every teacher should know about words and vocabulary instruction. *Journal of Adolescent & Adult Literacy, 50*(7), 528–537. doi:10.1598/JAAL.50.7.2

Fisher, D., & Frey, N. (2008). *Word wise and content rich: Five essential steps to teaching academic vocabulary.* Portsmouth, NH: Heinemann.

Fisher, D., Frey, N., & Lapp, D. (2008). Shared readings: Modeling comprehension, vocabulary, text structures, and text features for older readers. *The Reading Teacher, 61*(7), 548–556. doi:10.1598/RT.61.7.4

Graves, M. (2006). *The vocabulary book: Learning & instruction.* Newark, DE: International Reading Association.

Greenwood, C.R., Delquadri, J.C., & Hall, R.V. (1989). Longitudinal effects of classwide peer tutoring. *Journal of Educational Psychology, 81*(3), 371–383. doi:10.1037/0022-0663.81.3.371

Greenwood, S. (2004). Content matters: Building vocabulary and conceptual understanding in the subject areas. *Middle School Journal, 35*(3), 27–34.

Harmon, J.M. (2002). Teaching independent word learning strategies to struggling readers. *Journal of Adolescent & Adult Literacy, 45*(7), 606–615.

Harmon, J.M., & Hedrick, W.B. (2000). Zooming in and zooming out: Enhancing vocabulary and conceptual learning in social studies. *The Reading Teacher, 54*(2), 155–159.

Harmon, J.M., Hedrick, W.B., & Fox, E.A. (2000). A content analysis of vocabulary instruction in social studies textbooks for grades 4–8. *The Elementary School Journal, 100*(3), 253–271. doi:10.1086/499642

Juel, C., & Deffes, R. (2004). Making words stick. *Educational Leadership, 61*(6), 30–34.

Merriam-Webster's collegiate dictionary (11th ed.). (2007). Springfield, MA: Merriam-Webster.

Nagy, W.E., & Scott, J.A. (2000). Vocabulary processes. In M.L. Kamil, P.B. Mosenthal, P.D. Pearson, & R. Barr (Eds.), *Handbook of reading research* (Vol. 3, pp. 269–284). Mahwah, NJ: Erlbaum.

Ogle, D. (1989). The know, want to know, learn strategy. In K.D. Muth (Ed.). *Children's comprehension of text: Research into practice* (pp. 205–223). Newark, DE: International Reading Association.

Paivio, A. (1990). *Mental representations: A dual coding approach*. New York: Oxford University Press.

Pearson, P.D., Hiebert, E.H., & Kamil, M.L. (2007). Vocabulary Assessment: What we know and what we need to learn. *Reading Research Quarterly, 42*(2), 282–296. doi:10.1598/RRQ.42.2.4

Rasinski, T., Padak, N., Newton, R., & Newton, E. (2008). *Greek & Latin roots: Keys to building vocabulary*. Huntington Beach, CA: Shell Education.

Robb, L. (2000). *Teaching reading in middle school*. New York: Scholastic.

Stahl, S.A., & Fairbanks, M.M. (1986). The effects of vocabulary instruction: A model-based meta-analysis. *Review of Educational Research, 56*(1), 72–110.

Vygotsky, L.S. (1986). *Thought and language* (A. Kozulin, Trans.). Cambridge, MA: MIT Press. (Original work published 1934)

CHAPTER 6

Productive Group Work in Middle and High School Classrooms

Nancy Frey, Douglas Fisher, Aida Allen

KEY POINTS AND STRATEGIES

Five Principles for Cooperative Learning

Partner Talk

Reciprocal Teaching

Digital Collaborative Writing

Problem-Based Learning

> *"You know what they say: 'Two heads are better than one.' I might as well use his."*
>
> —Ben, age 15

Talk to nearly any secondary educator and he or she will speak eloquently about the way knowledge is built. He or she will recall the work of Vygotsky (1978), if not by name, then certainly through discussion of the zone of proximal development, which posits that a learner will accomplish more when given a bit of support, or scaffolding. In particular, he or she will note that learning is social—that it requires the interaction that comes from joint attention to a meaningful task. As Vygotsky (1978) wrote, "Every function in the child's cultural development appears twice: first, on the social level, and later, on the individual level; first, between people ... and then inside the child" (p. 57).

And yet, in too many middle and high school classrooms, students are expected to sit hour after hour, taking notes and answering the occasional question with little interaction with peers. Teachers, knowledgeable about their content and feeling the pressure to cover the standards that will be tested each spring, regress to the very practices they know are not effective. The social learning theories they studied in their preparation programs have been abandoned in favor of predominately lecture-based courses.

The fear, of course, is that the moment students are placed in any kind of group-work situation, chaos will ensue. Most teachers have good reason to be concerned, based on their own experiences as learners and as instructors. As

Adolescent Literacy, Field Tested: Effective Solutions for Every Classroom, edited by Sheri R. Parris, Douglas Fisher, and Kathy Headley. © 2009 by the International Reading Association.

learners, they have likely found themselves on the short end of the group-work stick—either given an unfair share of the work to do on everyone's behalf or crowded out of the process altogether while a Type-A personality took over. As teachers, they have seen the proverbial cocktail party occur when they have given a simple set of instructions to "turn to your partner and...." In the meantime, the principal is making notes about the noisy classroom. No wonder few middle and high school teachers want to go to the trouble of creating group assignments. Even in classrooms where teachers feels otherwise assured about their ability to manage the logistics of group work, there may be a hesitation to allow students to construct their own knowledge. After all, what if students don't learn what they are "supposed" to learn?

Truly productive group work should be about collaboratively building knowledge so that each member gains new understandings—what Scardamalia (2002) calls the "democratizing of knowledge" (p. 76). These are the skills that employers speak so highly of when describing the qualities they seek—the ability to work with others in ways that result in the successful resolution of problems for which there is no simple formula. In this chapter, we will discuss the conditions necessary for productive group work, the challenges of fostering more student responsibility, and our recommendations for future directions that will support adolescents' abilities to engage in these learning situations. We illustrate these principles by describing the teaching and learning practices Aida Allen (third author) uses in her ninth-grade earth science seminar.

Why Is Productive Group Work Essential for Learning?

The evidence on the effectiveness of collaborative group work is compelling, and it appears to positively affect the way students learn even when not with peers. Topping and Trickey (2007) followed up on high school students who had experienced one hour a week of collaborative inquiry over a 16-month period during middle school. They discovered that these students continued to outperform peers on a standardized measure of academic ability two years after the experience ended. In another study, middle school science students who wrestled with incomplete ideas reached new understandings when given the opportunity to figure them out with one another (Hogan, Nastasi, & Pressley, 1999). Interestingly, although they took longer to reach accurate conclusions than the teacher-directed groups, they benefited from the kind of persistence necessary for formal scientific thought.

Scardamalia (2002) found that constructing an interesting problem to draw learners together and allow them to build knowledge lies at the heart of productive group work. She also refers to the "collective cognitive responsibility" (p. 67) of high-functioning teams, like flight crews that require members to be experts at a specialized task but who are also able to take over for one another at a moment's notice. In particular, several conditions ensure that collective responsibility occurs:

- The work must be connected to real-world problems.
- The work must involve ideas that are improvable.
- The scope of work should not be overly prescriptive (groups find their own way).
- Group members should have shared responsibility for outcomes.
- The work should have embedded assessment that allows members to evaluate their own success. (Scardamalia, 2002, pp. 75–76)

These principles of knowledge building overlap with those described in the cooperative learning literature (Johnson, Johnson, & Holubec, 1993). Although many teachers first think of the social outcomes of cooperative learning, the research on the effectiveness of cooperative learning for content learning in secondary classrooms is persuasive (Slavin, 1996). There are five principles for an effective cooperative learning task (Johnson et al., 1993):

1. *Positive interdependence* of group members such that they need to rely on one another to solve the problem successfully—a sink-or-swim approach.

2. *Face-to-face interaction* to promote the personal investment group members have in one another, both academically and as people.

3. *Individual and group accountability* focused on goals and outcomes, so members are acknowledged for their individual contributions and their ability to be collectively responsible for the results.

4. *The teaching of interpersonal and small-group skills* to foster the social and academic skills needed to work together.

5. *Group processing* so members have opportunities to evaluate their products and determine how they might improve the ways they work together.

These principles of cooperative learning and the elements of knowledge building described by Scardamalia (2002) come together in the classroom through the use of effective instructional routines that foster productive group work. Although a full account of these practices is beyond the scope of this chapter, we have included the core instructional routines used in our classrooms every week. In the next section, we will describe how Aida Allen uses partner talk, reciprocal teaching, digital collaborative writing, and problem-based learning to build knowledge and academic learning in her ninth-grade earth science seminar course.

Instructional Practices That Work

The students enrolled in the earth science seminar have been learning about the natural resources and geology of their home state of California. This unit has proven to be particularly interesting because students get to use knowledge gained from their geography course to analyze topographical maps and assess for natural hazards such as earthquakes, landslides, and wildfires. The unit emphasizes the importance of water in the state and the need to conserve natural resources. In addition, students analyze the data of the state, including population demographics and density patterns as well as the relationship between natural resources and economics.

Ms. Allen's students are accustomed to collaborative learning in their class because she uses this as part of a gradual release of responsibility model of instruction (Fisher & Frey, 2008; see Chapter 16 of this book for more information). Her instruction includes many routines that foster the social and academic skills used for productive group work. Now, these things don't just magically occur when you bring a few kids together and tell them to work. It takes the same kind of careful planning as any other part of the lesson. In order for students to become adept at collaborative learning, they must be exposed to it on a regular basis.

Partner Talk

The basic unit of any collaborative learning experience is the exchange of information that occurs between two people. Although it may be tempting to dismiss the need to encourage adolescents to talk to one another any more than they already do, in truth most have had relatively little experience with doing this in the context of learning and knowledge building. There are two considerations in crafting useful partner talk occurrences: establishing procedures and designing meaningful questions.

Effective partner talk procedures include two elements—letting students know your time and noise level parameters. We find that using a timer that as an audible and visual signal is most useful. The one we like best is an overhead timer that projects onto the screen to display the amount of time remaining. After announcing the time limit, we set the device to count down to zero. The timer also buzzes, but we've noticed that our students keep an eye on the elapsed time to pace themselves. We also introduce the noise level expectations at the beginning of the year. Although students may roll their eyes at the sight of the noise meter (see Figure 6.1), we have found that it serves as a good reminder about what our expectations are for maintaining a voice level that doesn't interfere with the partner conversations occurring around them (Frey, 2007).

An effective procedure doesn't result in much learning if the task isn't designed well. The cognitive framework first proposed by Bloom (1956) is useful for thinking about good partner questions. Because we focus much of our productive group work on knowledge building, we find that application- and analysis-level questions are especially well suited for these short conversations.

Application-level question stems include the following:

- What would happen if …
- What would you have done …

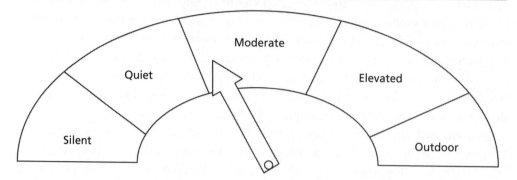

FIGURE 6.1
Noise Meter

Moderate

Quiet

Elevated

Silent

Outdoor

Silent—when we take a test
Quiet—when we read and work independently
Moderate—when we are working in partners
Elevated—when we are working in groups
Outdoor—not here!

Note. From Frey, N. (2007). *The effective teacher's guide: 50 ways for engaging students in learning* (2nd ed.). San Diego, CA: Academic Professional Development. Used with permission.

- If you were there, would you …
- How would you solve the problem …

Analysis-level question stems include the following:

- What would you have used …
- What other ways could …
- How are these things similar or different?
- What kind of person is … (Fisher & Frey, 2007, p. 44)

The easiest way to facilitate productive group work is to increase the amount of partner talk that occurs throughout each lesson. The goal in our classrooms is to provide a partner talk opportunity at least every 15–20 minutes. The combination of an effective instructional routine and an interesting question encourages students to think deeply about what they are learning while they are honing the social skills needed to exchange ideas with others. These routines pay off when using more formal instructional routines such as reciprocal teaching.

During an earth-science lesson, Ms. Allen posed several partner-talk questions to students. She shared information in the form of graphs on the differences between water availability and population size in northern and southern California, explaining that while one third of the state's population is in the north, almost two thirds of its water supply is there. Conversely, two thirds of the state's population reside in the south, but only one third of the water supply is there. She then asked students an analysis-level question and displayed it on the screen: "Talk to your science partner for the next three minutes about this question: Based on this information, what do you believe are the major problems in determining how and where water gets used in the state?" She then reminded them about the noise level, saying, "Don't forget to use a moderate voice so others can talk as well."

Students turned to one another to discuss the question. Ruth told Alexis (all student names are pseudonyms), "If I lived in the north, I'd be charging you a lot!" Alexis giggled, but then offered, "Yeah, but I have all the people. You know what that means—votes! I can make sure you don't get what you want unless you make a good deal with us. SoCal rules!" The girls debated for the next few minutes, building knowledge by consolidating information from this and other classes.

Reciprocal Teaching

We have as yet to encounter a secondary classroom where reciprocal teaching would not be useful. First developed by Annmarie Palincsar and Ann Brown in 1984, this instructional routine has been shown to be a powerful reading comprehension tool across grade levels (Rosenshine & Meister, 1994). Because every content area includes reading material necessary for concept development, reciprocal teaching can support comprehension for all students. This instructional routine is meant to foster comprehension through the use of four strategies: question generation, summarization, prediction, and clarification. In this regard, it is understood as a method for externalizing the processes a reader should use to understand text. A further strength of reciprocal teaching is that it fosters dialogue between students, so that they become more skilled at posing questions, requesting clarification, summarizing information within conversations, and making thoughtful predictions about what the author might disclose in upcoming passages.

Reciprocal teaching procedures can be complex for inexperienced students, so many teachers will build capacity by introducing and modeling one comprehension strategy at a time and coupling it with role assignments. Over time, these roles are absorbed into the overall dialogue, but they do serve the purpose of supporting novice users. Because it is early in the year, Ms. Allen's earth science reciprocal teaching groups are still driven by role assignments. After moving her class into groups of four heterogeneous partners, she asks them to choose their roles: questioner, clarifier, predictor, and summarizer. The students have practiced each of these roles in previous lessons and are growing more comfortable with the process. Ms. Allen explains to her students:

> We've been discussing natural disasters in California, mostly earthquakes. But there are other disasters that occur. I've got a newspaper article on the landslide in La Conchita in Ventura County a few years ago. Your groups are going to read and discuss the article.

Remember that it's not good enough that you get it. You need to make sure everyone in your group understands.

Ben, Ari, Andrew, and Sean quickly decide who'll be doing what and get down to the business of reading and discussing the article. Ben, the clarifier, asked what the word *slip* meant in the sentence "La Conchita is a slip of a town pressed between Highway 101 and a towering coastal bluff" (Wilson, 2005). "Does it have to do with sliding?" he asks.

"No, man, it means like a little...tiny town," says Andrew. "It's like an expression. It helps that it says 'pressed between Highway 101 and a towering coastal bluff.' That means it's squished. You know how tight PCH [Pacific Coast Highway] is to the shore."

Later in the same article, the boys talked about the connection between this disaster and the widespread effects of the storm in other parts of the region. Sean, serving as summarizer, pointed out that sinkholes, pipeline washouts, floods, school closings, and evacuations were mentioned at various points. "Even though the headline is about the landslide, the article's really about the damage the bad weather is causing all over the state."

Ari, the predictor for the group, offered, "I think the article will tell us more about the weather, since they said that this was part of the Pineapple Express... the bad weather from Hawaii."

Ms. Allen selected this reading not only because she wanted students to know about the La Conchita disaster, which claimed 10 lives and 36 houses, but also because she wanted them to make connections to their emerging knowledge of the topography of the state. The conversation the groups had helped many of them understand that this wasn't a situation unique to La Conchita, but rather a risk many Californians live with on the slopes of the state's mountains and bluffs.

Digital Collaborative Writing

With the rise of technologies, the practice of writing collaboratively has become infinitely easier. The best-known collaborative writing website is Wikipedia, the online encyclopedia visited by an estimated 683 million visitors annually (we learned this by reading the Wikipedia entry on Wikipedia on July 15, 2008). A version of Wikipedia, called Simple English Wikipedia, contains entries using the 2,000 or so most common words in English and is well-suited for younger readers, English-language learners, and anyone who benefits from more controlled vocabulary. Anyone can contribute information to existing entries or add new entries. Although Wikipedia does have its critics who argue that consensus but not necessarily accurate documents can result, many people have come to rely on it as a starting point for locating information. Wiki writing (*wiki* means "quickly" in the Hawaiian language) has drawn the interest of educators who are interested in finding new ways for students to jointly compose.

The purpose of collaborative writing is not the sequential editing that results when a paper is passed from one person to another, but rather that new knowledge is built from shared writing. Google Docs (docs.google.com) allows users to create a Word document on the Internet for use by other writers. Because one version of a developing paper or presentation exists in only one place, changes can be made and immediately seen by the other writers. In addition, there is a password protection system that ensures that only the writers, and not the entire digital world, can see the documents.

Collaborative writing can also occur within the discussion boards of course management systems such as Moodle, which is open source and free to any user. Discussion boards can be established by the classroom teacher to foster an online conversation about a topic or concept. Because students must be registered, they are not able to post comments anonymously, which reinforces the accountability for their work. The teacher determines the format and requirements, but a typical assignment is to reply to the question on an initial posting and then read the work of at least two other students and comment on their ideas.

During the unit of study on California's geology, Ms. Allen posted the following question for the students to consider: "After looking at the 'Keeping Water Resources Clean' website, think about ways in which the information you reviewed at this site will influence your own life. How does this alter your behavior or thinking?" Belinda wrote in her initial response,

> After reading the article I am more aware that small everyday things such as improper disposal and how they can cause major negative effects on the ocean. I am more aware that those everyday mistakes can be a leading cause to damage to the beach and the closing of the beach eventually. I am also more conscious as to what I personally can do to prevent eventual damage to out local beaches.

Charlotte replied to Belinda's post,

> I think there are many easy things that we could do to keep our water clean. One way is not polluting. When you pollute you expose everyone else in your community to the trash. Recycling is another big way we can keep our water clean. Many people throw bottles, and other plastic and aluminum objects into waterways. The bottles may get stuck in whales blow holes. I think protecting our environment is important if we want to keep it.

Maritza read both of these postings and replied,

> I agree with you on everything but we also have to keep our air clean.

Ms. Allen's purpose for fostering discussion-board conversations is to integrate the back-and-forth nature of digital communication with the academic language of formal thought. She wants her students to become fluent readers and writers who are accustomed to the synthesis, evaluation, explanation, and argumentation necessary in secondary writing. As well, she understands that this ability does not suddenly emerge when a term paper is assigned, but rather that student writers need lots of opportunities to read the writing of others, respond with their own ideas, and apply information accordingly.

Problem-Based Learning

Although problem-based learning (PBL) is typically thought of as emanating from the field of K–12 education, many are surprised to learn that it was originally designed as a method for increasing the learning of medical students who were faced with vast amounts of information to memorize, but little opportunity to apply it (Barrows & Tamblyn, 1980). It was quickly adopted by educators as a way of creating meaningful opportunities to build knowledge collaboratively. Once again, the principles of PBL dovetail easily with the guidelines for knowledge building and cooperative learning. An effective problem-based learning assignment should be structured such that (a) the students are responsible for their learning and the final product, (b) the task is deliberately ill-defined (hence, it is a problem), (c) it requires the full participation of all its members, (d) it reflects the type of problem seen outside the classroom, and (e) students are able to assess themselves (Barrows & Tamblyn, 1980). The following are examples of problem-based learning tasks:

- Developing a petition to change a local law or regulation
- Assigning a budget for the construction costs for a school addition
- Composing an editorial on an issue associated with alternative fuel sources

Ms. Allen introduces a problem-based task that students will use to coalesce and extend their understanding of issues related to the natural resources, geology, and economics of California they have been studying in this unit. Each group of four or five students will work as employees of a California county of their choice. They are to devise a plan for promoting the tourism and economic development opportunities for their county. Each group must research the demographic, topographical, and geological features of their area and complete an analysis of the county's potential in each of these areas. The students work with census data for population information, locate federal and state reports on watersheds, and evaluate the risks for a variety of natural and manmade hazards. They are also responsible for delivering a 10-minute PowerPoint presentation on their county to the other members of the class, and the presentation must include a trifold tourism brochure constructed using an online brochure tool (www.mybrochuremaker.com).

For example, Marco's group chose Imperial County and extolled the virtues of Mount Signal and Anza-Borrego Desert State Park in their brochure, but they also reported on the economic challenges facing this agricultural county as it competes for a diminishing water supply. The group noted in their economic report that the county's large area (4,600 square miles) and low population (142,000) presented social service agencies with unique challenges. The relative lack of population centers also made it difficult to attract large employers. They evaluated the natural resources of the county, describing the Quaternary sediments that make up most of the Colorado Desert (of which Imperial County is a part), and reported on the reopening of the Mesquite gold mine as a new source of economic development for the region. As a teacher, Ms. Allen was pleased to see that the groups had to consolidate information from a variety of content domains, including English and geography. The complexity of the task was such that the group needed the full involvement and expertise of each member. For instance, Derrick used his technology skills to lead the development of the PowerPoint presentation but needed the content from the other members to complete the task.

Overcoming Challenges

As we stated at the beginning of this chapter, there are challenges associated with implementing meaningful productive group work in middle and high school classes. The first is in introducing and reinforcing procedures and instructional routines that contribute to social and academic skills (Frey, 2007). It is not advisable to begin the school year with a large problem-based learning assignment, if for no other reason than you don't yet know enough about your students' skill levels to develop groups that will work well together. It is best to start with shorter and less complex tasks, such as partner talk, and observe the students' development. Within a few weeks, you will have a good sense of who might need additional support.

A second challenge is in the design process itself. Productive group work is more than just clumping students together. In order for it to be meaningful, there must be a knowledge-building component. Recall and recognition tasks are less engaging to adolescents, who relish the chance to ask, "When will we ever need this?" Well-designed collaborative learning can allow them to answer that question for themselves.

Looking Ahead

You probably have noticed that much of the productive group work described in this chapter relies on the availability of new technologies. There is little doubt that the sea change of digital communication and learning will continue to have an impact on our classrooms and in fact demand that we do things differently. Although it is not possible to predict the type of work our students will do as adults in the coming decades, we feel assured that the need for both face-to-face and virtual communication will be a common thread across professions. In the previous decade, the digital divide was characterized as the availability of hardware and software. As new technologies become integrated with our daily lives, we believe the digital divide will be about the relative ability to communicate effectively within and across groups. As the office cubicle disappears, will social networks take their place? We can't say, but whether it is leaning over a cubicle wall or managing a product team in another city, the value of working together productively will only increase.

EXTEND YOUR THINKING

▓ Complete a time sample of your classroom practices for a week to determine the average number of minutes per period when your students work together or discuss content. What patterns do you notice within and between periods? Establish a goal for increasing the time your students spend working collaboratively.

▓ What instructional routines and practices described in this chapter resonate with you? Are there some that would not be appropriate for your setting? What other methods not described here do you use?

▓ How do you evaluate productive group work? What assessment practices have you found to be the most useful?

REFERENCES

Barrows, H.S., & Tamblyn, R.M. (1980). *Problem-based learning: An approach to medical education.* New York: Springer.

Bloom, B.S. (Ed.). (1956). *Taxonomy of educational objectives, the classification of educational goals—Handbook I: Cognitive domain.* New York: McKay.

Fisher, D., & Frey, N. (2007). *Checking for understanding: Formative assessment techniques for your classroom.* Alexandria, VA: Association for Supervision and Curriculum Development.

Fisher, D., & Frey, N. (2008). *Better learning through structured teaching: A framework for the gradual release of responsibility.* Alexandria, VA: Association for Supervision and Curriculum Development.

Frey, N. (2007). *The effective teacher's guide: 50 ways for engaging students in learning* (2nd ed.). San Diego, CA: Academic Professional Development.

Hogan, K., Nastasi, B.K., & Pressley, M. (1999). Discourse patterns and collaborative scientific reasoning in peer and teacher-guided discussions. *Cognition and Instruction, 17*(4), 379–432. doi:10.1207/S1532690XCI1704_2

Johnson, D.W., Johnson, R.T., & Holubec, E.J. (1993). *Circles of learning: Cooperation in the classroom* (6th ed.). Edina, MN: Interaction.

Palincsar, A.S., & Brown, A.L. (1984). Reciprocal teaching of comprehension-fostering and comprehension-monitoring activities. *Cognition and Instruction, 1*(2), 117–175.

Rosenshine, B., & Meister, C. (1994). Reciprocal teaching: A review of the research. *Review of Educational Research, 64*(4), 479–530.

Scardamalia, M. (2002). Collective cognitive responsibility for the advancement of knowledge. In B. Smith (Ed.), *Liberal education in a knowledge society* (pp. 67–98). Chicago: Open Court.

Slavin, R.E. (1996). Cooperative learning in middle and secondary schools. *Clearing House, 69*(4), 200–204.

Topping, K.J., & Trickey, S. (2007). Collaborative philosophical inquiry for schoolchildren: Cognitive gains at 2-year follow-up. *British Journal of Educational Psychology, 77*(4), 787–796. doi:10.1348/000709907X193032

Vygotsky, L.S. (1978). *Mind in society: The development of higher psychological processes* (M. Cole, V. John-Steiner, S. Scribner, & E. Souberman, Eds. & Trans.). Cambridge, MA: Harvard University Press.

Wilson, J. (2005, January 10). Deadly landslide hits homes in stormy southern California. *San Diego Union-Tribune.* Retrieved July 15, 2008, from www.signonsandiego.com/news/state/20050110-1832-ca-californiastorm.html#

CHAPTER 7

New Literacies in the Secondary Classroom

Kelly Chandler-Olcott

KEY POINTS AND STRATEGIES

Blogging: Components, Conventions, and Criteria

Content-Specific Blogging

Digital Storytelling: Options and Methods

"I'd be removing my finger from their pulse [by not addressing new literacies].... I'd appear like a snail mail car salesman in a cyber-Jetson world."

—Caitlin, 10th-grade English teacher
(cited in Lewis & Chandler-Olcott, 2007)

The past 10 years have seen consensus emerge among scholars and educators about the importance of new literacies—ways of reading, writing, and communicating that are multimodal, multimedia, and often facilitated by digital technologies—in public and private life. Although research and journalism are illuminating this trend, teachers need look no further than the local mall to see its effects. During a recent shopping trip, I witnessed these new literacies:

- A 30-ish dad using his cell phone's camera to snap a picture of an item and sending it home to his wife's computer to ensure he was getting the right brand
- A teenage girl scrolling through her iPod to choose a playlist
- A 40-something woman in a business suit texting a message on her BlackBerry
- A preteen boy playing a video game on a handheld computer

As these examples show, new literacies are used by people of varying ages and profiles, although they have been particularly embraced by the generation of young people who grew up with the Internet, multimedia cell phones, and Xbox.

Adolescent Literacy, Field Tested: Effective Solutions for Every Classroom, edited by Sheri R. Parris, Douglas Fisher, and Kathy Headley. © 2009 by the International Reading Association.

The secondary classrooms where these youth go to learn each day have been slower to embrace new literacies than many workplaces and affinity groups (O'Brien & Bauer, 2005), but teachers have begun to recognize the potential of new literacies for classroom-based literacy learning (Kajder, 2007; S.M. Miller, 2007; Read, 2006, West, 2008; Witte, 2007). Teachers may not always be sure about their roles in such instruction, but they realize that addressing them in some way in the classroom has the potential to bridge students' often disparate worlds.

The purpose of this chapter is to describe what new literacies are and how they might be used to support adolescents' literacy development. More specifically, I do the following:

- Define new literacies and discuss how this construct has changed over time
- Provide extended examples of how two forms of new literacies—blogging and digital storytelling—can be implemented across the curriculum
- Consider typical challenges related to addressing new literacies in classrooms
- Suggest areas for future exploration around new literacies

Defining New Literacies

Early definitions of new literacies emphasized the role of information and communication technologies (ICTs), such as cellular telephones, personal computers, CD-ROMs, and especially the Internet, in shaping new forms of reading and writing. Take, for example, the following:

> The new literacies of the Internet and other ICTs include the skills, strategies, and dispositions necessary to successfully use and adapt to the rapidly changing information and communication technologies and contexts that continuously emerge in our world.... [They] allow us to use the Internet and other ICTs to identify important questions, locate information, critically evaluate the usefulness of that information, synthesize information to answer those questions, and then communicate the answers to others. (Leu, Kinzer, Coiro, & Cammack, 2004, n.p.)

This definition underscores the reciprocal relationships between changing technologies and emerging literacy practices, and it points out that new attitudes, not just new skills and strategies, are likely to be required by these changes. Recently, the term *Web 2.0* has been applied to new technologies such as blogs, podcasts, wikis, and videosharing sites that are more interactive and multimodal than those typically used when the Internet was first introduced to the public (Wilber, 2008). Although web searching and authorship remain important, this paradigm emphasizes collaboration and social relationships as driving forces for new literacies in addition to inquiry and communication.

Other scholars, such as Lankshear and Knobel (2003), acknowledge the presence of ICTs in many new literacies but broaden the term to include ways of creating meaning that are "comparatively new in chronological terms and/or that are (or will be) new to being recognized as literacies" (p. 25). In this view, technology-mediated practices such as podcasting and online gaming count as new literacies, but so does fanfiction, writing by fans that responds to or borrows from a media text. Although many fanfictions are shared and critiqued online, some are simply print-based. What makes the practice "new" is not the technology, but rather the assumption that popular culture is available for borrowing and the collaboration that arises from that assumption. Teachers who want to address new literacies must decide on their own definition of the term, as it will drive the instruction they design.

Instructional Practices That Work

Given limited space in this chapter as well as rapid changes in technology, I discuss just two new literacies here—blogging and digital storytelling—that I see as promising for classroom integration. Both have existed since the early 1990s, though neither has been widely adopted in schools. Both demonstrate aspects of what Wilber (2008) calls a Web 2.0 perspective, though I chose one (blogging) to highlight the centrality of interactivity to that concept and the other (digital storytelling) to illustrate the importance of multimodality. See Table 7.1 for current websites on these two topics.

Spotlight on Interactivity: Blogging

Read (2006) defines blogs, a shortened form of the term *web logs*, as "online journals—a series of archived Internet postings, some of which contain hypertext links to websites and other blogs" (p. 38). With entries typically in reverse chronological

TABLE 7.1
Helpful Websites for Exploring New Literacies

Topic	Websites
Blogging	• BlogScope: www.blogscope.net/ • Edublogs: www.edublogs.com • Technorati: www.technorati.com • Will Richardson's website: weblogg-ed.com/
Digital storytelling	• Center for Digital Storytelling: www.storycenter.org • DigiTales: The Art of Telling Digital Stories: www.digitales.us/ • Educational Uses of Digital Storytelling: www.coe.uh.edu/digitalstorytelling • Sara Kajder's website: www.bringingtheoutsidein.com

order, blogs vary in terms of their topic and their formality. They tend to be text-driven, although video blogs are becoming more common (see examples by news anchor Katie Couric at www.cbsnews.com and by a 12-year-old New Yorker at www.dylanverdi.com). Most blogs are personally authored, but they may also be produced by businesses or mass media companies. The majority of blogs by individuals reach a limited audience, but a few—for instance, the politically focused blog Daily Kos—have a national following. Media scholars contend that the blogosphere has an increasing influence on how people get and perceive their news (Tremayne, 2007). For this reason, teachers concerned with students' critical literacy skills must attend to blogs.

Moreover, blogs are a new literacy with which many students have out-of-school familiarity. Lenhart, Arafeh, Smith, and McGill (2008) recently found that 27% of teens keep an online journal or blog—a number increasing to 41% for girls aged 15 to 17. If you teach middle or high school students, you can expect that many will have read a blog, kept one, or both. At the same time, most students will not have had much, if any, experience formally analyzing blogging, nor are they likely to have blogged much about topics related to secondary curricula; preliminary studies suggest that youth mostly blog about personal experiences and popular media (Read, 2006).

I see three primary ways that we can promote adolescent literacy in schools by harnessing the considerable energy in contemporary culture around blogging: having students analyze patterns in blogs, modeling content-specific blogs, and asking students to blog.

Have Students Analyze Patterns in Existing Blogs. A few years ago, middle school English teacher Donna Mahar and I wrote an article arguing for genre study focused on digital texts such as webpages (Chandler-Olcott & Mahar, 2001). The questions we offered to guide this analysis were decidedly Web 1.0 in nature (for example, the questions assumed that the pages would not change much after construction), but the basic idea—that it can be fruitful to examine patterns in online communication—is just as relevant eight years hence. Blogs, because of their ubiquity and the range of topics on which they are written, are excellent for this sort of classroom inquiry.

To get started with critical analysis of blogs, ask students to select a topic of personal interest or one with content area connections (e.g., the U.S. Civil War in social studies) and use a search engine or a central blogging site to find a range of blogs on that topic. For example, when I used *New York Yankees*, my favorite baseball team, and *blog* as search terms, the first few results demonstrated differences in how blogs are authored, organized, and hosted:

- Pinstripe Alley, by multiple contributors, hosted by SB Nation, a network of more than 130 sports-related fan blogs

- Blogging the Bombers, by Mark Feinsand, a sportswriter for the New York *Daily News*, hosted by that newspaper
- Scott Proctor's Arm, by a 19-year-old fan and journalism student from Quinnipiac University, hosted by Blogger, Google's free service

Because blogs are meant to be read over time, students should select a few to track over two to four weeks. This way, they can see what topics are covered, how often these topics change, and how often readers comment. After students have had time to explore their blogs, invite them to talk or write in response to these questions:

- Components: What features did the blogs you investigated have? (e.g., they all have an "About" section)
- Conventions: What were the rules for contributing to those blogs? (e.g., links to commercial products are prohibited)
- Criteria: What makes blogs good? (e.g., the postings have a clear point of view)

As with most kinds of inquiry, I find it helpful to ask students to share in small groups prior to beginning a whole-class discussion. This provides more air time for individuals, encourages sharing of diverse perspectives, and helps students rehearse their ideas before expressing them in the more public, and often more intimidating, whole-class space.

Model a Content-Specific Blog. Many teachers now keep blogs about their classroom practice with other educators as their audience. Although this can support professional reflection, I am advocating a more curriculum-focused kind of teacher blog here. Many adolescents have little access to their teachers' ways of thinking and communicating within their disciplines. Teachers who keep and share content-specific blogs with students can provide windows to those ways of thinking.

Some of the best content-focused blogs I've seen belong to Darren Kuropatwa, a secondary mathematics teacher in Manitoba, Canada. His blogs include assignment reminders, sample problems with solutions, uploaded slides from lectures, summaries of student course evaluations, and even poems for graduating seniors. He also asks each student to serve as class scribe on a rotating basis, and their summaries are interspersed with his postings. More than just peripheral course supplements, Darren's blogs model a wide variety of mathematical genres.

In addition, teacher blogs can connect students to distant experts. For example, a science teacher might introduce students, at least in the virtual sense, to Clifford Johnson, a physics professor at the University of Southern California, who keeps a blog called Asymptotia. He explains that one of its purposes is to break down stereotypes associated with science:

> It is helpful to learn what scientists actually do in their jobs from day to day, and so I'll be telling you, as others do, a bit about what I do as a scientist. I hope that frequenting this or other blogs written by scientists you'll have several images with which to replace the usual cliches. (n.p.)

Teachers who link and respond to these portions of his site can help expand students' conception of the discipline as well as provide access to cutting-edge ideas about science—the kind not likely to make it into their textbooks. They can also use their own blog postings to provide explanatory commentary about difficult concepts or link to dictionary definitions for unfamiliar vocabulary. In this way, the blog becomes a responsive tool to mediate student understanding.

Ask Students to Blog. Perhaps the most obvious classroom application for blogging is to ask students to keep them, and many teachers are doing so (e.g., West, 2008; Witte, 2007). One impressive example on Elie Wiesel's Holocaust memoir, *Night*, has been collaboratively authored by high school students from New York and Michigan. As they read, students responded to prompts such as "What do you believe to be the most memorable passage in *Night*?" In one discussion, they posed questions about the Holocaust and Wiesel's life to a teacher fellow at the United States Holocaust Museum. In another discussion, they were provided with a link to an op-ed piece authored by Wiesel in *The New York Times* and asked to compare it to a specific section of *Night* before writing. As a whole, the blog supports Witte's (2007) claim that this form helps "prepare students to become citizens of a global society" (p. 96).

I suggest making the ground rules for blog participation explicit and revisiting these with students as needed. You should tell students how often they are expected to post, how long those postings should be, what kinds of language usage are acceptable (e.g., it's OK to use abbreviations and an informal tone but not to curse), and what your role will be in monitoring the discourse. Some teachers feel uncomfortable about censoring student contributions, while others intervene too much; I take my cues in this regard from bloggers in the public sphere, who typically make a statement about their responsibility as host of the blog to delete any offensive or off-topic responses but who also share their desire to do so on a very limited basis.

Although others might disagree, I think that blogging best serves adolescents' literacy development in school when it is focused on a curricular topic rather than being completely open-ended. Inexperienced writers may indeed improve their fluency by blogging about the details of their daily lives, but the benefits of such blogging are likely limited to just that. A blog that invites students to respond to a piece of literature, comment on daily news headlines, or critique an image from a new gallery show offers chances for students to personalize important concepts, use content area vocabulary in context, and explore differences in perspective. An overarching umbrella topic or open-ended prompts that change will also reduce boredom over time for both readers and writers.

From my perspective, it's fine and may even be desirable for school blogs and out-of-school blogs to represent different constructs to students. Such a distinction helps to prevent youth from feeling like their private pleasures have been simply imported into, and perhaps co-opted by, school. Not only does this give students clearer cues about what is appropriate to reveal in which context, but also it gives them practice in adjusting their tone for different audiences. Because blogs are interactive, they will get timely feedback from you and their peers on their success in this regard.

Spotlight on Multimodality: Digital Storytelling

From interactivity, let's turn to multimodality. Although blogs can and sometimes do incorporate other media beyond print, their message isn't usually dependent on the combination. In contrast, digital storytelling, my second example of a new literacy, relies on the relationships between and among image, text, and sound. Kajder (2007) defines digital storytelling as "the melding of human voice and personal narrative, using technologies only as tools that bring these elements together into one text" (p. 17). Pioneered by Joe Lambert and colleagues at the Center for Digital Storytelling (CDS), digital stories are typically between two and five minutes in length and combine written text with narrative voice-overs, music, still images, or video.

Lisa Miller (2007), a former journalist and current writing teacher, provides this rationale for teaching digital storytelling in secondary schools:

> We can't afford not to teach this kind of writing. Our students live in a world of digital storytelling.... They need to be visually literate ... so that they can look at a photograph that has a strong visceral kick and consider whether that photograph tells the whole story or only one side of the story. They need to be able to sort through the visuals and voices and text on the World Wide Web to find the stories they need and determine what is true. Moreover, if they're going to be active citizens of the world, they need to be able to tell their own stories using writing, visuals, and technology. (p. 174)

Studies of digital storytelling have revealed it to be motivating for students who have not traditionally been well served by school, partly because its use of multiple modes plays to their strengths and because it offers an interested audience for their work (Hull, 2003; Ranker, 2007).

Like these advocates, I see digital storytelling as a new literacy with enormous potential in today's society. I do not, however, believe that such storytelling is widely practiced, at least not to date, by youth outside of school. The required software (e.g., iMovie) may be available on many personal computers, but it seems safe to say that the percentage of youth who design multimedia texts with the precision characteristic of the best digital stories is significantly lower than the percentage of students who have blogged. For this reason, teachers have a key role to play in facilitating literacy learning with digital storytelling. Even when students are more adept than adults at manipulating images or downloading an audio file, most students will still need help organizing a storyboard, crediting their sources, and editing their narration for economy.

I see three ways that we can promote adolescent literacy in schools with digital storytelling: helping students tell their own stories, helping students tell class stories, and helping students tell other people's stories.

Help Students Tell Their Own Stories. Personal narratives are the most common kind of digital story, and they appear to be the easiest kind to tell, especially at first. Even the umbrella term *personal narrative*, however, reflects variety: the CDS website describes numerous subgenres, including those focusing on a key relationship, those about an important event or accomplishment, and those celebrating a special place. To generate ideas for digital stories, students can use the same kinds of tools—for example, a writer's notebook—that they use to generate ideas for print writing. Viewing multiple online exemplars will help them internalize, in ways that are difficult to replicate from exposure to print alone, what "size" story works best in two to five minutes.

One of my favorite personal narratives is "Breaking Free" by Griffin Kinnard, a young man who created his story in a Hunter College workshop for foster youth. His text (view it at the CDS website), combines still and video images of himself in his neighborhood with soft, subtle music playing in the background and the eloquent narration of such beautiful writing lines as "My family was two million miles from perfect." Because the story is just shy of three minutes long, it can be viewed multiple times, with students focusing on different elements each time and then finally considering how the elements work together to create a unified text. Not every student will face the personal challenges that Kinnard did, but his candor and reflectiveness demonstrate the power of the digital story in helping creators share whatever they learn from experience. I think you'll find that viewing and discussing a story like Kinnard's with young people will ignite interest in telling their own stories.

Help Students Tell Class Stories. Students can also tell stories about life and learning in their classes. Members working in small groups can take responsibility for specific tasks while providing feedback and support to one another in constructing a coherent text. One idea I find compelling is the creation of stories intended to orient students entering a class in subsequent years (e.g., "Getting Off to a Good Start in Ms. Gibson's Music Class"). Such stories help the authors synthesize and reflect on their learning, and they help make visible to new students the language, culture, and norms associated with success in a new subject area or grade.

Students can also create digital stories about discipline-specific processes, such as how to construct a proof in geometry or dissect a plant in biology. These creations stretch the label of "story" a bit—they are perhaps better described as expository text—but the combination of voiceover, soundtrack, and images will create interest in the topic as well as reinforce important content and skills for both the producers and viewers. If you pursue this option, you might have groups of students construct stories on the same topic, in which case they can compare their approach to others' and talk about the costs and benefits of particular strategies. Or, you might brainstorm different topics together as a class and then assign each group to address one, enriching the community's collective knowledge when they are publicly presented.

Digital stories can also be created in genres privileged in a particular subject area. For example, Suzanne Miller (2007) brought English teachers together for a summer class on digital storytelling where they made poetry videos of their own or published poetry, movie trailers to "advertise" short stories and novels, and news segments in the style of television newsmagazines. All three genres could be produced by adolescents (many of Miller's participants did ask their students to do so)—and each requires use of and metacognition about skills and strategies valued in English language arts. Relevant digital genres could be identified across the disciplines, including history narratives in the style of Ken Burns's popular documentaries or MTV-style videos for classical compositions in a general music class.

Help Students Tell Other People's Stories.

Students can also use digital storytelling to document others' experiences. In some cases, these stories might take the place of writing a conventional research paper. Art students, for instance, often research notable artists or movements in art history; the multimedia format of a digital story allows the incorporation of many visual texts in ways that a print document would not (see "Picasso: In His Own Words," a notable exemplar of this kind of story, at the University of Houston's website on educational uses of digital storytelling).

Students can also construct digital stories rooted in the community. After collecting oral histories from people who live in their neighborhoods, students might incorporate clips from these interviews in their stories or perform dramatic excerpts themselves from the transcripts. Either approach requires them to consider a perspective other than their own and to think about how the essence of that person's experience might be conveyed through more than just words. Community-based projects need not be limited to English and social studies classes, however. Students might use cameras or camcorders to capture images and footage related to local public art and architecture for a visual arts class or to document variables and patterns in everyday life for a middle school mathematics class. Such learning experiences will likely cause them to see both their communities and the curricular content from a new perspective.

Overcoming Challenges

Addressing new literacies such as blogging and digital storytelling in secondary classrooms presents a number of challenges. First, teachers may not know the technologies and thus may be fearful of integrating those tools with instruction. This is less of a concern with blogs because free blogging sites tend to have simple interfaces that will require little teacher support for most students. The multimedia packages used for digital storytelling do have a bit more of a learning curve and will require more experimentation to get a sense of their capabilities. That said, you can and should keep your initial digital storytelling projects simple, and many excellent tutorials exist online in addition to the help function within the software itself. Because a hallmark of new literacies is the ability to adapt to changing technologies and learn from them via exploration, teachers need to model this disposition themselves.

Another challenge may be limited or uneven access to equipment needed to facilitate these new literacies. You will need to decide whether you want students to pursue the bulk of their work in or out of class. If you require some work at home, not all students will have equal access to technology. If you have students pursue these projects during class, then you will likely be faced with the difficulty of reserving enough lab time, unless you are lucky enough to have classroom computers through which students can rotate. These issues should not dissuade you from beginning a project, but they will require you to think through your plans in advance. I suggest strategizing specifically about how to support students who might have less technology access at home, less experience using technology, or less developed writing skills.

A third challenge is students' potential tendency to reveal too much information about themselves. Both blogs and digital storytelling are designed to promote personal expression; at the same time, parents and administrators are understandably concerned about adolescents' privacy and safety. Witte (2007) reports that a blog between her middle schoolers and preservice teachers was shut down abruptly after an administrator felt that one student had provided identifying information about his neighborhood, despite writing under a pseudonym. Her experience points to the importance of setting clear guidelines for students about what is appropriate to share in a school-based blog or digital story and discussing ahead of time with various stakeholders how concerns might be addressed without sabotaging an entire project.

Looking Ahead

More and more teachers are writing about their experiences addressing new literacies in the classrooms, and I find their accounts, both on the Web and in the pages of our professional journals, to be inspiring and energizing. They demonstrate what is possible when adults take adolescents' perspectives seriously and work to align the world of school more closely with the other worlds their students inhabit. But we still know far too little about the impact this work has on adolescent literacy learners' attitudes and achievement. Much of the evidence we do have is better characterized as anecdotal rather than empirical. We need detailed case studies of how students of varying profiles respond to invitations to blog and create digital stories, we need interview and observational data about the instructional moves their teachers make to support meaning-making in these forms, and we need experimental studies that link those moves to student outcomes.

What's more, educators need to engage in conversation about definitions of new literacies and how these might change over time. What should we call a form of literacy, such as PowerPoint presentations, that is new to many K–12 teachers but has been used in business for a long time? How long does it take a literacy practice such as blogging to become "old," not new? If numerous teachers require students to construct digital stories, will those stories become the new five-paragraph essay to students—a rigid genre associated primarily with school—or will they become a familiar, comfortable way of representing complex ideas across contexts? Pondering questions like these will help us think about *why* to address new literacies in our teaching, not just *how* to do so, in ways that will serve our students well as they confront Web 3.0 practices—those we cannot imagine now—in their literate futures.

EXTEND YOUR THINKING

- Find an adolescent who uses a new literacy discussed here and ask him or her (a) what is most appealing about these practices and (b) what was easy and hard to learn about them. What do the student's responses suggest about integrating new literacies with your teaching?

- Select a new literacy and unpack it in terms of the skills it requires, using Table 7.2 as a guide. Given both sets of skills, what minilessons would benefit your students most?

TABLE 7.2 Literacy Skills Required for Blogging		
New Literacy	**"Old" Literacy Skills Required**	**"New" Literacy Skills Required**
Blogging	• How to construct an opening that orients and interests readers • How to credit material from a source • How to edit written text conventionally	• How to use comments to guide future postings • How to read postings in sequence • How to insert a link to a website • How to chunk text for on-screen reading

■ Brainstorm the ways "insiders" to your discipline read, write, and communicate, then identify those you see as new literacies. Which might help students learn content or processes valued in your discipline, and why?

REFERENCES

Chandler-Olcott, K., & Mahar, D. (2001, November). Considering genre in the digital literacy classroom. *Reading Online, 5*(4). Retrieved June 9, 2008, from www.readingonline.org/electronic/elec_index.asp?HREF=/electronic/chandler/index.html

Hull, G. (2004). At last: Youth culture and digital media: New literacies for new times. *Research in the Teaching of English, 38*(2), 229–233.

Kajder, S.B. (2006). *Bringing the outside in: Visual ways to engage reluctant readers.* Portland, ME: Stenhouse.

Lankshear, C., & Knobel, M. (2003). *New literacies: Changing knowledge and classroom learning.* Philadelphia: Open University Press.

Lenhart, A., Arafeh, S., Smith, A., & McGill, A.R. (2008). *Writing, technology and teens.* Washington, DC: Pew Internet and American Life Project. Retrieved June 9, 2008, from www.pewinternet.org/pdfs/PIP_Writing_Report_FINAL3.pdf

Leu, D.J., Jr., Kinzer, C.K., Coiro, J., & Cammack, D.W. (2004). Toward a theory of new literacies emerging from the Internet and other information and communication technologies. In R.B. Ruddell & N. Unrau (Eds.), *Theoretical models and processes of reading* (5th ed., pp. 1570–1613). Newark, DE: International Reading Association.

Lewis, E., & Chandler-Olcott, K. (2007, November). *Secondary English teachers' perspectives on incorporating new literacies into their pedagogy.* Paper presented at the annual meeting of the National Reading Conference, Austin, TX.

Miller, L. (2007). Space to imagine: Digital storytelling. In T. Newkirk & R. Kent (Eds.), *Teaching the neglected "R": Rethinking writing instruction in secondary classrooms* (pp. 172–185). Portsmouth, NH: Heinemann.

Miller, S.M. (2007). English teacher learning for new times: Digital video composing as multimodal literacy practice. *English Education, 40*(1), 61–83.

O'Brien, D.G., & Bauer, E.B. (2005). New literacies and the institution of old learning. *Reading Research Quarterly, 40*(1), 120–131. doi:10.1598/RRQ.40.1.7

Ranker, J. (2007). A new perspective on inquiry: A case study of digital video production. *English Journal, 70*(1), 77–82.

Read, S. (2006). Tapping into students' motivation: Lessons from young adolescents' blogs. *Voices From the Middle, 14*(2), 38–46.

Tremayne, M. (2007). *Blogging, citizenship, and the future of media.* New York: Routledge.

West, K.C. (2008). Weblogs and literary response: Socially situated identities and hybrid social languages in English class blogs. *Journal of Adolescent & Adult Literacy, 51*(7), 588–598. doi:10.1598/JAAL.51.7.6

Wilber, D.J. (2008). iLife: Understanding and connecting with the digital literacies of adolescents. In K.A. Hinchman & H. Sheridan-Thomas (Eds.), *Best practices in adolescent literacy instruction* (pp. 57–77). New York: Guilford.

Witte, S. (2007). "That's online writing, not boring school writing": Writing with blogs and the Talkback Project. *Journal of Adolescent & Adult Literacy, 51*(2), 92–96. doi:10.1598/JAAL.51.2.1

CHAPTER 8

Best Literacy Practices for Secondary English Language Arts Classrooms

Pamela Sissi Carroll, Rachel De Luise, Tiffany Howard

At the heart of [a Learning Society] is the commitment to a set of values and to a system of education that affords all members the opportunity to stretch their minds to full capacity, from early childhood through adulthood, learning more as the world itself changes. (A Nation at Risk, National Commission on Excellence in Education, 1983, p. 6)

Today's English language arts classrooms, like today's adolescents, are shaped by changes in the ways that literacy is defined and applied to teaching and learning. In the 19th and 20th centuries, teaching was clearly the job of adults, and learning was the task of students. Today, educators recognize that adolescents experiment with literacies in school, home, and community settings, among friends, family members, and even strangers. We know that what adolescents learn in their English language arts classes needs to be applicable and transferable to home and community settings. Today's secondary English language arts classes have moved away from the traditional tripod of instruction in language, composition, and literature to include attention to helping students become literate in the 21st century. "Reading" may involve the interpretation of graphic novels, "writing" can include sending enigmatic "tweets" to friends, and "language" instruction is likely to focus on the power of language and the languages of (social) power.

In their homes, adolescents generate and receive information from a variety of sources, including informational websites and social networks, text messages and "tweets" from friends, podcasts, print texts, visual advertisements, and radio broadcasts. Teens' familiarity with electronic gadgets, interactive television programs, communicative code, and Second Life participation often mark generational boundaries that separate them from adults and children. As participants in community life, adolescents need to be able to demonstrate clarity, precision, and propriety in spoken

Adolescent Literacy, Field Tested: Effective Solutions for Every Classroom, edited by Sheri R. Parris, Douglas Fisher, and Kathy Headley. © 2009 by the International Reading Association.

and written language, but they also must be able to navigate an increasingly complex territory of literacy demands from virtual and actual sources, sometimes making sense of symbol systems that they may not have been directly taught. These cultural and social changes in the ways that literacy is practiced have a profound influence on the role of the teacher in the 21st-century secondary English language arts class.

In February 2008, the National Council of Teachers of English (NCTE) Executive Committee adopted a definition of 21st-century literacies:

> Literacy has always been a collection of cultural and communicative practices shared among members of particular groups. As society and technology change, so does literacy ... the twenty-first century demands that a literate person possess a wide range of abilities and competencies, many literacies. These literacies—from reading online newspapers to participating in virtual classrooms—are multiple, dynamic, and malleable. As in the past, they are inextricably linked with particular histories, life possibilities and social trajectories of individuals and groups. Twenty-first century readers and writers need to
>
> • Develop proficiency with the tools of technology
> • Build relationships with others to pose and solve problems collaboratively and cross-culturally
> • Design and share information for global communities to meet a variety of purposes
> • Manage, analyze and synthesize multiple streams of simultaneous information
> • Create, critique, analyze, and evaluate multi-media texts
> • Attend to the ethical responsibilities required by these complex environments

Definitions and Practices

Relying on the NCTE (2008) concept of "multiple, dynamic" literacies that are necessary for navigation of the 21st century and terms we borrowed from Tatum (2006), we began to think about ways that teachers in secondary English classes need to address students' in-school and out-of-school literacy lives. In-school literacy demands are relatively easy to express and measure: primarily they include the ability to read and write with comprehension. These are the literacy skills that are measured on standardized tests and for which teachers and schools are most often held accountable in terms of student growth. They are also most closely associated with the literacies that we teachers typically focus on in lessons: formal instruction in vocabulary development, direct instruction in reading skills that distinguishes between implied and explicit meaning, and focused instruction on the intricacies of proper citation of research paper references in middle or high school language arts and English classes, for example.

The demands that adolescents face in terms of out-of-school literacy practices are much broader and more complex than those that we teachers typically zero in on as our territory within classrooms. The out-of-school literacies demand that adolescents develop the ability to use what O'Brien (2006) refers to as "multimediating," which means that they can "move seamlessly in and out of the real world and virtual worlds, rapidly and automatically using various technologies that they embrace as extensions of themselves" (p. 36). Outside of school, in homes and the community, adolescents are often the technological experts. They become quickly adept at taking advantage of social networking sites, enjoying electronic gaming, and locating information of all kinds. For adolescents, the information itself is almost a living and breathing organic creature, not the stuffy, moldy monster that we, as adults, had to dig for under layers of dust when we, too, were teens.

Overcoming Challenges

Yet adolescents' expertise with technology, their adroit ability to manipulate the technological communication tools of the 21st century, makes many of us uneasy, doesn't it? We are not used to acknowledging adolescents as experts. We tend to interpret their ease with text messaging and downloading songs and television shows on their iPods as insouciance instead of a kind of intelligence. We step away from their communications technology and reject the messages and the means as fads.

Secretly, isn't our resistance due, in part, to the fact that we don't yet know how to incorporate the tools and the products of adolescents' out-of-school worlds into our comfort zones—the in-school worlds in which we still hold power and set standards? Even when we rail against too many standardized tests, too many forms of accountability, too many impositions from administrators and others in positions of power above us, we are railing against recognizable foes. We feel comfortable making arguments against them, because they are familiar arguments, familiar battle lines. We continue to teach and evaluate learning in the same way as we have been taught to teach and evaluate learning: as though today's adolescents are receiving information and making meaning in the same ways as they did one, two, or more generations ago—as though they do not rely on visual messages, instant texting, and abbreviated language for their communication. We turn our backs, our eyes, and our ears to the truth: The differences are enormous between the in-school literacies that we privilege through our instruction, assessment, evaluation, and grading and the out-of-school literacies that we admit into our classrooms only during special projects or extra-credit assignments. These differences must be both recognized and reconciled if school is to continue to be relevant to adolescents' lives as learners.

What might a secondary English language arts classroom look like if a systematic concern for improving links between in-school and out-of-school literacies informed unit and lesson decisions? We envisioned an English classroom that might include nine-week units of film studies, with students as film creators and reviewers (in-school literacies of expository writing, critical thinking, research reading and writing, and synthesis of ideas, and out-of-school literacies including interpretation of popular culture within the larger social context, intertextual connections, and so on, would be possible areas of focus), or it might include units exploring the Web, with students as Web advertisement executives and critics (in-school literacies that focus on critical thinking and collaborative problem solving juxtaposed with out-of-school literacies including clear, direct communications with a variety of audiences would be possible). Other in-school and out-of-school possibilities that could be developed include units on cartoons, cartoonists, and cartoon reading—units in which graphic novels were read as the primary texts in a study of social satire.

But we began to wonder and ask ourselves: Where would we find a place within such a nontraditional, contemporary classroom to teach Shakespeare, the Brontë sisters, and Walt Whitman? Weren't experiences reading these texts—thick print volumes—responsible at least in part for our decisions to become teachers of English, and later, to become English teacher educators? We grew nervous as we reviewed the evidence of a mismatch between our own experiences as literacy learners in English classes of the past, what we knew about the demands of today's world, and the impact those demands have on today's adolescents. Today's classrooms simply cannot look, sound, or function like they did a generation ago.

Eventually, we discovered that we could, indeed, blend the traditions that brought us to the field with new literacies. Langer's (2002) longitudinal study, *Effective Literacy Instruction: Building Successful Reading and Writing Programs*, helped convince us that secondary English language arts instruction can reach across adolescents' school, home, and community lives to develop their literacy and to allow them to participate as members of society in the 21st century. The study reveals that, in schools across four states—New York, Florida, Texas, California—in which teachers were doing an excellent job of literacy instruction, the instructional characteristics that are constant are these three:

1. Separated instruction—This style is similar to direct instruction: A teacher tells the students rules, conventions, facts, vocabulary, and so on. The goal is covering the curriculum or highlighting a particular skill or item. During separated instruction, a teacher treats "a lesson, exercise, or drill apart in time from larger units of meaning or use," (Langer, 2002, p. 13). For example, a teacher might introduce the concept of appositives by providing students with a list of sentences, each of which has an appositive, as in this sentence: *Mark, the boy in the blue shirt, is older than the other players.* The students are asked to underline the appositive phrase. The lesson is a drill in which students practice their ability to recognize appositives when they see them in sentences. The sentences are not connected to any work of literature, student writing, or other literacy lesson.

2. Simulated instruction—This style involves the application of concepts and rules within a targeted unit of reading, writing, or oral language. The teacher uses self-made or prepackaged material, and the purpose is to practice

a skill or a concept of focus. It allows students to refer back to previously learned material. For example, that same student who learned to identify appositives might reinforce that skill in a lesson in which he or she is asked to identify instances in which an author uses appositives to add information that provides useful information to describe a key character in a story.

3. Integrated instruction—This style requires students to use their skills and knowledge "within the embedded context of a large and purposeful activity, such as writing a letter, report, poem, or play for a particular goal (not merely to practice the skill), or planning, researching, writing, and editing a class newspaper" (Langer, 2002, p. 14). The goal is completing the activity well, not just demonstrating knowledge of the skill itself. In other words, students need to demonstrate their ability to use the skill, not just their recognition of the skill or their ability to use it in isolation for the skill's sake. For example, to continue the example that began with the student learning to identify an appositive in a sentence, then learning to spot an author's purposeful use of an appositive phrase to add meaningful information about a character, the teacher might now ask the student to write a character sketch and include in it an effective appositive phrase, one that adds useful information about a main character. In this way, the information is being applied within the context of a meaningful activity.

The six major findings that Langer (2002) reports, based on analysis of five years of data related to the 25 schools and 44 teachers in her study, have further influenced our determination to bring attention to the distance between teachers' definitions of literacy and students' literacy practices:

1. In effective schools, learning and instruction related to English learning and high literacy involve all three approaches in balance (separated, simulated, and integrated); in typical schools, each approach might be used, but one dominates (pp. 14–16). This finding defies the common idea that there is no place in today's schools for separated instruction.

2. In effective schools, test preparation equals a focus on underlying knowledge and skills needed to do well in course work and life as well as on the test. This is not true in typical schools, where test preparation is synonymous with test practice and occurs during its own time in the curriculum, apart from the rest of the year's work and goals (pp. 17–23).

3. In effective schools, connections between knowledge and skills are made constantly across lessons, classes, and grades and across in-school and out-of-school applications. In typical schools, connections are often implicit or unspoken if they exist at all. More often, units are disconnected entities (pp. 23–28).

4. In effective schools, students are taught thinking strategies overtly. In typical schools, the focus is on content and skills, without attention to teaching students how to think, plan, organize, complete, or reflect on content (pp. 28–32).

5. In effective schools, English teachers move students beyond the original goals toward deeper understandings and toward helping students generate more ideas. In typical schools, once students exhibit understanding or skill knowledge, teachers move on to the next lesson (pp. 32–35).

6. In effective schools, English learning and high literacy are treated as social activities, with depth evolving through students' "interactions with present and imagined others" (p. 36), often mirroring out-of-school settings. In typical schools, students usually work alone or interact with the teacher or, if in groups, work together to answer a set of questions rather than to collaboratively engage in problem solving or sharing multiple perspectives (pp. 35–39).

Teaching and Evaluating Literacy in English and Language Arts Classrooms

What do Langer's (2002) findings mean for a group of teachers seeking insights about the impact of the evolution of literacy on in-school and out-of-school practices? Broadly speaking, her findings highlight the importance of connecting in-school literacies with out-of-school literacies. Langer's study demonstrates that we are on the right track when we seek ways to bring to the surface the intersection between the kinds of practices that traditionally have held significance in schools, such as separated instruction and discrete test preparation, and other kinds of instruction, such as simulated instruction, in which students are challenged to apply what they are learning to mock or even real situations, both in and beyond school settings. It also points to the need for teachers to consider carefully how today's students use visual, nonprint, and print texts when they engage in thinking and to explicitly incorporate adolescents' methods and materials into classroom lessons on critical thinking strategies that are designed to serve students who are multimediators.

Imagine, for a moment, the possibilities offered in the final finding describing a classroom in which interactions with "present and imagined others" are included in instruction. In this classroom, a teacher might ask students to write to a school administrator (a "present" other), if he or she wants to have them engage in a traditional writing assignment, but the teacher could also create an assignment in which students incorporate the use of podcasts, blogs, the Web, and social networks such as Facebook to interact with electronically present and imagined others as well, thus expanding the opportunities for their audience dramatically. The school assignment then takes on meaning in this intersection of in-school and out-of-school literacy practice. The barriers to this kind of innovation rest with teachers, not students: Instructional activities that include these technological applications are often reserved for students who finish their work early or for those who are engaged in special projects.

The goal of English language arts then, extends the definition of in-school literacy (the ability to read and write) and begins to link literacy to social and cultural connections. We argue that today's realities urge us to make connections between in-school and out-of-school literacies. When new literacies are added to the set of expectations that teachers of English take into our middle and high school classrooms, we draw on the traditional tripod of literature, composition, and language, and we enhance those with elements that we take directly from the lives of students—movies, music, computers, iPods and podcasts, blogs, and Facebook—the tools and the visual and print images that today's adolescents use to create and receive information, the input and output that they use to negotiate meaning as they make sense of their world. Have we created classrooms that encourage learning among adolescents by recognizing, valuing, and incorporating the tools through which they interact with the world—hardware including computers, iPods, and cell phones and software and communication aides such as movies, DVDs, computer games, webcasts, YouTube, and blogs? Do we evaluate their literacy growth in terms of their abilities in multimediating as well as the more traditional and easily isolated and graded skills of reading and writing? It is the integration of the elements from students' lives as curricular components, as new literacies, that will enhance the students' imaginations; relate to their own customs, ideas, and values; and encourage them to think critically and carefully about today's life, today's culture, their own lives, and about tomorrow as well.

Instructional Practices That Work

Finally, and perhaps most meaningfully, we considered various literacy instruction practices that teaching colleagues are implementing in classrooms where students are showing intense interest in learning. Here are some ways that teachers are meeting the challenge of bringing out-of-school literacies into the school setting, where they can be practiced, developed, and valued:

- Sergio's (all names are pseudonyms) ninth-grade students used the persuasive skills that they had learned during a writing activity and worked collaboratively to compose an essay in which they tried to persuade him that he needed a Facebook profile, and then helped him develop the profile. They became his first "friends" on the new site.

- Janine's middle school students collaborated with students at another school using the Web and text messaging. Each student took a role as a character in one of several young adult novels from a list of choices. He or she paired up with one or more partners at the other school who chose the same novel. Using the Web, the partners wrote back and forth as characters in the book would have written to each other. A few pairs were caught busily text messaging their partners at the other school during lunchtime—still in character. Jeanine had to admit that she was impressed by their lightning-fast fluency in the use of the abbreviated language of text messages, a dialect that seems to be generationally exclusive. She then developed a complete activity related to the study of a novel that involved text messaging, based on their enthusiasm for the technology.

- Rachel commented on the music that her adolescent students readily exchanged on their iPods and how they teach one another the intricacies of using those technologies with clarity, accuracy, and speed, but without formal instructions. She noted, too, that many of her seniors refer to the lyrics of songs when they respond to the themes and topics that catch their attention in the canonical texts that she has them read in advanced placement classes. This point suggests that they are making connections between the contemporary world of the music that they listen to and share and the world of traditional and even classic literature.

- Heather considered literacy issues from a language perspective. She found students were reluctant to use their own language in school, because they had been told in previous school situations that it was "incorrect" to speak using their home dialect. Students who used American Black English Vernacular (ABEV) and those who are English-language learners are often reluctant participants in literature lessons because they would rather abstain from discussions than have their speech corrected for "grammatical errors." The notion of dialectal patterns as differences to be studied and celebrated instead of as deficiencies to be corrected and condemned is one that is still not widely taught but is a new aspect of literacy in the 21st century that Heather is beginning to explore. She is using oral storytelling among secondary students as a vehicle for welcoming all students into her classroom discussions and conversations by allowing students to share digitally recorded stories in class podcasts.

- Jennifer's language concerns were slightly different. She wondered which language still applied to students who would be entering the work force of the early 21st century. Would they be expected to honor the standards that demand that if a sentence uses "everyone" or "somebody" followed by a pronoun, those pronouns must be the awkward use of a pair of singular pronouns ("he and she" or "him and her," and so on), or have the standards in the workplace become more relaxed than those reflected in the textbooks that teachers of English rely on in today's classrooms? This question raises for Jennifer, and all of us, a larger question regarding the fit or possible mismatch between what society accepts and what we teach as appropriate and correct in terms of language usage in the 21st century. A closely related question asks how popular media shapes acceptable and correct language and how long differences must exist before they are accepted. Her students became language detectives, collecting examples from television shows and advertising and bringing them in using a variety of formats ranging from video recordings to handwritten quotes.

- Tiffany was able to show her students how to tap into their potential as writers by having them write for a variety of audiences and purposes. One such writing situation included the production of a digital story, in which students wrote about a childhood memory, selected images to illustrate their memory, and produced digital movies of their stories. They presented the movies for one another, with popcorn, during class sessions that were highlights of the academic year for the students and the teacher.

- Brandi and Laura were both interested in branching out beyond traditional areas of literacy in the English language arts class to explore the place of film and video—from the perspective of both generating and actively viewing and critiquing film/video.

Looking Ahead

We have not yet analyzed the literacy gains, per se, of students who have completed class activities like those listed here—activities that are enhanced with new literacies familiar to students because they are important in students' out-of-school lives. But if student engagement is a predictor of student learning, then we are on the right track, because our students have been more attentive and involved in these lessons than in the previous "read, write, and turn your work in to the teacher" lessons that were more common. We will continue to explore the possibilities of incorporating new literacies with our teaching and learning.

As educators surrounded by adolescents who display the tools and talents of multimediating, we quickly realized, from our comfortable academic distance, what many of our adolescent students have learned too well through experience: the only separation between in-school and out-of-school literacy is one that exists in the minds of the teachers, not in the minds of adolescents. Yet it is the teachers who are the ones who broker the power of language and who enforce, as representatives of the adult world and society, what counts as the language of power. The lesson that many adolescent students learn, once in school, is that their most effective literacy practices, including their home dialects and languages as well as the technologies and practices that they use for communicating, are not valued inside the classroom. If they believe what they learn in school, these adolescents will become convinced that the literacy practices that work for them during their out-of-school lives—the text messaging, the YouTubing and podcasting, the abbreviated language use and visual meaning making—are useless or even irrelevant elements in classrooms. Students will assume that teachers, and perhaps, by extension, most adults, see electronic communication tools and nonprint media as toys, as distractions from the serious and carefully measured business of reading and writing as they have been practiced in American schools since the late 1600s. This lesson will be reinforced until the adolescents have classes with teachers who understand the value of incorporating iPods and webcasts, DVDs and social networking into lessons to promote literacy development.

Our next challenge is a huge one: the ways that we communicate will continue to change rapidly, and teachers will always be separated from adolescents by their generational barriers. However, teachers who will make positive differences in the lives of adolescent learners in the 21st century will rise to the challenge of learning to use the new tools of communication, to understand adolescents' ways of making sense of the world, and to continue to find the common ground that we share as humans. As a group of teachers, we are beginning to recognize our place in a field in which we always must be ready and willing to engage in the exciting activity of "learning more as the world itself changes" (National Commission on Excellence in Education, 1983, p. 6).

EXTEND YOUR THINKING

▦ Track the ways that you communicate with others for a designated portion of a day by recording each different interaction on a simple chart. List the time, purpose, format (e.g., text message, printed note, conversation), and length of each communication interaction. Rate your satisfaction level for each communication event from 1 to 5 using this scale: 1 = did nothing for me; 2 = slightly better than eating cold spinach; 3 = functional but not memorable; 4 = it was fun while it lasted; 5 = Wow! That really worked! Now, review your list and write a brief statement about what your chart and ratings might indicate about how you communicate. Think about how these ideas might apply to your teaching of adolescents in secondary English language arts classes.

▦ What are some ways that you might use contemporary communication tools to bring classic works of literature to life for secondary students in your English language arts classes?

▦ Composition, language, and literature compose the traditional tripod of the English language arts curriculum. What changes in the tripod are required by 21st century definitions of literacy? How do you feel about your role as a teacher (and as a learner!) in this newly conceptualized classroom?

REFERENCES

Langer, J.A. (2002). *Effective literacy instruction: Building successful reading and writing programs.* Urbana, IL: National Council of Teachers of English.

National Commission on Excellence in Education. (1983). *A nation at risk: The imperative for educational reform. A report to the nation and the secretary of education.* Washington, DC: U.S. Government Printing Office.

National Council of Teachers of English Executive Committee. (2008). *The NCTE definition of 21st-century literacies.* Retrieved August 7, 2008, from www.ncte.org/positions/statements/21stcentdefinition

O'Brien, D. (2006). Struggling adolescents' engagement in multimediating: Countering the institutional construction of incompetence. In D.E. Alvermann, K.A. Hinchman, D.W. Moore, S.F. Phelps, & D.R. Waff (Eds.), *Reconceptualizing the literacies in adolescents' lives* (2nd ed., pp. 29–46). Mahwah, NJ: Erlbaum.

Tatum, A.W. (2006). Adolescents' multiple identities and teacher professional development. In D.E. Alvermann, K.A. Hinchman, D.W. Moore, S.F. Phelps, & D.R. Waff (Eds.), *Reconceptualizing the literacies in adolescents' lives* (2nd ed., pp. 65–79). Mahwah, NJ: Erlbaum.

CHAPTER 9

Content Area Literacy in Mathematics and Science Classrooms

Roni Jo Draper, Daniel Siebert

"One of my main goals is to help create a science-literate citizenry. In a democracy, we are called upon to make science-related decisions ranging from health concerns to environmental issues, and it is important that decisions are made based on sound scientific evidence and not emotional gut reactions. To accomplish this, my curriculum focuses … [on] finding relevant credible information, analyzing this information, and making decisions based on [those] conclusions and [students'] own personal values. To me, this is the essence of scientific literacy."

—Sharon Miya, Middle School Science Teacher, Nebo School District

With the increasing importance of technology in society, more emphasis is being placed on science and mathematics learning. At the same time, educational leaders recognize that the scientific and mathematical knowledge needed to function as either a citizen or an expert in a technological area has changed. Now that calculators, computers, and access to the Internet are commonplace, there is no longer such a strong need for people to act as storehouses of facts or to be quick at complex computations. Instead,

Adolescent Literacy, Field Tested: Effective Solutions for Every Classroom, edited by Sheri R. Parris, Douglas Fisher, and Kathy Headley. © 2009 by the International Reading Association.

people need to be able to engage in the practices of science and mathematics. These include the ability to form hypotheses and test them, understand and critique scientific and mathematical results, build and use theories to organize experience and to model and make sense of the world, understand and compensate for the limitations of mathematical and scientific models, and flexibly apply scientific and mathematical processes to solve real-world problems. Although some factual knowledge and computational skill will still be necessary to successfully engage in these practices, it is the ability to participate in the practices of mathematics and science and not the factual knowledge or computational skills by themselves, which is of most value in our technological society.

Current reform movements in science and mathematics education are aimed at helping students become adept at the practices of science and mathematics. The *Inquiry and the National Science Education Standards* (National Research Council [NRC], 1996) call for the teaching of scientific inquiry and other general, unifying principles and processes in science. The *Principles and Standards for School Mathematics* (National Council of Teachers of Mathematics [NCTM], 2000) emphasize general processes necessary for doing mathematics, such as solving problems, reasoning and justifying, communicating ideas, and forming connections. Both of these important reform documents promote the vision of students engaging with the discipline as discipline experts—as scientists or mathematicians—rather than merely repositories of facts or skilled human calculators. They also identify general processes and visions for teaching these processes to help students become scientists and mathematicians.

Content area literacy instruction can complement and strengthen current reform efforts aimed at helping students become adept at doing science and mathematics. To achieve this goal, however, the literacy instruction must attend to more than just reading and writing texts about science and mathematics. If students are going to be able to engage in the practices of science and mathematics, they must become fluent in reading and writing the texts that are used in these fields while participating in these practices. The texts that are used to do science and mathematics are often highly specialized, so it is unlikely that students will know how to read and write these texts without help. Thus, if science and mathematics teachers hope to enable their students to engage in the practices of science and mathematics, they will need to provide literacy instruction to help their students read and write the texts that are used while participating in these practices. Content area literacy instruction is both a complementary and necessary component of good science and mathematics instruction.

In this chapter, we discuss four general instructional principles aimed at helping students become literate in the texts used in the practices of science and mathematics. Rather than focus on specific instructional strategies that may have limited application, we have selected general instructional principles that are applicable to most, if not all, instances of science and mathematics teaching. We also discuss problems teachers might face as they attempt to implement these instructional principles. Lastly, we present some issues that we think are important for educators to consider and address in the future.

Instructional Principles That Work

Engage Students in Inquiry and Problem Solving

In order for students to learn how to become literate with the texts used in mathematics and science, it is first necessary to make sure that mathematical and scientific practices are occurring in the classroom. Research has shown that literacy skills and strategies learned separately from the context in which they are to be used generally do not transfer well (Alvermann, 2002). Consequently, literacy instruction that is focused on developing fluency with the texts that are written and read while doing science and mathematics is not likely to be successful unless that instruction occurs within the context of having students do science and mathematics.

Students in science classrooms can engage in the practices of doing science by participating in the process of inquiry. Note the many different scientific practices that are included in the definition of inquiry given in *Inquiry and the National Science Education Standards* (NRC, 1996):

> Inquiry is a multifaceted activity that involves making observations; posing questions; examining books and other sources of information to see what is already known; planning investigations; reviewing what is already known in light of experimental evidence; using tools to gather, analyze, and interpret data; proposing answers, explanations, and predictions; and communicating the results. Inquiry requires identification of assumptions, use of critical and logical thinking, and consideration of alternative explanations. Students will engage in selected aspects of inquiry as they learn the scientific way of knowing the natural world, but they also should develop the capacity to conduct complete inquiries. (p. 23)

For science teachers, inquiry is not just a method for helping students learn scientific concepts and understand the nature of science but also a means for teaching students how to engage in the practices of doing science.

In mathematics classrooms, teachers often engage their students in problem solving so they can participate in the practices of doing mathematics. Students start with tasks for which they do not already have a well-established solution method. These tasks may involve a problem situated in either a real-world setting or a purely mathematical context. For example, when students begin learning about division of fractions, rather than memorizing and practicing the procedure for dividing fractions, they might instead start with a task that involves division of fractions, such as finding how many bows can be made from 1½ yards of ribbon if each bow takes ¼ yard to make, a real world context for 1½ ÷ ¼. Because this problem is given before students have a ready-made solution for dividing fractions, it requires students to engage in problem solving. Working individually or in small groups, students develop solutions to the problem. They share these solutions in whole-class discussions where they attempt to understand one another's solution methods. They also discuss the correctness, uniqueness, efficiency, generality, and elegance of the different solutions. As part of the problem-solving process, they make connections to other mathematical ideas, create and critique representations, communicate ideas, generate and test hypotheses, and develop justifications. Through participation in problem solving, mathematics students are able to engage in the practices of doing mathematics.

For science and mathematics teachers, the instructional principles of engaging students in inquiry and problem solving are key to providing good content area instruction, which is why science and mathematics teachers attend to this instructional principle in their teaching. However, inquiry and problem solving are also a crucial part of good literacy instruction in science and mathematics classes. When students are engaged in the processes of inquiry and problem solving, they are participating in the practices of doing science and mathematics, respectively. Consequently, they are necessarily reading and writing the texts, such as graphs, explanations, hypotheses, and mathematical expressions that naturally arise in the context of engaging in these practices. These are the very texts that literacy instruction must focus on to prepare students to function as citizens and experts in a technological society. This makes the contexts of inquiry and problem solving ideal for content area literacy instruction in science and mathematics.

Promote Sense Making

A second important principle for literacy instruction in science and mathematics is that it should focus on understanding and sense making. Current reforms in both disciplines reject instruction that promotes rote memorization of facts and procedures. Although knowing information and being able to perform certain procedures still have value in both subject areas, the goal in science and mathematics is that students will learn these facts and procedures with understanding. In other words, they will know why the facts and procedures are correct, when they are applicable, and how they relate to other facts and procedures (NCTM, 2000; NRC, 1996). For example, a student who is learning to measure mass in a science lab needs to connect this procedure to other essential ideas, such as significant digits and their importance, the unavoidable presence of measurement error, and the limitations of theoretical models in predicting real-world phenomena. It is this type of knowledge that is of the most use and has the largest chance of being applied outside the classroom.

Understanding is always a result of sense-making activities. Learners interpret what they hear and see based upon their prior experience. Thus knowledge, no matter how carefully it is conveyed, cannot be transferred directly from teacher to student; whatever object, utterance, or motion the teacher creates to communicate the knowledge must be interpreted by learners (von Glasersfeld, 1995). For example, a teacher might tell students that an object that is tied to a string and swung around in a circle would move in a direction tangent to the circle if the string suddenly broke. The teacher might even explain the theory for why this is the case. Nevertheless, the students might continue to believe that the object would move in a circular direction if the string broke unless they have the opportunity to make this belief explicit, design a way of testing the belief, collect data, and come to see that the data contradicts this belief. For students to develop deep understanding, they must be provided with the richest opportunities for sense making. Teachers who wish to have their students develop understanding provide their students with many opportunities to form ideas, reflect, make thinking explicit, and test the understandings they have formed. Inquiry and problem solving are ideal activities in which to do this type of sense-making work.

Educators who wish to incorporate literacy instruction and science and mathematics classrooms must promote understanding and sense making for two reasons. First, as noted earlier, understanding and sense making are important in the disciplines of science and mathematics. If literacy instruction does not foster understanding and sense making, particularly the kind valued in these disciplines, it will likely be viewed as antithetical to the goals of good science and mathematics instruction, and thus be rejected by science and mathematics teachers. Second, and perhaps even more important, is that understanding and sense making are a vital part of any literacy activity. In fact, one cannot be said to be literate unless one understands and is making sense of what is being read and written. By emphasizing understanding and sense making, literacy educators can both win the cooperation of science and mathematics teachers and further support science and mathematics students' reading and writing of the texts found in their disciplines.

With that said, it is important to note that a literacy specialist who is working with a science or mathematics teacher must be careful with his or her recommendations when attempting to foster understanding and sense making. This is because literacy specialists often lack the background to know what concepts are important in these disciplines, how different concepts and procedures are related, and what type of sense students should be making of different concepts and procedures. For example, literacy specialists may not know that there are two different ways of modeling division and that each model leads to a distinct way of conceptualizing the slope of a line. Rather than trying to dictate to science and mathematics teachers the things that their students should be understanding, literacy specialists should try prompting these teachers to consider what they want their students to understand. Asking teachers why a particular concept or procedure is important, to what other concepts or procedures it is related, how they want their students to be able to use the concept or procedure, and how they plan to help their students develop these understandings of the concept or procedure are just some of the useful ways that literacy specialists can help science and mathematics teachers reflect on their teaching.

Address All Texts

Traditionally, when literacy educators have discussed literacy they have described meaning-making activities associated with traditional print texts consisting of words and paragraphs. If science and mathematics teachers define texts narrowly, they will erroneously believe that the only literacy instruction they need provide will be in conjunction with textbooks and word problems. Furthermore, they may believe that learning how to decode these traditional print texts should simply be the responsibility of English or language arts teachers.

Recently, literacy educators have embraced a broader notion of text to include nonprint sources such as conversations, film, theatrical performances, graphs, charts, photographs, and models (Neilsen, 1998; Wade & Moje, 2000). Therefore, graduated cylinders, manipulatives, diagrams, charts, equations, proofs, explanations, discussions, various forms of electronic media, and other objects central to scientific and mathematics activities must be considered as texts. Indeed, texts include anything that people imbue with meaning and then use to represent and communicate ideas. For example, learners in a mathematics classroom might arrange algebra tiles or other manipulatives in such a way as to represent the result of squaring an algebraic binomial. In this instance, the students have imbued the tiles with mathematical meaning, and others can *read* the arrangement of the tiles and understand the meaning the tiles represent. Thus, the algebraic tiles are an important mathematics text used to reason and communicate mathematics.

However, students in mathematics and science classrooms are not going to be able to effectively use these texts simply because they have seen them used. Instead, because mathematical and scientific texts consist of a range of sign systems with which adolescents may be unfamiliar, they must be provided instruction that helps them meaningfully negotiate and create such texts. For example, consider the text $f(x) = x^2$. This text must be decoded, and to be comprehended, the reader of the text must be familiar with the mathematical ideas represented by the symbols. This instruction is best provided by a mathematics teacher who understands both how this text works and the content this text represents. Similarly, a student in a science classroom will likely need assistance to successfully negotiate the periodic table of elements. Indeed, to effectively use this text, readers must understand the abbreviations used to denote the various elements and that the color of the print and even the location or placement of the symbol on the table denotes particular meanings.

Adopting a broadened definition of text requires a rethinking of literacy and literacy instruction. Rather than define literacy as simply the ability to read and write print texts, literacy must be conceptualized as the ability to meaningfully use and create a range of texts. Thus, literacy instruction must include supporting students as they learn to negotiate, create, and critique a wide variety of texts. In mathematics and science classrooms, this means that students must have access to the full range of mathematics and science texts. However, access alone is not sufficient to enable students to become competent text users. Mathematics and science teachers must also provide instruction that allows learners to meaningfully use and create the texts central to the disciplines.

In mathematics and science classrooms, literacy instruction will support learners as they become proficient with a variety of mathematical and scientific texts. For example, learners in mathematics and science classrooms will certainly need help creating tables of data and converting those tables to graphs. Without explicit instruction, learners may erroneously believe that values are placed arbitrarily along either the horizontal or vertical axes of a graph. Moreover, they may not realize that different types of graphs are more appropriate for different kinds of data. Indeed, without instruction, students may believe that a particular set of data can be just as appropriately represented by a line graph as a bar graph.

Unfortunately, although a handful of educators have begun investigating the literacies associated with scientific and mathematical texts (e.g., Draper & Siebert, 2004; Hand, Prain, Lawrence, & Yore, 1999; Lemke, 2004), specific literacy instructional practices for supporting students' ability to negotiate and create mathematical and scientific texts have not been developed. Therefore, teachers must design instruction that supports learners' abilities to use the full range of texts that are found in mathematics and science classrooms. As previously discussed, adopting a problem-solving or inquiry approach to classroom instruction will introduce a range of texts that are like the texts used and created by mathematicians and scientists. In addition, teachers must take time to recognize that students will have to be taught how to negotiate, create, and critique these texts.

Support Explanation and Justification

Attending to a range of texts in mathematics and science classrooms will include print texts. However, these print texts must also conform to disciplinary conventions established for print mathematics and science texts. For example, science print texts created by students to explain scientific phenomena must consist of argumentation and justification (Hand et al., 1999). Without argumentation and justification grounded in scientific evidence, print texts in science classrooms run the risk of consisting of mere descriptions or chronologies of phenomena or processes. Although this difference may seem minor, the difference is significant if students are going to be prepared to meaningfully interact with scientific texts. Similarly, in mathematics classrooms, students may be asked to create print texts that consist of explanations of the mathematics they are learning. It is important that these explanations consist of more than mere descriptions of the steps involved in computations. Instead, the explanations must include reasons particular computations were made. Indeed, students in mathematics classrooms must realize that their explanations must answer the question: "Why does that work?" Furthermore, their justifications and refutations must be based on evidence other than, "Because my sister told me" (NCTM, 2000).

Consider the following writing prompt: Explain how to find the midpoint of a line segment with a compass and a ruler. This prompt, as written, will likely result in a written description of the steps one might follow to bisect a line segment. In their enthusiasm to support literacy in mathematics classrooms, mathematics teachers (and literacy specialists) may be satisfied with the prompt and the response. However, on closer inspection, this response would not be consistent with the kinds of explanations created by mathematicians, because it merely lists steps without providing a justification for each step or an explanation as to why each step is mathematically sound. To solicit explanations that include justifications, mathematics teachers must be mindful of the writing prompts they create. For example, students are more likely to write a response that includes justification for the following writing prompt: Describe the steps involved in finding the midpoint of a line segment and explain why each step works.

Using writing prompts that solicit mathematical and science explanations that include arguments and justification is a fine start. However, writing prompts in and of themselves may be insufficient to ensure that students write explanations that are consistent with disciplinary norms. Instead, mathematics and science teachers must provide instruction that assists students in learning how to write good explanations. This instruction will likely mirror good writing instruction. First, teachers should share models of and the criteria for good explanations. This will require teachers to be clear on the requirements for writing good explanations. The models and criteria could be followed up with opportunities for students to read one another's explanations and offer advice on how the author could improve the explanation to meet the standards for good explanations. Finally, students should be given opportunities to revise their writing to create polished scientific and mathematical arguments.

A beneficial outcome of this kind of writing instruction would be improved reading competence. While students learn to create scientific and mathematical argument and as they read and critique the written explanations of their peers, they learn to question the explanations created by others. Indeed, students must be taught to ask questions such as Has the author provided proper evidence and justification? And this begins with giving opportunities to ask such questions of student authors. Once students have had experience bringing these questions to the writing of their peers, they should be taught to bring these questions to other print texts—even the print texts they may encounter in textbooks.

Overcoming Challenges

There are two main challenges that educators face in facilitating students' fluency with the texts that naturally occur during the practices of doing science and mathematics. The first is overcoming students' expectations about what they should be doing in science and mathematics classrooms. In particular, students expect a teacher-delivered curriculum focusing on memorization and drill. Second, limited research has been done on the literacies associated with the practices of doing science and mathematics. Thus, little is known about exactly what types of texts are central to these practices, how these texts are used while engaging in the practices of science and mathematics, and how to foster literacy with these texts. We suggest the following approaches to address these challenges.

Establish Classroom Norms

Teachers who plan to engage their students in inquiry or problem solving cannot assume that students have had prior experiences with these processes. Teachers can help students acclimate to the new classroom culture by taking a few steps to establish classroom norms that are supportive of inquiry and problem solving. First, teachers can explicitly discuss and model classroom norms with the students. For example, a science teacher can talk about and demonstrate what it means to develop theories and models, to test models by collecting and analyzing data, to share findings with others, to listen to the theories and findings of others, and to adjust theories based on the evidence collected and the findings of others. Second, teachers can gradually introduce classroom norms or increase the amount of inquiry or problem solving expected of the students. A gradual increase in the students' responsibilities for learning can help offset students' initial discomfort at not being spoon-fed the content. Third, teachers can reinforce classroom norms by adjusting assessments so that the assessments require students to engage in inquiry and problem solving. Unless this is done, there is no need for students to buy into the classroom norms. Finally, teachers can resist students' demands to reduce the difficulty of tasks or investigations. If students are consistently able to pressure the teacher to give answers or solutions, there is no need for them to engage in inquiry or problem solving.

Form Collaborations

Because little is known about which specific literacy instructional strategies are useful in improving students' fluency with the texts that naturally arise while participating in the practices of science and mathematics, teachers who wish to promote the literacy of their students with these kinds of texts face severe challenges. In our own efforts to implement literacy instruction in science and mathematics classrooms, we have found that collaborations between content area teachers and literacy specialists are particularly helpful in addressing the challenge of designing appropriate instructional intervention. Content area teachers bring with them a sense of the important issues and processes in the discipline. They are best at identifying what texts are important, how those texts should be read and written, and what instructional practices fit well with the nature of the discipline. Literacy specialists, on the other hand, bring with them a sense of the history of literacy education as well as an arsenal of specific literacy strategies. Together, content area teachers and literacy specialists have all of the skills and knowledge necessary to identify which texts are being used while students participate in the practices of doing science and mathematics, how those texts are being used, and which literacy instructional strategies might be beneficial to improving students' reading and writing of those particular texts. Through collaboration and a certain amount of trial and error, content area teachers and literacy specialists can develop specific literacy instructional strategies that are suitable for scientific and mathematical texts.

Looking Ahead

Interest in discipline-specific literacies and instruction has increased in recent years (Draper & Siebert, 2004; Shanahan & Shanahan, 2008). However, much work remains to be done. In the meantime, we trust that thoughtful teachers working with literacy specialists can create content and literacy instruction that helps students learn content, reason, communicate, and participate within the disciplines of science and mathematics. We caution teachers and literacy specialists to design instruction that adheres to the principles that we have outlined in this chapter. We have seen recommendations made to teachers that, if followed, would undermine the opportunities for adolescents to learn content (Siebert & Draper, 2008). For example, literacy specialists and science teachers may collaborate and create ways to improve students' reading of a chapter from a science textbook about simple machines. But if this reading instruction is provided at the cost of having students experience simple machines or design inquiries to discover how simple machines work, the consequences for adolescents' learning could be compromised. This is not to say that science textbooks should be abandoned. Instead, science teachers and literacy specialists must work together to ensure that the use of the textbook fits with the aims of science instruction. In this case, it would make better sense to have students design inquiries with levers and inclined planes and then use their textbooks to compare their conclusions with those found in the book.

Similarly, literacy specialists may believe that reading in mathematics classrooms should focus on helping learners become more facile at reading and interpreting word problems found in mathematics textbooks. In their zeal to be useful to mathematics teachers, literacy specialists may recommend ideas for improved reading of traditional word problems that either reduce the reading of word problems to the translation of English words to mathematical computations or simply enhance students' ability to memorize mathematical algorithms (Siebert & Draper, 2008). The problem with instruction designed to help students read traditional word problems and improve their memorization of algorithms is that this kind of instruction has been deemphasized by framers of mathematics reform (NCTM, 2000). Instead, emphasis is being placed on helping students read and solve problems for which they do not already have well-formed solution methods. Typically, these problems cannot be reduced to a simple algorithm or translated directly into arithmetic operations. To solve them, students will need to learn to identify quantities, construct relationships between quantities, create representations that clarify these relationships and suggest new ones, and operate on quantities to produce the desired outcome. Only literacy instruction that supports these processes will be truly beneficial to mathematics students.

To avoid poor mathematics and science instruction in the name of literacy, collaborators must take into consideration recommendations made to science and mathematics teachers via standards documents (e.g., NCTM, 2000; NRC, 2000). Therefore, we recommend that collaborations between literacy specialists and science and mathematics teachers include familiarization with both literacy and content education literature.

We realize that the recommendations we have made here will not make the work of mathematics and science teachers easier. Indeed, what we are suggesting will likely result in significant changes to instruction and will require a considerable investment of time on the part of science and mathematics teachers. However, we know that teachers who are interested in helping adolescents learn both the content and processes associated with mathematical and scientific understanding will do well to consider the ideas we have presented here. Moreover, collaborating with other teachers and literacy specialists provides a way of sharing the load and, thus, increases the likeliness that valuable changes will take place. We are sure that collaborative activities that result in instruction that adheres to the principles we've outlined—engaging students in inquiry and problem solving, promoting sense making, addressing all texts, and supporting explanation and justification—will encourage adolescents' acquisition and learning of content and related literacies. Indeed, we trust that these principles will be useful reflective tools for teachers and literacy specialists as they redesign and evaluate mathematics and science instruction.

EXTEND YOUR THINKING

- Consider a lesson you have given in the past and instructional routines associated with the lesson (e.g., lectures, demonstrations, activities). How can your instructional routines be altered to provide more problem-solving and inquiry experiences for learners?

- Consider an upcoming lesson you plan to teach. What do you want students to understand (as opposed to memorize)?

■ Reflect on several recent days of instruction or perhaps an entire unit. What texts occurred as part of the lessons? Be sure to consider the texts that students had to create to aid their reasoning and the texts you created and used as part of instruction. Now consider one of the nonprint texts; what do learners need to know and do to meaningfully interact with that text?

■ Consider another text you identified as part of the exercise in the item above. How is a text like it used by disciplinary experts? How can you help learners use and create texts in discipline-appropriate ways?

REFERENCES

Alvermann, D.E. (2002). Effective literacy instruction for adolescents. *Journal of Literacy Research*, *34*(2), 189–208. doi:10.1207/s15548430jlr3402_4

Draper, R.J., & Siebert, D. (2004). Different goals, similar practices: Making sense of the mathematics and literacy instruction in a standards-based mathematics classroom. *American Educational Research Journal*, *41*(4), 927–962. doi:10.3102/00028312041004927

Hand, B., Prain, V., Lawrence, C., & Yore, L.D. (1999). A writing in science framework designed to enhance science literacy. *International Journal of Science Education*, *21*(10), 1021–1035. doi:10.1080/095006999290165

Lemke, J.L. (2004). The literacies of science. In E.W. Saul (Ed.), *Crossing borders in literacy and science instruction: Perspectives on theory and practice* (pp. 33–47). Newark, DE: International Reading Association.

National Research Council. (1996). *National science education standards: Observe, interact, change, learn*. Washington, DC: National Academy Press.

National Research Council. (2000). *Inquiry and the national science education standards: A guide for teaching and learning*. Washington, DC: National Academy Press.

National Council of Teachers of Mathematics. (2000). *Principles and standards for school mathematics: A guide for mathematicians*. Reston, VA: Author.

Neilsen, L. (1998). Playing for real: Performative texts and adolescent identities. In D.E. Alvermann, K.A. Hinchman, D.W. Moore, S.F. Phelps, & D.R. Waff (Eds.), *Reconceptualizing the literacies in adolescents' lives* (pp. 3–26). Mahwah, NJ: Erlbaum.

Shanahan, T., & Shanahan, C. (2008). Teaching disciplinary literacy to adolescents: Rethinking content-area literacy. *Harvard Educational Review*, *78*(1), 40–59.

Siebert, D., & Draper, R.J. (2008). Why content-area literacy messages do not speak to mathematics teachers: A critical content analysis. *Literacy Research and Instruction*, *47*(4), 229–245.

von Glasersfeld, E. (1995). *Radical constructivism: A way of knowing and learning*. London: Falmer.

Wade, S.E., & Moje, E.B. (2000). The role of text in classroom learning. In M.L. Kamil, P.B. Mosenthal, P.D. Pearson, & R. Barr (Eds.), *Handbook of reading research* (Vol. 3, pp. 609–628). Mahwah, NJ: Erlbaum.

CHAPTER 10

Adolescent Literacy Assessment: Finding Out What You Need to Know

Faye Brownlie

> *"Can we meet in groups again with our responses and the criteria? It's just like being the teacher! It's fun, and I am getting better and better!"*
>
> —*Julia*

Classroom assessment practices are the billboard for learning in the classroom. They signal to everyone—the outside community of parents and public and the inside community of learners—what counts in that room. On my billboard, I want my assessment targets clear, my assessment practices transparent and supportive, and my opportunities for student success wide and varied. I want my assessment practices to reflect current assessment research—which says that assessment can have a profound impact on student learning—and I want that impact to be positive and inclusive. What I assess, how I assess, and how I use the assessment information reflects what I value in learning.

There are two different types of learning assessment: assessment *of* (summative) and assessment *for* (formative). These assessments have different purposes, different audiences, different timings, different forms, and, especially, different impacts on student learning. The differences between assessment of learning and for learning are summarized in Table 10.1.

In an effective classroom, both forms of assessment are occurring: Assessment for learning (AfL) supports and enhances student learning, and assessment of learning (AoL) ensures that the classroom instruction is making a difference to

Adolescent Literacy, Field Tested: Effective Solutions for Every Classroom, edited by Sheri R. Parris, Douglas Fisher, and Kathy Headley. © 2009 by the International Reading Association.

TABLE 10.1
Assessment Contrast Chart

	Assessment of Learning (AoL)	Assessment for Learning (AfL)
Purpose	Reporting out, summative assessment, measuring learning	Guiding instruction, improving learning
Audience	Parents and public	Teachers and students
Timing	At the end	Minute by minute, day by day, at the beginning
Form	Letter grades, rank order, percentages, scores	Descriptive feedback

student learning, that standards are being maintained, and that the public contract is being realized. The research is very clear. If we want to have the greatest impact on student learning, we will spend less time measuring the learning *of* and more time supporting the learning *for* (Black, Harrison, Lee, Marshall, & William, 2003; Black & William, 1998; Hattie & Timperley, 2007).

Instructional Practices That Work

In this chapter, I will address two AFL practices we have found to be effective when working with adolescent literacy learners. ("We" represents a network of teachers, administrators, and staff developers in British Columbia with whom I work. We are connected through provincial networks such as the District Assessment of Reading Team [DART] and the Leadership for Learning Academy.) The first AfL practice is a set of six strategies that weave into the daily fabric of the classroom. The second AfL practice is a key event to inform teaching. Teachers design and use performance-based assessments that focus on assessing what is important—thinking skills, comprehension strategies, and students' perceptions of their own understanding and of their own performance.

Daily AfL Strategies

What does AfL look like in a classroom? We began with the work of the Assessment Reform Group (1999) and melded this with research and practice (Black et al., 2003; Butler, Schnellert, & Cartier, 2008; Cameron, Gregory, Politano, & Paquin, 2004; Clarke, Owens, & Sutton, 2006; Gregory, Cameron, & Davies, 1997; Hattie & Timperley, 2007; Stiggins, 1997; Wiggins, 1998). From this we developed six target AfL strategies that we work to incorporate in a continual way in our teaching: (1) learning intentions, (2) criteria, (3) descriptive feedback, (4) questioning, (5) self-assessment and peer assessment, and (6) ownership.

Learning Intentions. At the beginning of a lesson, a sequence of lessons, or a unit, teachers state what is intended to be learned. These intentions are stated as "I" statements, as it is the learner who is the most important consumer of this information. For example, in a seventh-grade English class, the students are beginning a unit on poetry. There are three learning intentions for the students:

1. I can read a variety of poems and explain my thinking about the poems in a small group.
2. I can write a personal response to a poem.
3. I can self-assess my work in the small group and my response using cocreated criteria.

These learning intentions are posted and discussed at the beginning of the unit. The expectations are clear to everyone and are referred to throughout the unit. No one is left wondering, What am I supposed to be doing? or How do these activities fit in with what I am supposed to be learning? Imagine traveling with a group of friends. You are in Europe but head in different directions for a few days. You arrange to meet again. But the group leader doesn't explicitly tell you the location. Your chances of reconnecting are slim at best! We would never arrange travel this way, but too often students have a sense of wandering through the curriculum, not knowing where they are headed and certainly not knowing when they have arrived.

Criteria. Criteria help students know when they have arrived. They describe what a powerful performance or product will look like. Criteria are best developed *with* students, using examples either of published work or of the students' work. In the same seventh-grade English class, the following process was used for building criteria (Brownlie, Feniak, & Schnellert, 2006):

1. Four student responses to poetry were examined as a class. These were chosen from a diverse range of students, each sample exhibiting different strengths. The discussion focused only on strengths, never on criticism.
2. Individually, students wrote the criteria they thought were most important to include in a written response.
3. Students chose their top three criteria.
4. In groups of three or four, students decided on three common criteria.
5. Students presented their group's top criteria.
6. The criteria were categorized and made into a class list. (Note: The teacher can add additional criteria if the students have not identified an aspect of the curriculum that needs to be addressed.)
7. Students and teacher worked with the criteria for several days to ensure they had a working model.

8. Students kept a copy of the criteria in their poetry response journals.

9. Students used the criteria during their work with poetry responses to self-evaluate, peer evaluate, and set goals.

Table 10.2 shows the criteria generated by this class.

Descriptive Feedback. The backbone of AfL is finding out what you need to know, when you need to know it. As a learner, descriptive feedback answers three questions: (1) What's working? (2) What's not? and (3) What's next? These questions guide our interactions with our students as we meet with them individually in a side-by-side conference, in a small group, or as a class.

In the seventh-grade English class, the students receive descriptive feedback from the teacher as she reads their poetry responses. She moves around the class as they are working, with a highlighter in hand. The students signal when they would like a quick chat with her—when they want some descriptive feedback. She asks if there is something in particular they want her to notice. With this student guidance in mind, she highlights several examples of "what's working" in one student's response. Then she helps him decide on *one* aspect that is not working, and together they negotiate a quick plan for "what's next" to deal with the "what's not."

The teacher also collects those responses she has not yet seen. She responds in writing in the same way to these responses, so all students receive descriptive feedback as quickly as possible, when they can still use the advice. If she notices a pattern in the "what's not" category, she teaches a minilesson the next day to either the whole class or to the small group of students who need this instruction. Her response is guided by the established learning intentions and the coconstructed criteria. Everything is explicit. Students practice responding and working with the

TABLE 10.2
Student-Developed Criteria for Response to Poetry

Criteria	Details
Connections	• Relating self to the poem • Showing how the poem changes your thinking
Opinions	• Expressing likes and dislikes about the poem, with evidence • Asking questions of the poem or the poet
Emotions	• Explaining why you feel the way you do about the poem and how you think the author feels about his or her subject
Image	• Commenting on the image formed in your mind upon reading the poem
Response style	• Using descriptive words • Using quotes from the poem • Suggesting improvements to the poem, if needed

criteria many times before any grade is given. When the grade is given, it is based on the criteria. There are no surprises.

Questioning. In a classroom that focuses on assessment for learning, teachers' questions are open ended and invite reasoning. Teachers listen in a deeply respectful way, intent on understanding the student's thinking and in engaging in actual discourse. Students are invited to question themselves, to use their questions to guide their learning, and to kindle their curiosity.

In the seventh-grade English class, the students write questions they have about the poem—around the actual text of the poem—before entering their small-group conversations. These questions are their entry into the conversation. They also pose questions about their responses, using the criteria. They, too, are reflecting on their work, considering, what's working, what's not, and what's next? Consider the teacher's question, "What should I notice about your response today?" This gives ownership to the student, invites his or her participation in the assessment process, and leaves the control with the learner. The learner is leading the learning, and the teacher is following the learner's lead, mapping a learning journey to a common goal.

Self-Assessment and Peer Assessment. Students need to be involved as much as possible in the work of becoming the best learners they can be. This requires that they clearly understand the task, the learning intention, and what achievement will look like—the criteria. When these are explicit to the students and the teacher models how to work with the criteria, with descriptive feedback, and with open-ended questioning, students can successfully peer assess. They follow the same guidelines that the teacher has been modeling: work with the end in mind, use the criteria as a reference point for what it needs to look like, frame the descriptive feedback around the same three questions, invite a conversation with a peer, and do not take control and tell. As students work with peer assessment, the teacher is there to guide the practice and coach as necessary. Student conversations are authentic and helpful, so performance improves as each student now has many more opportunities for feedback. When all feedback comes from the teacher, the odds of getting enough, when you need it, are not great! Ultimately, the students are self-assessing as they work, which is where the real locus of learning is—carrying with them the ability to tell if what they are doing is getting them what they want.

In the seventh-grade class, the teacher began by having all peer assessment happen simultaneously, after each student had received two quick conferences with her and after they had examined her descriptive feedback. Students understood the process and were able and keen to participate. With their continued practice, their poetry responses improved and their ability to pinpoint for the teacher and for their peers where they would like feedback—in other words, "What should I notice?"—became more and more precise.

Ownership. The agent of learning is the student. When students are clear about the expectations, know how to participate, and recognize that their voices are valued in the process and that they are the ultimate consumer, they work harder. All of the AfL strategies are geared toward inviting students in, giving them informed control, and working with them to help them be the best they can be. The strategies help students of differing abilities participate more fully in the lessons. Differentiation is easily addressed. It is no wonder that more students are experiencing more success. They are more engaged and more confident and critical readers and thinkers as they become more reflective.

In the seventh-grade class, the teacher uses the question, "What do you want me to notice about your work?" to center the conversation on the student. The student owns the learning. The teacher's job is to help. The message is "We are in this together." Ownership is also evident when the students choose the written response they want to hand in for grading.

Performance-Based Assessment

At the beginning of a semester or a term, teachers are working to get to know their students—their strengths and their stretches—as advised by the International Reading Association's Adolescent Literacy Position Statement (Moore, Bean, Birdyshaw, & Rycik, 1999). A whole-class, performance-based assessment can assist in this process. Our assessment, called the Standard Reading Assessment, is one we have been using for almost 20 years (Brownlie & Feniak, 1998, Brownlie et al., 2006). It is based on the beliefs that reading is thinking, that comprehension instruction matters, and that adolescents need to be able to learn through reading, writing, and talking (Butler, Schnellert, & Cartier, 2005; Fielding & Pearson, 1994; Keene, 2008; Beers, Probst, & Rief, 2007; Wilhelm, Baker, & Dube, 2001). We use it to get a snapshot of independent, thoughtful reading. We most frequently use it with content reading. The chosen passage for the assessment is not tied directly to the content that is currently being taught, but is content specific—for example, in a science classroom the text is from a grade-appropriate science text. The intent is to see if students are independently and thoughtfully applying the skills and strategies of reading that are required to gain meaning from the text they are going to be reading, and if not, to focus instruction on what is missing. It is *not* an assessment for grades. It is intended to guide learning, not measure learning.

The teacher constructs the assessment by choosing a piece of text (often from a text he or she is going to be using) and designing a series of open-ended questions. The teacher administers the assessment, looks for patterns in the students' work, sees what they can do and what is missing, and uses this information to design instruction. This is part of a cyclical process. Once a class goal has been established, the students are informed, and opportunities to practice toward improved performance in this goal infuse the classroom. At the end of a set period of time—perhaps six weeks, in advance of the next reporting period, or at the end of a term or semester—the assessment is repeated with a new piece of text. The teacher reassesses to see if the instruction has made a difference in student learning and to set a new goal. Again, this information is shared with the students.

So how does this work? A classroom social studies teacher and her resource teacher chose a two-page passage from the social studies text, which included several text features. They posed several open-ended questions:

- Connections—How does what you read connect with what you already knew?

- Summarizing—Choose a way to show the main ideas and details in what you read.

- Making inferences—Read between the lines to find something that you believe to be true, but that is not explicitly said. Explain your reasoning.

- Vocabulary—Here are three challenging words from the text. Explain what you think they mean and the strategies you used to determine their meaning.

- Reflecting—Was this passage easy or hard to understand? How did you help yourself understand?

The text portion was called "The Rise of Islam." Before the students began, the teachers had the students talk with their learning partners about what they knew about Islam. This information was shared in the class. The questions were read aloud before the students began to read to establish a purpose for reading. As the students then read and responded to the questions, the teachers moved throughout the class, listening to each student read aloud a portion of the text that he or she had already read and practiced, and coding on the student's paper what they noticed about the students' reading (an abridged running record). Each student was also asked the main idea of the text and how it connected with what he or she already knew. A compliment about his or her oral reading was written on each student's paper. This process took the full class period of 60 minutes.

After the class ended, the two teachers sat down with their running records, their interview responses, and the students' written responses and coded them by highlighting the appropriate descriptors from the provincial standards for reading for information (British Columbia Ministry of Education, 2002). They looked for patterns in what the students could and couldn't do. The students had several different note-making strategies. They made good use of their background knowledge. However, they had few strategies for determining unknown words and for providing details to support main ideas. These became their comprehension strategy targets for the term. The teachers shared this information with the students and targeted their instruction to include more explicit teaching of vocabulary strategies and supporting detail. They reassessed two months later and saw definite growth in both areas.

In some schools, all incoming students (grade 8 or grade 9) are assessed in reading science and social studies. The responses are coded (descriptors highlighted, no grades given) by the entire staff, and the literacy committee helps examine the data and choose the goals. The results are reported to the staff and each department considers how they can support these students in achieving improved performance within their subject area—for example, How can we support learners making inferences in science, in social studies, in home economics, in information technology, in math, and in English? The students are reassessed at the end of the semester or year. The results of the teaching—the changes in learning—are reported, and new targets are set.

Looking Ahead

Initially, what is most difficult in using AfL strategies is letting go of collecting more and more grades and trusting that a change in assessment focus is going to work. We have found that taking one step at a time—trying one AfL strategy again and again until it is common practice—is a useful beginning. Also incredibly important is to not work alone, but to have a teaching/learning partner or group to help you think, problem solve, reflect, and design. It is challenging to stay strength-oriented, to use words to describe rather than numbers, letters, or grades, and to believe in your students' abilities to set their own goals and to reflect on their own progress. The bar is set high. By using strategies such as those discussed here, all students can become agents of their own learning and, in so doing, become more effective learners.

The Carnegie Foundation's *Reading Next* report (Biancarosa & Snow, 2004) identifies 15 focus areas for improvement. It also states that without a focus on professional development, assessment of learning, and assessment for learning, we would see no long-term significant change in student achievement. We know how to improve our performance in assessment for learning. By improving these practices, student success—as measured by assessment of learning—will improve. Now is the time to put into practice what we know, to make a difference for all learners.

EXTEND YOUR THINKING

■ What is your first step in implementing more assessment-for-learning practices in your classroom?

■ Who will help you?

■ How will you know your efforts are making a difference?

REFERENCES

Assessment Reform Group. (1999). *Assessment for learning beyond the black box*. Cambridge, England: University of Cambridge School of Education.

Beers, K., Probst, R.E., & Rief, L. (2007). *Adolescent literacy: Turning promise into practice*. Portsmouth, NH: Heinemann.

Biancarosa, G., & Snow, C.E. (2004). *Reading next: A vision for action and research in middle and high school literacy. A report to Carnegie Corporation of New York*. Washington, DC: Alliance for Excellent Education.

Black, P., Harrison, C., Lee, C., Marshall, B., & Wiliam, D. (2003). *Assessment for learning: Putting it into practice*. Maidenhead, England: Open University Press.

Black, P., & Wiliam, D. (1998). Inside the black box: Raising standards through classroom assessment. *Phi Delta Kappan, 80*(2), 139–148.

British Columbia Ministry of Education and Ministry Responsible for Multiculturalism and Human Rights. (2002). *B.C. Performance Standards for Reading and Writing* (revised ed.). Victoria, BC: Student Assessment and Program Evaluation Branch. Retrieved June 18, 2008, from www.bced.gov.bc.ca/perf_stands/

Brownlie, F., & Feniak, C. (1998). *Student diversity: Addressing the needs of all learners in inclusive classrooms*. Markham, ON: Pembroke.

Brownlie, F., Feniak, C., & Schnellert, L. (2006). *Student diversity: Classroom strategies to meet the learning needs of all students* (2nd ed.). Markham, ON: Pembroke.

Butler, D.L., Schnellert, L., & Cartier, S.C. (2005). Adolescents' engagement in "reading to learn": Bridging from assessment to instruction. *BC Educational Leadership Research, 2*. Retrieved December 2, 2005, from slc.educ.ubc.ca/eJournal/index.htm

Butler, D.L., Schnellert, L., & Cartier, S.C. (2008, March). *Educational change and layers of self-regulation: Teachers working strategically to improve practice so as to foster student self-regulation*. Paper presented at the 2008 meeting of the American Educational Research Association, New York, NY.

Cameron, C., Gregory, K., Politano, C., & Paquin, J. (2004). *Voices of experience series: Practical ideas to start up the year, grades 4–8*. Winnipeg, MB: Portage & Main.

Clarke, P., Owens, T., & Sutton, R. (2006). *Creating independent student learners: Practical guides to assessment for learning for grades 7–9*. Winnipeg, MB: Portage & Main.

Fielding, L., & Pearson, P.D. (1994). Reading comprehension: What works. *Educational Leadership, 51*(5), 62–68.

Gregory, K., Cameron, C., & Davies, A. (1997). *Setting and using criteria*. Merville, BC: Connections Publishing.

Hattie, J., & Timperley, H. (2007). The power of feedback. *Review of Educational Research, 77*(1), 81–112. doi:10.3102/003465430298487

Keene, E.O. (2008). *To understand: New horizons in reading comprehension*. Portsmouth, NH: Heinemann.

Moore, D.W., Bean, T.W., Birdyshaw, D., & Rycik, J.A. (1999). *Adolescent literacy: A position statement for the Commission on Adolescent Literacy of the International Reading Association*. Newark, DE: International Reading Association.

Stiggins, R.J. (1997). *Student-centered classroom assessment* (2nd ed.). Upper Saddle River, NJ: Merrill.

Wiggins, G.P. (1998). *Educative assessment: Designing assessments to inform and improve student performance*. San Francisco: Jossey-Bass.

Wilhelm, J.D., Baker, T.N., & Dube, J. (2001). *Strategic reading: Guiding students to lifelong literacy 6–12*. Portsmouth, NH: Heinemann.

PART II

Literacy Instruction With Special Populations

CHAPTER 11

Literacy Interventions for Adolescent Struggling Readers

Michael F. Hock, Irma F. Brasseur-Hock

"One of my hopes as a learner is that I won't continue to get frustrated reading books. I get so frustrated when I read and don't understand what I just read."

—*Veronica, ninth-grade student*

In the United States, there is a subtle but unmistakable realization that the competitive edge that drives the nation's economy is in jeopardy. International comparisons show that U.S. students are no longer in the academic top tier, as students from other nations have surpassed ours in critical literacy and higher order thinking skills (Organisation for Economic Cooperation and Development, 2007). Recently, this challenge has become central to policy discussions that target educational reform. Business, political, and educational leaders have responded by calling for renewed focus on preparing our most able students to compete globally. This focus is welcome and necessary. However, the fact that many adolescents in America have yet to attain even basic academic literacy skills is cause for concern. Like Veronica, a sizeable population of adolescents is faced with the dual task of mastering basic literacy skills *and* preparing to compete in a knowledge-based society (National Center for Educational Statistics, 2007). Thus, adolescents who struggle with reading need interventions that are effective and powerful enough to both close the literacy gap and help them become proficient in reading to learn.

The focus of this chapter is on the exploration of research-based literacy interventions for adolescent struggling readers (ASRs) that have been found to be

Adolescent Literacy, Field Tested: Effective Solutions for Every Classroom, edited by Sheri R. Parris, Douglas Fisher, and Kathy Headley. © 2009 by the International Reading Association.

effective in closing the achievement gap experienced by ASRs. In support of this goal, we will explore three main questions:

1. Who are adolescent struggling readers?
2. What is their reading component skill profile?
3. How can we close the academic literacy gap?

Who Are Adolescent Struggling Readers?

ASRs are a diverse group, generally characterized as students who struggle with academic reading demands. They are sometimes described as youth with reading or learning disabilities (LD), or as students who are unmotivated and disengaged from school (Deshler & Hock, 2007). ASRs include students in grades 4 through 12 who are reading two or more years below grade level (Torgesen, 2005). In short, ASRs are students who, for a variety of reasons, are unable to meet the school-related reading demands required for them to learn successfully.

Recently, some states and researchers have begun to define ASRs as students reading at the 40th percentile and below. This definition reflects the desire to describe ASRs in terms of the federal government's guidelines for No Child Left Behind (2002), which sets the expectation and standard that all children and youth will be at least average readers and read at grade level. Thus, students who are not reading at the proficient or average level and are not making adequate yearly progress (AYP) are sometimes included in the ASR category. For the purpose of this chapter, adolescent struggling readers are defined as those students who are not making AYP gains in reading and who are reading at the 40th percentile or lower as determined by AYP or standardized reading measures.

What Is the Reading Component Skill Profile of Adolescent Struggling Readers?

Within the broad category of ASRs described earlier is the reality that ASRs are a very diverse group in terms of reading achievement. In an effort to more precisely describe the reading skills of ASRs, researchers recently found that many ASRs lack the basic and foundational reading skills necessary to support comprehension. In a descriptive study designed to identify the reading component skill profile of adolescent readers (Hock et al., 2009), 345 eighth and ninth graders were administered a battery of reading tests. Specifically, the tests measured student achievement in a variety of reading skills identified as essential for proficient reading by the National Reading Panel (National Institute of Child Health and Human Development, 2000). Participants were assessed in the domains of word-level skills (word identification and word attack), fluency (accuracy and rate for words and passages), vocabulary (receptive and expressive), and comprehension.

Analysis of the results found that 61% of the ASRs had significant deficits in all of those reading component skills. They scored a full standard deviation or more below average in *all* of the reading component skills assessed. Some subgroups of ASRs showed even more severe patterns. For example, students with LD scored significantly below the levels of the ASRs group as a whole. In contrast, most proficient readers scored high on all measures of reading, with above average reading skills in word level, vocabulary, and comprehension. The lowest skill area for the proficient reader group was fluency, where they scored at the average level. Implications for policy and instructional programming suggest that literacy interventions for ASRs need to respond to the component reading skill needs of this group. That is, instruction must include both word level and comprehension skill instruction. To ignore one area will, in all likelihood, limit overall reading achievement.

Using a subset of the data described above, a latent class analysis (LCA) was conducted to further define the ASR group. LCA is a form of cluster analysis that groups individuals on the basis of their performance on multiple measures. The analysis essentially clusters groups of readers that present statistically distinct profiles that are unique to the cluster (Lubke & Muthén, 2005).

In the LCA, results indicated heterogeneity within the population of ASRs, and researchers found five distinct clusters of ASRs (Kieffer, Hock, Brasseur, Biancarosa, & Deshler, 2008). The cluster that performed lowest on all reading measures was designated as *Readers With Global Weaknesses*. This cluster contained 14.4% of the below-average comprehenders, and they scored low on all reading measures. Additionally, they were more than two standard deviations below national norms on oral reading passage accuracy, phonemic decoding efficiency, and word attack skills.

The second-lowest performing cluster was designated *Sight Word Readers*. This cluster contained the largest percentage of below-average comprehenders (36.4%). Like the class of *Readers With Global Weaknesses*, this class demonstrated below average performance on all measures, with particular weaknesses on tasks involving decoding of pseudowords (phonemic decoding efficiency), tasks involving passage fluency, and tasks involving language comprehension. As a cluster, they were about one standard deviation below the expected mean on all measures. It is important to note that these two clusters together (slightly more than 50% of the below average comprehenders) exhibit significant deficits in *all* critical reading component skills.

The third cluster of ASRs was designated as *Dysfluent Readers*. This cluster contained 29.2% of the subsample. Although students in this class demonstrated language comprehension and word reading accuracy skills in the average range, their fluency skills (at both the word and passage levels) fell significantly below average.

The fourth cluster of ASRs was designated as *Weak Language Comprehenders*. This group contained 10.8% of the subsample. Students in this class demonstrated word reading accuracy and fluency skills in the average range but weakness in listening comprehension.

Finally, the fifth and smallest class, designated as *Weak Reading Comprehenders* (containing 9.2% of the subsample), had component reading skills in the average range but were weak in reading comprehension tasks. It is important to note that this cluster may have weaknesses in skills not assessed in this battery of component skills. For example, they might have difficulties with the processing of extended text, limited experience with particular text types, or limitations in the background knowledge necessary for comprehension.

The LCA supports the findings of the descriptive study and lends additional support for the notion of balanced reading instruction. Clearly, there are five distinct groups of ASRs with profiles that call for some level of differentiated instruction. Thus, to respond to the unique skill profiles identified in these studies, practitioners need to be able to provide instruction in word-level skills (advanced phonics, decoding, and word identification), fluency (rate and accuracy), vocabulary, and reading comprehension. We believe this balanced approach to literacy instruction for ASRs is necessary if we are to close the academic literacy gap.

How Can We Close the Academic Literacy Gap?

Because the literacy needs of ASRs are so diverse, the most effective literacy programs offer support and instruction at various levels of intensity (Alliance for Excellent Education, 2004). It is necessary that comprehensive support and instruction involve all teachers in a school if we are to improve literacy outcomes. For example, some students, including ASRs, benefit when teachers use graphic organizers to help them master critical subject-matter content; others benefit from reading strategies instruction taught in the context of core classes using content material (Lysynchuk, Pressley, & Vye, 1990; Palincsar & Brown, 1984; Rosenshine & Meister, 1995; Taylor & Frye, 1992). In a comprehensive approach to literacy, all teachers have an important role to play in ensuring that students are prepared to participate in a knowledge-based society. The following are instructional frameworks and practices that have been shown to be effective with ASRs.

Tiered Instructional Continuums

One comprehensive approach to literacy involves a tiered continuum of instructional services. Within such a continuum, specialized and supplemental instruction is provided to students who do not benefit from instruction in core classes alone. The intent of tiered intervention models is to support instruction that meets the needs of all students, including ASRs and students with disabilities (Deshler, Schumaker, & Woodruff, 2004).

A primary example of a tiered instructional continuum is Response to Intervention (RTI). In RTI models, levels or tiers of instruction follow a sequential approach to providing increasingly targeted instruction for students who are struggling with learning. At the first level, instructional strategies are designed to benefit all students in the entire class. Enhanced instruction at this level is designed to boost the academic progress of all students but particularly those students who may need more explicit instruction. This level can be referred to as an enhanced classroom approach. The goal of this level is to increase the number of students who are successful with important content in their core classes.

The second tier of instruction in RTI models includes supplemental intervention (e.g., reading instruction) that is clearly linked to core classroom instruction. This level of instruction consists of intensive small-group instruction, practice, and feedback tailored to the academic needs of the students who haven't responded to first-level instruction. This level of instruction is designed to address gaps in the students' knowledge and skills that prevent acquisition of content knowledge and skills.

Finally, the third tier of RTI instruction includes regularly scheduled and intensive specialized instruction for students considered severely at risk and those whose needs were not met at the second level. This level of instruction responds to students generally referred to as needing special education services and with reading skill profiles like those found in the LCA for Readers With Global Weaknesses and Sight Word Readers.

Another example of a tiered instructional continuum is the Content Literacy Continuum (CLC; Lenz, Ehren, & Deshler, 2005). The CLC also recognizes that some students require more intensive, systematic, and explicit instruction of content, strategies, and skills than other students, and that each school staff person has a unique but important role when it comes to literacy instruction. The CLC framework has five levels. These include Level 1: Enhanced content instruction in general education core classes (mastery of critical content for *all* students regardless of literacy levels); Level 2: Strategy instruction in general education core classes and with content class materials (routinely weave strategies within and across content classes using large-group instructional methods); Level 3: Intensive strategy instruction (mastery of specific strategies using intensive-explicit instructional sequences in special classes other than core content classes); Level 4: Intensive basic skill instruction (mastery of entry-level literacy skills at the fourth-grade level); Level 5: Therapeutic intervention (mastery of language underpinnings of curriculum content and learning strategies).

Together, the multiple levels of the tiered instructional continuum most often referred to as RTI and the similar CLC constitute systematic instructional frameworks that support multiple levels of intervention that respond to the distinct clusters of ASRs identified in the studies previously discussed.

Component Reading Skills

In response to the ASR clusters or distinct profiles identified in the LCA, an intervention framework that highlights evidence-based interventions that correspond to the critical reading components skills should be considered. A review of the critical reading component skills and supporting research on ASRs is provided below.

Word-Level. Interventions that target word-level skills have been found to be effective for ASRs. Word-level interventions teach students fundamental reading skills such as phonemic awareness, phonological decoding, syllabication, structural analysis, and word identification (Abbott & Berninger, 1999; Bhat, Griffin, & Sindelar, 2003; Bhattacharya & Ehri, 2004; Penney, 2002). ASRs who have reading skill profiles like Readers With Global Weaknesses and Sight Word Readers benefit from word-level instruction.

Fluency. Interventions that focus on reading words accurately with good rate and prosody have been found to be somewhat effective for ASRs. Although studies in which repeated reading and cues to read with accuracy and increased rate have been more effective than comparison conditions, the effect sizes of these studies has been comparatively small (Allinder, Dunse, Brunken, & Obermiller-Krolikowski, 2001; Conte & Humphreys, 1989; Homan, Klesius, & Hite, 1993; O'Shea, Sindelar, & O'Shea, 1987). Thus, fluency interventions in and of themselves may not be effective in closing the achievement gap. The utility of fluency interventions may be as methods to ensure automaticity of word-reading accuracy and efficiency of reading rate.

Vocabulary. Vocabulary has been found to be highly correlated with reading comprehension (Cromley & Azevedo, 2007). Thus, interventions that increase vocabulary seem to warrant instructional time with ASRs. Vocabulary interventions found to be effective focus on analysis of semantic features, computer-based drill and practice, using visual or pictorial mnemonics, and using keywords (Anders, Bos, & Filip, 1984; Johnson, Gersten, & Carnine, 1987; Mastropieri, Scruggs, Levin, Gaffney, & McLoone, 1985; McLoone, Scruggs, Mastropieri, & Zucker, 1986; Veit, Scruggs, & Mastropieri, 1986). The effect size for these studies is large, with most studies showing gains well over one standard deviation with outcome measures for the mastery of the words taught during the intervention.

Comprehension. The ultimate outcome for reading instruction is comprehension that integrates understanding of text and the reader's prior knowledge of the content being read. Comprehension of this nature has been characterized as the construction of knowledge among reader, text, and context. Reading comprehension interventions have been found to have a substantial impact on the reading comprehension skills of ASRs. In general, ASRs have made significant gains on standardized measures of reading, with effect sizes that are in the moderate to large range when ASRs have been taught to use reading strategies (i.e., questioning, summarization, paraphrasing) and when the strategies have been taught explicitly (Alfassi, 1998; Boyle, 1996; Chan, 1991; Gajria & Salvia, 1992; Jitendra, Hoppes, & Xin, 2000; Klingner & Vaughn, 1996; Moore & Scevak, 1995; Snider, 1989; Wilder & Williams, 2001; Williams, Brown, Silverstein, & deCani, 1994).

Comprehensive Programs

Content Enhancement: A Way to Teach Content. Teaching content to ASRs, including adolescents with LD, has been the focus of much of the work conducted at the University of Kansas Center for Research on Learning. Content Enhancement (CE), a Level 1 or Tier 1 intervention, is composed of planning and teaching routines for use by general education content teachers. These routines include ways to select and plan for content instruction, plus ways to explicitly teach content to diverse groups of students. CE teaching routines have been validated with adolescents in secondary school settings (e.g., Bulgren & Lenz, 1996). Findings from these studies show that critical content can be taught to students in classes characterized by diversity. One of the key outcomes of explicit instruction using CE has been the significant growth of content knowledge or knowledge of the world by all students in these classes (Bulgren, Deshler, & Schumaker, 1997).

Studies provide data to support CE routines. For example, Bulgren, Deshler, Schumaker, and Lenz (2000) extended the research in a study (using random assignment of classes) of conceptual learning through analogies. They found that students who participated in the experimental condition for the Concept Anchoring Routine earned significantly higher scores than students in the control condition on measures of content knowledge. This routine also supports content area instruction that builds on prior knowledge, vocabulary, and summarization.

Fusion Reading: An Example of a Comprehensive Reading Course. In an attempt to bring together the instructional interventions found to be effective for ASRs at the high school level, researchers developed, tested the feasibility, and studied the effects of a reading program called Fusion Reading (Brasseur-Hock, Hock, & Deshler, 2008a). Fusion Reading is a comprehensive, multiyear reading course comprised of three major elements: motivation, classroom management, and reading instruction.

Motivation is built into Fusion Reading in several ways. First, students are provided with engaging literature to read, thereby increasing their motivation to read even more. Teachers and students report that they like to read the literature that makes up Fusion Reading. Second, students learn specific reading strategies, which enable them to experience learning success. The result of success with reading increases their motivation to read more. Finally, students are introduced to a program that shows them how to create visions of themselves in the future. These visions are goal oriented and personally motivating (Markus & Nurius, 1986). The connection between students' positive visions of the future and academic skills and learning is made concrete. By having such a vision, motivation to learn increases even further.

Because a supportive learning environment is foundational to effective instruction, classroom management is an integral component of Fusion Reading. Thus, in Fusion Reading, teachers explain classroom learning expectations and routines, have students observe models of appropriate learning behavior, and have students practice those skills and behaviors throughout the course. In addition, learning expectations and personal behaviors are reinforced through reading instruction. Specifically, students read and discuss texts that highlight the value of high expectations, partnership commitment, and both positive and negative consequences. The lessons about high expectations and discipline are translated into the context of the reading classroom.

Reading instruction is the heart of Fusion Reading. That instruction is built upon the two primary components of the Simple View of Reading: word recognition and language comprehension. The first component, word recognition, involves two main programs: Thinking Reading and the Bridging Strategy.

With Thinking Reading, students participate in oral reading and the discussion of highly engaging text. Initially, the teacher leads this activity by reading aloud, modeling cognitive and metacognitive strategies used by expert readers, and engaging students in conversations about how to effectively navigate various text demands. Eventually, students take more and more responsibility for reading and asking questions. They also begin to use strategies independently as they read. Specific reading strategies that are explicitly taught during another instructional segment of the class are also discussed and applied to the reading selection during Thinking Reading. Thus, strategies are taught within the immediate context of highly engaging literature and informative or expository text.

With the Bridging Strategy (Brasseur-Hock, Hock, & Deshler, 2007), students learn advanced phonics, decoding, word recognition, and fluency skills and strategies. In a unique fashion, instruction in advanced phonics is presented to adolescents using the metaphor of athletic and musical warm up activities. That is, students learn and practice phonics skills in brief (5–7 minute) warm-up activities, much as athletes stretch, train, and scrimmage before an actual game. Thus, students learn, practice, and build word-level fluency with short but intense and explicit learning activities that occur on a regular basis. Additionally, students apply advanced phonics skills when they learn effective decoding and word recognition strategies. Finally, through rereading fluency strategies, students integrate advanced phonics, decoding, and word recognition skills, which in turn enhance comprehension.

The second component, language comprehension, involves a continuation of Thinking Reading, plus three other elements: the Vocabulary Strategy, the

Prediction Strategy, and the Summarization Strategy. Thinking Reading is essentially the same as it was during the word recognition component. Now, however, students see the teacher modeling vocabulary and reading comprehension strategies. Eventually, word identification, vocabulary, and comprehension strategies are all included in Thinking Reading. With the Vocabulary Strategy (Brasseur-Hock, Hock, & Deshler, 2008b), students learn a process that helps them understand vocabulary through individual work and rich class discussion of words in the context of course materials. In the Prediction Strategy (Hock, Brasseur-Hock, & Deshler, 2007a), students learn strategies for finding clues about what they are about to read, make predictions about what they are about to learn, read to confirm or modify predictions, summarize what they have learned, and continue to engage with reading material in the same fashion. In the Summarization Strategy (Hock, Brasseur-Hock, & Deshler, 2007b), students learn to read informational text, locate main ideas and important details, and paraphrase those main ideas and details. Students also learn strategies for summarizing complete sections of text by integrating text-based information with the reader's knowledge of the subject matter.

A random assignment experiment was conducted at two urban high schools to test the effectiveness of Fusion Reading. Students were divided into two groups: a control condition that received instruction in a well-established, evidence-based reading program for struggling readers, and an experimental group that received instruction in Fusion Reading. Students who participated in Fusion Reading significantly increased their reading comprehension scores an average of 5.05 standard score points (⅓ of a standard deviation) as measured by the Group Reading and Diagnostic Evaluation reading measure, a standardized measure of Listening, Comprehension, Vocabulary, Sentence Comprehension, and Passage Comprehension (Williams, 2001). In contrast, students in the control condition actually *decreased* their reading comprehension scores to -0.8 standard score points. The difference between the Fusion Reading student scores and the control reading program student scores is statistically significant at the 0.05 level. Thus, Fusion Reading students narrowed the achievement gap.

Explicit and Intensive Strategy Instruction

Teaching students strategies for reading, writing, and remembering important information has been found to be effective for ASRs, including adolescents with LD. These strategies include the cognitive processes efficient readers employ when they read narrative and expository text, and the metacognitive and self-regulatory strategies they use when they select, monitor, and evaluate their understanding of text (e.g., Deshler & Schumaker, 1988; Gersten, Fuchs, Williams, & Baker, 2001; Swanson, 1999; Swanson & Hoskyn, 1999; Vaughn, Gersten, & Chard, 2000).

Central to teaching strategies to ASRs is the need for explicit instruction. Explicit instruction is characterized by clear explanations of specific skills and strategies, supported by expert models of the skills or strategies in the context of tasks familiar to students. In addition, extensive practice of skills and strategies in context with scaffolded support has been found to be effective in guided, partner, and independent structures (Swanson & Hoskyn, 1999). Practice is further enhanced when students are provided with positive, corrective, elaborated feedback (Kline, Schumaker, & Deshler, 1991).

Looking Ahead

Effective instruction for ASRs requires that specific skills and strategies be taught with instructional explicitness and intensity. The following list highlights the significant challenges that may prevent the implementation of interventions:

- The nature of ASRs—ASRs are a heterogeneous group comprising at least five different subgroups that require substantially different instruction. Districts and schools must find ways to provide instruction that is responsive to student needs. This may require that multiple interventions be made available to students and that teachers become proficient with practices that support them in providing differentiated instruction within heterogeneous classrooms.

- Instructional explicitness—Teaching ASRs requires that instruction be explicit in nature. Explicit instructional methods need to be learned and applied by secondary teachers who have little or no background in this type of instruction. Significant professional development (and ongoing instructional coaching) in explicit instruction must be available to teachers.

- Instructional intensity—Intensity of instruction or issues of "dosage" are major challenges for teachers, students, parents, and administrators. Instructional intensity is determined by class size (e.g., 1 to 35, 1 to 15, 1 to 1, etc.), duration (e.g., one semester, one year, multiple years, 50 minutes, 90 minutes, every day, or every other day, etc.), and instructional engagement in learning activities. Unfortunately, limited resources often force educators to provide services that lack research-based instructional intensity attributes.

- Professional development—The professional development required to support the delivery of explicit, intense, and evidence-based interventions is great. Fidelity of implementation without professional development and ongoing instructional coaching is difficult to attain.

Although there is much to learn about instruction for ASRs, there are instructional practices and interventions that produce significant gains in learner outcomes. As a field, we should work toward the goal of delivering instruction to ASRs that has a strong research base or carefully evaluating interventions when no such research base exists.

EXTEND YOUR THINKING

▨ Given the heterogeneous reading skill profile of ASRs discussed in this chapter, what specific reading interventions should you be prepared to deliver in middle and high schools? Start by considering one student or class. What specific interventions could you employ?

▨ Research seems to support explicit instruction as an effective component of reading interventions for ASRs. How would you characterize the main features of explicit instruction? Consider one text you commonly teach and design a lesson using explicit instruction for a reading strategy that is helpful for comprehending that text.

▨ The instructional needs of ASRs are significant. What roles do content and support teachers currently play in your school in addressing the needs of this population? What support structures might need to be added in order for teachers at your school to systematically close the achievement gap experienced by ASRs?

Note

The research on Latent Class Analysis and Fusion Reading reported here was supported by the Institute of Education Sciences, U.S. Department of Education, through Grant R305G04011 to The University of Kansas Center for Research on Learning. The opinions expressed are those of the authors and do not represent views of the institute or the U.S. Department of Education.

REFERENCES

Abbott, S.P., & Berninger, V.W. (1999). It's never too late to remediate: Teaching word recognition to students with reading disabilities in grades 4–7. *Annals of Dyslexia, 49*(1), 221–250. doi:10.1007/s11881-999-0025-x

Alfassi, M. (1998). Reading for meaning: The efficacy of reciprocal teaching in fostering reading comprehension in high school students in remedial reading classes. *American Educational Research Journal, 35*(2), 309–332.

Allinder, R.M., Dunse, L., Brunken, C.D., & Obermiller-Krolikowski, H.J. (2001). Improving fluency in at-risk readers and students with learning disabilities. *Remedial and Special Education, 22*(1), 48–54. doi:10.1177/074193250102200106

Anders, P.L. Bos, C.S., & Filip, D. (1984). The effect of semantic feature analysis on the reading comprehension of learning-disabled students. In J.S. Niles & L.A. Harris (Eds.), *Changing perspectives on reading/language processing and instruction* (pp. 162–166). Rochester, NY: National Reading Conference.

Bhat, P., Griffin, C.C., & Sindelar, P.T. (2003). Phonological awareness instruction for middle school students with learning disabilities. *Learning Disability Quarterly, 26*(2), 73–87. doi:10.2307/1593591

Bhattacharya, A., & Ehri, L.C. (2004). Graphosyllabic analysis helps adolescent struggling readers read and spell words. *Journal of Learning Disabilities, 37*(4), 331–348. doi:10.1177/00222194040370040501

Biancarosa, G., & Snow, C.E. (2004). *Reading Next: A vision for action and research in middle and high school literacy. A report to Carnegie Corporation of New York*. Washington, DC: Alliance for Excellent Education.

Boyle, J.R. (1996). The effects of a cognitive mapping strategy on the literal and inferential comprehension of students with mild disabilities. *Learning Disability Quarterly, 19*(2), 86–98. doi:10.2307/1511250

Brasseur-Hock, I.F., Hock, M.F., & Deshler, D.D. (2007). *The bridging strategy*. Lawrence: The University of Kansas, Center for Research on Learning.

Brasseur-Hock, I.F., Hock, M.F., & Deshler, D.D. (2008a). *The fusion reading curriculum: A comprehensive two-year reading course for struggling adolescent readers*. Lawrence: The University of Kansas, Center for Research on Learning.

Brasseur-Hock, I.F., Hock, M.F., & Deshler, D.D. (2008b). *The vocabulary strategy*. Lawrence: The University of Kansas, Center for Research on Learning.

Bulgren, J.A., Deshler, D.D., & Schumaker, J.B. (1997). Use of a recall enhancement routine and strategies in inclusive secondary classes. *Learning Disabilities Research & Practice, 12*(4), 198–208.

Bulgren, J.A., Deshler, D.D., Schumaker, J.B., & Lenz, B.K. (2000). The use and effectiveness of analogical instruction in diverse secondary content classrooms. *Journal of Educational Psychology, 92*(3), 426–441. doi:10.1037/0022-0663.92.3.426

Bulgren, J.A., & Lenz, B.K. (1996). Strategic instruction in the content areas. In D.D. Deshler, E.S. Ellis, & B.K. Lenz (Eds.), *Teaching adolescents with learning disabilities: Strategies and methods* (2nd ed., pp. 409–473). Denver: Love.

Chan, L.K. (1991). Promoting strategy generalization through self-instructional training in students with reading disabilities. *Journal of Learning Disabilities, 24*(7), 427–433.

Conte, R., & Humphreys, R. (1989). Repeated readings using audiotaped material enhances oral reading in children with reading difficulties. *Journal of Communication Disorders, 22*(1), 65–79. doi:10.1016/0021-9924(89)90007-5

Cromley, J.G., & Azevedo, R. (2007). Testing and refining the direct and inferential mediation model of reading comprehension. *Journal of Educational Psychology, 99*(2), 311–325. doi:10.1037/0022-0663.99.2.311

Deshler, D.D., & Hock, M.F. (2007). Where we are, where we need to go. In M. Pressley, A.K. Billman, K.H. Perry, K.E. Reffitt, & J.M. Reynolds (Eds.), *Shaping literacy achievement: Research we have, research we need* (pp. 98–128). New York: Guilford.

Deshler, D.D., & Schumaker, J.B. (1988). An instructional model for teaching students how to learn. In J.L. Graden, J.E. Zins, & M.J. Curtis (Eds.), *Alternative educational delivery systems: Enhancing instructional options for all students* (pp. 391–411). Washington, DC: National Association of School Psychologists.

Deshler, D.D., Schumaker, J.B., & Woodruff, S.K. (2004). Improving literacy skills of at-risk adolescents: A school wide response. In D.S. Strickland & D.E. Alvermann (Eds.), *Bridging the literacy achievement gap grades 4–12* (pp. 86–104). New York: Teachers College Press.

Gajria, M., & Salvia, J. (1992). The effects of summarization instruction on text comprehension of students with learning disabilities. *Exceptional Children, 58*(6), 508–516.

Gersten, R., Fuchs, L.S., Williams, J.P., & Baker, S.K. (2001). Teaching reading comprehension strategies to students with learning disabilities: A review of research. *Review of Educational Research, 71*(2), 279–320. doi:10.3102/00346543071002279

Hock, M.F., Brasseur-Hock, I.F., & Deshler, D.D. (2007a). *The prediction strategy*. Lawrence: The University of Kansas, Center for Research on Learning.

Hock, M.F., Brasseur-Hock, I.F., & Deshler, D.D. (2007b). *The summarization strategy*. Lawrence: The University of Kansas, Center for Research on Learning.

Hock, M.F., Brasseur, I.F., Deshler, D.D., Catts, H.W., Marques, J., Mark, C.A., et al. (2009). What is the reading component skill profile of adolescent struggling readers in urban schools? *Learning Disability Quarterly 32*(1), 21–38.

Homan, S.P., Klesius, J.P., & Hite, C. (1993). Effects of repeated readings and nonrepetitive strategies on students' fluency and comprehension. *The Journal of Educational Research, 87*(2), 94–99.

Jitendra, A.K., Hoppes, M.K., & Xin, Y.P. (2000). Enhancing main idea comprehension for students with learning problems: The role of a summarization strategy and self-monitoring instruction. *The Journal of Special Education, 34*(3), 127–139. doi:10.1177/002246690003400302

Johnson, G., Gersten, R., & Carnine, D. (1987). Effects of Instructional design variables on vocabulary acquisition of learning disabilities students: A study of computer-assisted instruction. *Journal of Learning Disabilities, 20*(4), 206–213.

Kieffer, M., Hock, M.F., Brasseur, I., Biancarosa, G., & Deshler, D.D. (2008, July 11). *Latent class analysis of adolescent struggling readers' component skills.* Paper presented at the Society for Scientific Study of Reading, Asheville, NC.

Kline, F.M., Schumaker, J.B., & Deshler, D.D. (1991). Development and validation of feedback routines for instructing students with learning disabilities. *Learning Disability Quarterly, 14*(3), 191–207. doi:10.2307/1510849

Klingner, J.K., & Vaughn, S. (1996). Reciprocal teaching of reading comprehension strategies for students with learning disabilities who use English as a second language. *The Elementary School Journal, 96*(3), 275–293. doi:10.1086/461828

Lenz, B.K., Ehren, B., & Deshler, D.D. (2005). The content literacy continuum: A school-wide framework for improving adolescent literacy for all students. *Teaching Exceptional Children, 37*(6), 60–63.

Lubke, G.H., & Muthén, B.O. (2005). Investigating population heterogeneity with factor mixture models. *Psychological Methods, 10*(1), 21–39. doi:10.1037/1082-989X.10.1.21

Lysynchuk, L.M., Pressley, M., & Vye, N.J. (1990). Reciprocal teaching improves standardized reading-comprehension performance in poor comprehenders. *The Elementary School Journal, 90*(5), 469–484. doi:10.1086/461627

Markus, H., & Nurius, P. (1986). Possible selves. *American Psychologist, 41*(9), 954–969. doi:10.1037/0003-066X.41.9.954

Mastropieri, M.A., Scruggs, T.E., Levin, J.R., Gaffney, J., & McLoone, B. (1985). Mnemonic vocabulary instruction for learning disabled students. *Learning Disability Quarterly, 8*(1), 57–63. doi:10.2307/1510908

McLoone, B.B., Scruggs, T.E., Mastropieri, M.A., & Zucker, S.F. (1986). Memory strategy instruction and training with learning disabled adolescents. *Learning Disabilities Research, 2*(1), 45–52.

Moore, P.J., & Scevak, J.J. (1995). The effects of strategy training on high school students' learning from science texts. *European Journal of Psychology of Education, 10*(4), 401–410.

National Center for Educational Statistics. (2007). *The nation's report card: Reading 2005.* Washington, DC: U.S. Department of Education.

National Institute of Child Health and Human Development. (2000). *Report of the National Reading Panel. Teaching children to read: An evidence-based assessment of the scientific research literature on reading and its implications for reading instruction* (NIH Publication No. 00-4769). Washington, DC: U.S. Government Printing Office.

No Child Left Behind Act of 2001, Pub. L. 107-110, 115 Stat. 1425 (2002).

O'Shea, L.J., Sindelar, P.T., & O'Shea, D.J. (1987). The effects of repeated readings and attentional cues on the reading fluency and comprehension of learning disabled readers. *Learning Disabilities Research, 2*(2), 103–109.

Organisation for Economic Cooperation and Development. (2007, December). *PISA 2006: Science competencies for tomorrow's world, briefing note for the United States.* Paris: Author.

Palincsar, A.S., & Brown, A.L. (1984). Reciprocal teaching of comprehension-fostering and comprehension-monitoring activities. *Cognition and Instruction, 1*(2), 117–175. doi:10.1207/s1532690xci0102_1

Penney, C.G. (2002). Teaching decoding skills to poor readers in high school. *Journal of Literacy Research, 34*(1), 99–118. doi:10.1207/s15548430jlr3401_4

Rosenshine, B., & Meister, C. (1995). Direct instruction. In L. Anderson (Ed.), *International encyclopedia of teaching and teacher education* (2nd ed., pp. 143–148). Oxford: Elsevier Science.

Snider, V.E. (1989). Reading comprehension performance of adolescents with learning disabilities. *Learning Disability Quarterly, 12*(2), 87–96. doi:10.2307/1510724

Swanson, H.L. (1999). Instructional components that predict treatment outcomes for students with learning disabilities: Support for a combined strategy and direct instructional method. *Learning Disabilities Research & Practice, 14*(3), 129–140. doi:10.1207/sldrp1403_1

Swanson, H.L., & Hoskyn, M. (1999). Definition X treatment interactions for students with learning disabilities. *School Psychology Review, 28*(4), 644–658.

Taylor, B.M., & Frye, B.J. (1992). Comprehension strategy instruction in the intermediate grades. *Reading Research and Instruction, 32*(1), 39–48.

Torgesen, J.K. (2005). Remedial interventions for students with dyslexia: National goals and current accomplishments. In S. Richardson & J. Gilger (Eds.), *Research-based education and intervention: What we need to know* (pp. 103–114). Boston: International Dyslexia Association.

Vaughn, S., Gersten, R., & Chard, D.J. (2000). The underlying message in LD intervention research: Findings from research synthesis. *Exceptional Children, 67*(1), 99–114.

Veit, D.T., Scruggs, T.E., & Mastropieri, M.A. (1986). Extended mnemonic instruction with learning disabled students. *Journal of Educational Psychology, 78*(4), 300–308. doi:10.1037/0022-0663.78.4.300

Wilder, A.A., & Williams, J.P. (2001). Students with severe learning disabilities can learn higher order comprehension skills. *Journal of Educational Psychology, 93*(2), 268–278. doi:10.1037/0022-0663.93.2.268

Williams, J.P., Brown, L.G., Silverstein, A.K., & deCani, J.S. (1994). An instructional program in comprehension of narrative themes for adolescents with learning disabilities. *Learning Disability Quarterly, 17*(3), 205–221. doi:10.2307/1511074

Williams, K.T. (2001). *GRADE: Group reading assessment and diagnostic evaluation.* Circle Pines, MN: American Guidance Service.

CHAPTER 12

Helping Struggling Secondary Students Make Connections to Literature

Joan F. Kaywell

> *"When the going gets tough, the tough get a librarian."*
>
> —*Jenna (cited in Bauer, p. 141)*

The term *struggling secondary student* can mean different things to different people. Because this chapter is about reading, one could assume that the term *struggling* refers to a secondary student who has difficulty when reading literature. Another interpretation—the one that I think is often overlooked but is of major importance—is that the term refers to a secondary student who is having difficulty or is struggling with life, and, as a result, does not read. Mikulecky (1978) coined the term *aliteracy* to refer to students who can read but don't, and Beers (2003) identified them as students who simply choose not to read. I, however, refer to these students as those "struggling to survive," the ones who find school curriculum meaningless when they are trying to negotiate the situations wreaking havoc in their daily existence. The premise of this chapter is that this latter group, struggling to survive (STS) secondary students, *must* be led to literature as a means to cope with—and perhaps even save—their lives.

Who are these secondary students? Secondary students are typically middle and high school students, ranging in age from 12 to 18 years of age. During these teenage years, or adolescence, young adults are experiencing major physical, emotional, cognitive, and behavioral changes and growth (Allen & Land, 1999). I've yet to meet an adult who wanted to repeat those years even under the best of

Adolescent Literacy, Field Tested: Effective Solutions for Every Classroom, edited by Sheri R. Parris, Douglas Fisher, and Kathy Headley. © 2009 by the International Reading Association.

circumstances, but STS adolescents are often dealing with situations beyond what we educators would consider "normal." For those living in less-than-desirable circumstances, their lives can be full of turbulence, abuse, and emotional upheaval. A conservative estimate is that 25% of secondary school students can be categorized as STS because they are victims of their parents' poor choices, resulting in poverty, abuse, bullying, alcoholism, divorce, foster care, homelessness, and death (Kaywell, 1993, 1999, 2004, 2005, 2006).

Because these students are "neither children nor adults" (Pipher, p. 52), they have no control over where they live or who raises them. Like the "normal" presented to them in their dysfunctional lives, many of these STS students make unhealthy choices for themselves and continue the cycle, thus repeating the pattern for their own children or ending life entirely. Consider the following startling statistics from the Centers for Disease Control and Prevention (CDC) about the risky behavior many students experience during their young lives:

- 26% of high school students engage in episodic heavy drinking, with 23.8% reporting they drank alcohol for the first time before age 13 (CDC, 2007a).

- 22.3% were offered, sold, or given an illegal drug by someone on school property (CDC, 2007a).

- 62% of 12th graders and 33% of 9th graders have had sexual intercourse (CDC, 2004).

- In 2004, suicide was the third-leading cause of death for U.S. 10–24-year-olds; this translates into 4,599 deaths (CDC, 2007b).

- In 2005, 14% of U.S. 10–24-year-olds were victims of homicide (CDC, 2006).

We must teach STS students that choosing literature is perhaps the best way they can both momentarily and healthily escape their emotional pain until they reach adulthood, when they will be more able to address their issues. Additionally, by improving their own skills as readers, STS students can acquire the ability necessary to read the texts that can help them learn to break the cycle for their own families. To accomplish this, we must motivate students to read, match books with readers, and help students develop their reading proficiency.

Instructional Practices That Work

Although "it is not well understood how adolescents can be motivated to read" (National Institute for Literacy, 2002, Rationale section, ¶ 4), research conducted by Curtis (2002) suggests that time spent reading, diversity in text selection, and text choice contribute to students' reading motivation. For STS students, a frank discussion on the importance of reading in today's world is a must. It can be as simple as listing the pros and cons for persons who can read versus persons who cannot read. The point is that STS students know that it is important to be skilled readers and all of them really want to be skilled readers, but often the reading required of them in school is either too difficult or meaningless to warrant their giving it the time. By getting them to revisit reading's value to them individually, they will be more apt to make and keep the goals they set for themselves in making time to read.

A related but often overlooked discussion should also be held about the importance of reading literature, especially fiction. At this particular time in history, there is an emphasis on reading nonfiction and informational text, which speaks to one's head rather than to one's heart. I worry at times that without heart at the center of reading, we may produce "educated Eichmanns" whose primary means of acquiring story is through film without conversation. Because the results of this discussion may be less obvious than the outcomes on why we read, I offer a list of reasons for teaching and studying literature (see Figure 12.1). The following sections describe several ways to facilitate this important study of literature to bring our STS students into the world of reading.

FIGURE 12.1
Why Teach and Study Literature?

Teach and study literature because literature …

- Provides escape
- Increases vocabulary
- Elicits mental stimulation
- Establishes awareness of self
- Provides awareness of and sensitivity to other people (individuals, cultures, countries, etc.) and situations (history, dilemmas, etc.) outside of the realm of the reader
- Presents moral values that can be objectively accepted or rejected so people can deal with their worlds in a responsible manner
- Offers universal truths about the human condition for objective consideration
- Broadens one's experience, both simple (a Floridian "seeing" snow) and complex (a priest meeting a murderer), through vicarious experience
- Allows us to test and clarify our own values
- Stimulates analytical and critical thought about the society in which we live
- Ties our social fabric together by providing a cultural frame of reference
- Reviews cultural heritage
- Enables us to objectively study other cultures
- Reviews literary biography and history
- Enables us to peruse the future, its possibilities, and its mystery
- Promotes the discussion of ideas by providing something to talk about with others
- Helps people become better writers through the study of various styles, rhetorical devices, modes of discourse, and so on
- Helps students become independent readers
- Exposes students to art and beauty through the skillful use of language
- Adds to our store of knowledge which helps make our lives richer and fuller
- Entertains us and gives us pleasure

Setting a Goal and Making the Time to Read

Sustained silent reading practices are advocated and encouraged in schools but often fail when students are given the time to read without any instruction. Have STS students select anything they want to read for an experiment that will gauge how long they can focus on a selection. Record the time and have them begin reading. Ask them to look at the clock individually and record their respective times as soon they notice they either stopped comprehending what they were reading or their minds drifted off the selection. Have STS students individually record their focus time and set their next focus goal. Do the same with the class as a whole, starting with a five-minute period. As soon as the entire class can read with focus and without interruption for five minutes, incrementally increase the class's goal by five minutes until the entire class can independently read for an entire class period. By modeling what is expected as a class goal, students can set their individual goals, commit to developing a habit of reading (see Figure 12.2), and track their progress (see Figure 12.3).

Getting Parents Involved

Obviously, teachers can learn a lot about their students' attitudes toward reading by getting information—or not—from their parents. By asking parents to respond to a few basic questions, teachers can get plenty of information to assist in their efforts to increase students' literacy and find the right books for them to read. For those students who insist their parents won't comply, have them answer the questions themselves. I also advocate the use of regular progress reports to serve as reading reminders for all concerned (see Figure 12.4).

Finding and Choosing the Right Young Adult Texts

Matching a reader with the right book is key to helping STS students connect with literature (Beers, 2003; Lesesne, 2003). Young adult (YA) literature, or "books either written for or read by YA readers," (Lesesne, 2003, p. 54) is the best resource for making a good match. The best way to familiarize yourself with this literature is to join the professional organizations that provide you with the best resources.

Finding Good Young Adult (YA) Literature. There are several ways to find literature written specifically for young adults, but there are few journals that both review and feature this particular kind of literature. The International Reading Association's *Journal of Adolescent & Adult Literacy* (*JAAL*) is a literacy journal published specifically for teachers of older students, featuring a regular column called Books for Adolescents. Within IRA is a special interest group called the Network on Adolescent Literature that publishes the journal *SIGNAL*. *SIGNAL* contains an extensive review section on books of interest to secondary

---

FIGURE 12.2
Improving Your Reading

Name: _____

READING/WRITING REQUIREMENT: Obviously, if you want to get better at something, you must practice. For the next couple of months, you are to read for one half hour every night (excluding weekends). In other words, you are to spend 2.5 hours each week reading a book on your own. If, for example, something comes up and you are unable to read one day, then you may make up that time either by doubling up on another day or by reading on the weekends. The point is that you develop a habit of reading regularly. You will need to write at least a half of a page each time you read to prove that you read and understood your book.

PROVING YOUR READING: To give you credit for practicing your reading, I need to see that you reflected or thought about what you read. This is different than answering a bunch of questions at the end of a chapter. Instead, I would like you to copy your favorite line or section of the book and explain clearly why it was your favorite part. Additionally, to help me help you, I need you to complete what time you started reading and what time you ended, followed by how many pages you read.

GRADING: The credit you receive for this is pretty straightforward. By reading for 2.5 hours and writing 2.5 pages each week, you will earn an "A." Reading only 2 hours with 2 pages of writing will earn you a "B." Reading 1.5 hours with 1.5 pages of writing will earn you a "C." Reading for 1 hour and writing 1 page will earn you a "D," and reading for half an hour and writing a half a page will earn you an "F." If you do nothing, you will earn nothing; zeroes are devastating to your grade.

SELECTING A BOOK TO READ: There are three requirements: (1) You may read only a book you want to read (I will help you with your selection); (2) You may not read a book that is required in another class; and (3) You may not read a book that will get me in trouble.

What is your personal reading goal for this term? _____

Title of Book: _____

Author: _____ Number of Pages: _____

Date Begun: _____ Date Finished (finishing times will vary):_____

My parents/guardians have read my reading goal, know what is expected of me, have approved the book I am reading, and have agreed to help me in reaching my reading goal.

_____
Parents' or Guardians' Signatures

---

readers as well as teaching strategies and author interviews on how to teach them. More information about these journals can be found at IRA's website, www.reading.org.

The National Council of Teachers of English (NCTE) has two publications that provide regular information about YA literature and how to use it: *Voices From the Middle*, like *JAAL*, also has a column entitled Books for Adolescents, and *English*

FIGURE 12.3
Tracking Your Reading Progress

Name: _____ Date: _____

Title of Book: _____ Author: _____

       Time Began: _____ Time Ended: _____ (Total Time Read: _____)

       Beginning Page: _____ Ending Page: _____ (Total Pages Read: _____)

My half-page response:

_____

_____

_____

_____

_____

An example of what this might look like:

Name: _____ Joan F. Kaywell _____ Date: _____ August 15, 2008 _____

Title of Book: _ *Staying Fat for Sarah Byrnes* _ Author: _ Chris Crutcher _

       Time Began: __ 9:45 A.M. __ Time Ended: __ 10:25 A.M. __ (Total Time Read: 40 minutes total)

       Beginning Page: __ 13 __ Ending Page: ____ 25 ____ (Total Pages Read: 12 pages total)

What you may write about: Write those things from the book that you want to remember, especially as the material relates to your own life. As your teacher, I will be looking that you actually read, understood, and thought about your reading. If you get stuck, think about the following things about which to write:

- Copy a part of the book you like and comment on why you liked it so much.
- Relate what you've read to something that you've either learned or experienced.
- Offer advice or words of wisdom for the character or characters.
- Do you love or hate reading the book? When you read this book, does time get away from you because you just can't put it down? Do you want to stop reading the book because it makes you uncomfortable, or because the vocabulary is too difficult for you to understand? What makes you feel the way you feel?
- Write any questions you have about the book, either in terms of what confuses you or what the book makes you wonder about. In that way, I can help you as your teacher.

Journal has a column entitled Bold Books for Teenagers. NCTE's website, www. ncte.org, gives information about these two journals. Within the NCTE is the Assembly on Literature for Adolescents (ALAN; www.alan-ya.org), which publishes *The ALAN Review*. In it, teachers can find information and current research about YA literature and its teaching, interviews with authors, and most important, a section of reviews of new YA books.

FIGURE 12.4
Help Me Help Your Child Read and Write Better

Teacher's Name: _____

Please print your child's name: _____

Please print your name and phone number: _____

Please answer these questions about your child as a reader and writer at home. Your responses will help inform my teaching:

1. Did you regularly read to your child as an infant and toddler?

    If yes, please tell me when you started reading to your child, and list the books you enjoyed together (as many as you can remember).

2. What is the first chapter book that your child read without your help? List other books that he or she has read to your knowledge.

    If your child has never read a book from cover to cover, please write "none."

3. In your opinion, does your child like to read?

    If yes, what types of material does he or she read?

    If no, why do you suppose he or she doesn't enjoy reading?

4. As a parent, what do you wish I could get your child to do as a reader and writer?

5. How many hours of TV does your child watch on average daily? _____ What kinds of things occupy his or her time?

6. Is there anything you would like me to know about your child that I did not ask, especially if you think it will help me in developing your child's literacy?

Progress Report

Dear Parents/Guardians:

As a reminder, students are supposed to read for a half an hour every weekday and respond to their reading by writing one paragraph for each day. In other words, students are to read for 2.5 hours and write 2.5 pages each week. In order for reading to become habitual, this is a combined effort between you, your child, and me. If there's anything I can do to help, please let me know. You can help by reminding your child to read and by signing his or her reading log every week.

Parents' or Guardians' Signatures: _____

The American Library Association (ALA; www.ala.org) is mostly a professional organization that caters to media specialists, and teachers interested in YA literature may want to join their Young Adult Library Services Association for the wealth of information this organization provides on YA literature. ALA's *Booklist* magazine reviews thousands of YA titles each year. The ALA also annually awards the Newbery Medal to the author of the most distinguished contribution to American literature for children and the Michael L. Printz Award, sponsored by *Booklist*, to a book that exemplifies literary excellence in young adult literature. Although Scarecrow Press is not officially affiliated with the ALA, it caters to librarians and publishes *Voices of Youth Advocates* (www.voya.com), which is the only privately published magazine devoted exclusively to intellectual freedom and the informational needs of adolescents.

Now referred to as "the goddess of YA literature," Teri Lesesne has published two wonderful resources in *Making the Match* (2003) and *Naked Reading* (2006). Hundreds of award-winning YA novels are briefly annotated in these two reader-friendly texts. Another must-have text for finding quality YA literature is Jim Blasingame's (2007) *Books That Don't Bore 'Em*, which includes annotated lists of YA books organized by theme, genre, and degree of difficulty.

Why Realistic Fiction Is Recommended. According to the American Psychological Association (2004), "Resilience is the process of adapting well in the face of adversity, trauma, tragedy, threats, or even significant sources of stress—such as family and relationship problems.... It means 'bouncing back' from difficult experiences" (p. 1). Based on the results of three studies, Dennis Charney, MD, PhD, Dean of Research, and a professor of psychiatry at Mt. Sinai School of Medicine, believes that resilience can be increased in 10 ways, one way being exposure to resilient role models in heroic figures (Milne, 2007). Because such training affects what type of adults young people develop into, Charney further recommends that youth be engaged both emotionally and intellectually. We can do this by exposing students to realistic fiction that shows young adult protagonists dealing with adversity through positive outlets. Healthy escape options include participation in arts or crafts, music or dance, spirituality, athletics, service, and reading and writing (Kaywell, 2005). The following are a few examples of such YA literature:

- Choosing arts or crafts—In *Speak* (Anderson, 2001), Melinda is raped and metaphorically conquers "the beast" in her life through a tree sculpture.
- Choosing music or dance—In *The Big Nothing* (Fogelin, 2004) 13-year-old Justin Riggs has abandonment issues because of his depressed mother. Justin eventually learns that playing the piano is much more preferable than delving into nothingness as a way to cope.

- Choosing spirituality—Perhaps the very best book about forgiveness ever written is *What Daddy Did* (Shusterman, 1993). Based on a true story, Preston has to learn to love his father again after his father murders Preston's mother.

- Choosing athletics—Any of Chris Crutcher's award-winning novels will show YA protagonists constructively using sports as a way of coping, but *Ironman* (1995) is a personal favorite. Bo Brewster has a verbally abusive and controlling father, and Bo both bikes and writes letters as his way of managing anger.

- Choosing service—*Touching Spirit Bear* (Mikaelsen, 2002) illustrates the concept of "what goes around, comes around." Cole, a victim of an abusive family, turns violent and is sent to an island after nearly beating a peer to death. According to Native American Circle Justice, Cole must heal himself as well as the community.

- Choosing reading and writing—*Chinese Cinderella: The True Story of an Unwanted Daughter* (Mah, 2001) shows how books were the author's best companions while growing up as an unwanted daughter. *Push* (Sapphire, 1997) is probably the meanest book ever written and yet is one of the most brilliant. Precious Jones is an illiterate, sexually and physically abused 16-year-old whose writing saves her life. This latter book clearly illustrates STS students and why teachers must read the books they offer to students.

Because of space considerations, I listed only my best recommendations of books that address current issues affecting teenagers, books with teen protagonists who choose wisely in spite of their circumstances. For those interested in delving deeper into this topic, please refer to any of the six volumes of the series *Using Literature to Help Troubled Teenagers Cope With [Various] Issues* (Greenwood Press). The issues addressed in the series are *Family* (Kaywell, 1999), *Societal* (Carroll, 1999), *Identity* (Kaplan, 1999), *Health* (Bowman, 2000), *End-of-Life* (Allen, 2001), and *Abuse* (Kaywell, 2004). In this series, literacy experts are paired with counselors to provide therapy for YA protagonists in YA novels. Another book specifically designed to encourage teenagers to choose reading as a way to escape emotional pain is *Dear Author: Letters of Hope* (Kaywell, 2007), in which authors of YA books write letters directly to teenagers to offer them hope and new perspectives in dealing with life's difficulties. For those who like what a particular author has to say, information about the author, annotations of three of his or her books, and a website address are included. For a list of authors who wrote letters with the topic that was addressed in her or his respective letter, please refer to Table 12.1.

Topic	Author

TABLE 12.1
Topics of Letters Written by Authors in *Dear Author: Letters of Hope*
(Kaywell, 2007)

Topic	Author
Date rape	Laurie Halse Anderson
Alienation	Sandy Asher
Death of self	T.A. Barron
Alcoholic parent	Joan Bauer
Guilt/divorce	Marion Dane Bauer
Eating disorders/self-image	Cherie Bennett
9/11 prejudice	Edward Bloor
Depression	Sue Ellen Bridgers
Sexual abuse	Chris Crutcher
Racism/prejudice	Christopher Paul Curtis
Death, drugs, and murder	Lois Duncan
Teasing/anger	Alex Flinn
Lesbian love	Nancy Garden
Death of mother	Patricia Hermes
Eating disorders/suicide	Sara Holbrook
Divorce/identity Issues	Anne C. LeMieux
Life's choices	Chris Lynch
Poverty	Janet McDonald
Death of mother/father in prison	Rodman Philbrick
Teen pregnancy	Marilyn Reynolds
Domestic violence	John H. Ritter
Mother murdered by father	Neal Shusterman
Bad neighborhood/violence	Jerry Spinelli
Cutting	Shelley Stoehr
Sexual abuse	Ann Turner
Loneliness/prejudice	Ellen Wittlinger

The Book Pass

Originally developed by Carter and Rashkis (1980), the book pass has evolved into an instructional strategy that successfully matches books with readers. After acquiring multiple titles of YA books that will appeal to STS students and making sure that there are enough books so that each STS student has a different book, you are ready to begin the book pass. The directions are simple:

1. Give each student a different book and have them write down the book's title and author on a piece of paper.
2. Give students 2–4 minutes to preview their books by reading the information on the book's jacket and by beginning to read page one. Gauge the time by observing your students' concentration levels.

3. Have students rate the book on a scale of 1 to 5, with 1 being "No way will I read this book!" 3 being "I'd read it if I had to," and 5 being "I HAVE to read this book."

4. Have students jot one to three words to describe why they liked the book—or not—and then pass the book to the next person; the teacher decides the logical order.

5. Do this for about eight rotations and ask for a show of hands of those students who do not have any ratings of 5. If it's a small number, you can address those students individually. If it's a large number, then continue with the book pass.

6. Distribute the books to students, beginning with those students who only have one rating of 5, then two 5s, then three 5s, and so on until every single student has a book they rated 4 or higher.

Once students have selected their books, have them respond to their reading (see Figure 12.3 on p. 148) using methods espoused by reading theorist Rosenblatt (1995) to get them to transact or have an emotional engagement with the text.

The Book Talk

The book talk is a 2–5 minute presentation of a book with the sole intention of getting others to read it. There are three basic rules to giving a book talk: (1) book talk only books you have read; (2) book talk only books you enjoyed; and (3) never, under any circumstances, tell the ending. Students are familiar with how they persuade their peers to watch a movie they've seen, and it is basically the same thing. For those wishing to develop book talking skills, refer to the website "Booktalks—Quick and Simple" developed by Nancy Keane and located at nancykeane.com/booktalks/.

Overcoming Challenges

It is important to acknowledge that we are literacy teachers, not therapists or guidance counselors. With that said, however, we all need to recognize the signs when our STS students are at risk and to whom they should be referred. By law, teachers must refer to the administration those students they believe are either being abused or are at risk to themselves or others. The not-for-profit website www.helpguide.org offers comprehensive information about abuse, including information about neglect and emotional, physical, and sexual abuse. The Screening for Mental Health Website at www.mentalhealthscreening.org offers two youth programs, one for the middle school level and the other for the high school level, called the Signs of Suicide (SOS). These programs use "an action-oriented approach instructing students how to ACT (Acknowledge, Care, and Tell) in the face of a mental health emergency" (Signs of Suicide, main page). It is common practice that teachers receive training on recognizing those warning signs, but it is less common that teenagers are provided with information.

Teachers will undoubtedly be concerned about censorship issues, too, especially because the list of books in print is analogous to the list of censored books. The bottom line is that any book is potentially censorable by someone, somewhere, for some reason. Usually the reason is that it doesn't square with someone's personal beliefs, and in a country as diverse as ours, it is no wonder that censorship cases abound. First and foremost, parents have the right to choose what is appropriate for their own children to read, but censorship problems arise when parents want to decide what is appropriate for other people's children to read. Second, by following three simple rules, teachers can avoid censorship cases. Tell your STS students that their self-selected books must be books (1) that they want to read, (2) that are not required for another class, and (3) that will not get you, the teacher, in trouble. Your students know their parents better than you do, and what will be fine with one set of parents might not sit well with someone else's parents.

Looking Ahead

STS students need help in connecting to literature that relates to their lives and circumstances. Teachers need to know their students and the available YA literature to make the match between reader and book. By reminding STS students of the importance of reading and literature, by offering them an array of engaging YA books, and by giving them choices in what they read and encouraging individual goal setting, teachers can help these STS students make life-changing connections to the literature.

Because I firmly believe that "teachers, librarians, and authors are often the unsung heroes of children on the brink of self-destruction" (Kaywell, 2006, p. 311), I would love to see more research done in the area of bibliotherapy. Perhaps school guidance teachers can be taught strategies for improving literacy skills and offer group therapy for those STS students who are 14 going on 40. Perhaps the pendulum will swing back to a more qualitative approach rather than the scientific empirical approach to present a balanced view as to the value of literature in students' lives. Perhaps books really do save lives.

EXTEND YOUR THINKING

▦ Involve your students in designing your own record-keeping system for an individualized reading program.

▦ Model book-talk strategies with your students and teach them how to give book talks to their peers.

- Involve your students in selecting a topic of interest for them to study and together build a list of related books with increasing sophistication and difficulty.

- Ask your students to ask three important adults in their lives two questions: What is your favorite book of all time, and why? Compile a bulletin board of the results.

REFERENCES

Allen, J. (Ed.), & Kaywell, J.F. (Series Advisor). (2001). *Using literature to help troubled teenagers cope with end of life issues.* Westport, CT: Greenwood.

Allen, J.P., & Land, D. (1999). Attachment in adolescence. In J. Cassidy & P.R. Shaver (Eds.), *Handbook of attachment: Theory, research, and clinical applications* (pp. 319–335). New York: Guilford.

American Psychological Association. (2004). *The road to resilience.* Retrieved August 18, 2008, from www.apahelpcenter.org/featuredtopics/feature.php?id=6&ch=2

Beers, K. (2003). *When kids can't read: What teachers can do.* Portsmouth, NH: Heinemann.

Blasingame, J. (2007). *Books that don't bore 'em.* New York: Scholastic.

Bowman, C.A. (Ed.), & Kaywell, J.F. (Series Advisor). (2000). *Using literature to help troubled teenagers cope with health issues.* Westport, CT: Greenwood.

Carroll, P.S. (Ed.). & Kaywell, J.F. (Series Advisor). (1999). *Using literature to help troubled teenagers cope with societal issues.* Westport, CT: Greenwood.

Carter, C., & Rashkis, Z. (1980). *Ideas for teaching English in the junior high and middle school.* Urbana, IL: National Council of Teachers of English.

Centers for Disease Control and Prevention. (2004). Youth risk behavior surveillance—United States, 2003. *Morbidity and Mortality Weekly Report, 53*(SS-2). Retrieved August 14, 2008, from www.cdc.gov/mmwr/PDF/SS/SS5302.pdf

Centers for Disease Control and Prevention. (2006). Youth risk behavior surveillance—United States, 2005. *Morbidity and Mortality Weekly Report, 55*(SS-5). Retrieved August 14, 2008, from www.cdc.gov/mmwr/PDF/SS/SS5505.pdf

Centers for Disease Control and Prevention. (2007a). *The youth risk behavior surveillance system (YRBSS): 2007.* Retrieved August 14, 2008, from www.cdc.gov/HealthyYouth/yrbs/slides/yrbs07_tobacco_alcohol_other_drugs.ppt#1136

Centers for Disease Control and Prevention. (2007b). Suicide trends among youths and young adults aged 10–24 years—United States, 1990–2004. *Morbidity and Mortality Weekly Report, 56*(35), 905–908. Retrieved August 14, 2008, from www.cdc.gov/mmwr/preview/mmwrhtml/mm5635a2.htm

Curtis, M.E. (2002). Adolescent reading: A synthesis of research. In *Adolescent literacy—research informing practice: A series of workshops.* Retrieved August 15, 2008, from www.nifl.gov/nifl/webcasts/transcripts/NIFL_Introduction.doc

Kaplan, J. (Ed.), & Kaywell, J.F. (Series Advisor). (1999). *Using literature to help troubled teenagers cope with identity issues.* Westport, CT: Greenwood.

Kaywell, J.F. (1993). *Adolescents at risk: A guide to fiction and nonfiction for young adults, parents, and professionals.* Westport, CT: Greenwood.

Kaywell, J.F. (Ed.). (1999). *Using literature to help troubled teenagers cope with family issues.* Westport, CT: Greenwood.

Kaywell, J.F. (Ed.). (2004). *Using literature to helped troubled teenagers cope with abuse issues.* Westport, CT: Greenwood.

Kaywell, J.F. (2005). Teachers offering healthy escape options for teenagers in pain. *Voices From the Middle, 12*(4), 31–36.

Kaywell, J.F. (2006). There's hope in a book: Saving our students with literature and laughter. *Voices of Youth Advocates, 29*(4), 311–316.

Kaywell, J.F. (Ed.). (2007). *Dear author: Letters of hope.* New York: Philomel.

Keane, N. (2008). *Booktalks—quick and simple.* Retrieved December 9, 2008, from nancykeane.com/booktalks.

Lesesne, T.S. (2003). *Making the match: The right book for the right reader at the right time, grades 4–12*. Portland, ME: Stenhouse.

Lesesne, T.S. (2006). *Naked reading: Uncovering what tweens need to become lifelong readers.* Portland, ME: Stenhouse.

Mikulecky, L. (1978, May). *Aliteracy and a changing view of reading goals.* Paper presented at the 23rd annual meeting of the International Reading Association, Houston, TX. (ERIC Document Reproduction Service No. ED157052)

Milne, D. (2007). People can learn markers on road to resilience. *Psychiatric News, 42*(2), 5.

National Institute for Literacy. (2002). *Adolescent literacy—research informing practice: A series of workshops.* Retrieved August 15, 2008, from www.nifl.gov/partnershipforreading/adolescent/summary.html

Pipher, M. (1995). *Reviving Ophelia: Saving the selves of adolescent girls.* New York: Ballantine.

Rosenblatt, L.M. (1995). *Literature as exploration* (5th ed.). New York: Modern Language Association.

Screening for Mental Health. "SOS Signs of Suicide." Retrieved January 13, 2009, from www.mental healthscreening.org/schools/

LITERATURE CITED

Anderson, L.H. (2001). *Speak.* New York: Puffin.

Crutcher, C. (1995). *Ironman.* New York: Dell Laurel-Leaf.

Fogelin, A. (2004). *The big nothing.* Atlanta, GA: Peachtree.

Mah, A.Y. (2001). *Chinese Cinderella: The true story of an unwanted daughter.* New York: Dell Laurel-Leaf.

Mikaelsen, B. (2002). *Touching spirit bear.* New York: Scholastic.

Sapphire. (1997). *Push.* New York: Random House.

Shusterman, N. (1993). *What daddy did.* New York: HarperTeen.

CHAPTER 13

Successful Teachers Share Advice for Motivating Reluctant Adolescents

Cheryl Taliaferro, Sheri R. Parris

"What we do as teachers is intimately connected to why we are here on earth. We become teachers because we believe each child is special— each child—and deserves the best academic, social, and emotional support we adults can offer. It really is that simple."

—*Justin Smith, recipient of 2007–2008 Princeton University Distinguished Secondary School Teaching Award*

I n an ideal world, secondary classrooms would be filled with students excited about their assignments and eager to learn more. Although some classrooms come close to realizing this ideal, it unfortunately is not the reality that many teachers face. According to the National Council of Teachers of English (2006), fewer than 75% of students in the United States graduate from high school. Although factors influencing this high drop-out rate are certainly complex, one factor that plays a pivotal role is related to students' experiences in school.

What motivates some students to remain in school and to excel at academic tasks while others languish or give up completely? As Turner and Paris (1995) note, "Motivation does not reside solely in the child; rather it is in the interaction between students and their literacy environments" (p. 672).

Adolescent Literacy, Field Tested: Effective Solutions for Every Classroom, edited by Sheri R. Parris, Douglas Fisher, and Kathy Headley. © 2009 by the International Reading Association.

The purpose of this chapter is to identify instructional routines that have proven to be effective in helping to motivate reluctant adolescent readers. To help us determine what those practices are, we interviewed award-winning secondary teachers from across the United States. Following are the most common practices that they cited as being helpful in their classrooms.

Select Texts on the Basis of Students' Interests and Needs

To engage the reluctant adolescent reader, teachers need to align materials and assignments to students' interests and needs. Researchers have noted that a mismatch often exists between what students want to learn and what they are required to learn in school, and this mismatch is further evidenced by discrepancies between many students' in-school literacy activities and their out-of-school literacy activities (Ivey & Broaddus, 2001; Newkirk, 2002; Smith & Wilhelm, 2002). In other words, students often have skills that schools and teachers ignore. Mary Schlieder, 2008 Nebraska Teacher of the Year, reminds us, "You have to find a way to help [students] find their strengths and know they are capable. Everyone is good at something, even if it's not an area we teach and test during the school day."

To motivate reluctant readers, teachers should begin by recognizing and working with students' strengths and then scaffold instruction to include a wider range of literacy activities. John Kline Jr., 2008 New Jersey Teacher of the Year, describes the way he uses this approach in his classroom:

> For adolescents with reading difficulties, start with something they're good at and enjoy. For example, a football player who's having difficulty reading—give him a *Sports Illustrated* and find articles that he enjoys reading.... After a few months of *Sports Illustrated*, move up to a *New York Times* sports page.

Build Relationships

To select materials and activities based on students' interests and needs, teachers need to know what those interests and needs are. They need to build relationships with their students. According to the teachers we interviewed, the best way to create these relationships is to take a personal interest in each student in the classroom. Adolescents know when their teachers care about them and when they don't, and students are more likely to work for teachers who show an interest in them as individuals (Smith & Wilhelm, 2002). Student–teacher relationships can be fostered in myriad ways: teachers can greet their students at the door before they enter the classroom; attend their students' extracurricular activities, including sports games, drama performances, musical recitals, and academic competitions; and talk to students about their interests.

In their qualitative study of adolescent boys throughout the United States, Smith and Wilhelm (2002) found that many boys alluded to an implicit social contract that exists between students and their teachers. This social contract includes the following features:

1. A teacher should try to get to know me personally.
2. A teacher should care about me as an individual.
3. A teacher should attend to my interests in some way.
4. A teacher should help me learn and work to make sure that I have learned.
5. A teacher should be passionate, committed, work hard, and know his or her stuff. (p. 99)

Unfortunately, many of these boys expressed that their teachers had reneged on this contract; therefore, the boys were not willing to do their part in class. However, when they did encounter teachers who met even one of the conditions outlined in the contract, they were willing to work hard for him or her. The power that teachers have in this regard can be instrumental in motivating students. By showing an interest in students as individuals and by recognizing the skills and strengths that students bring to the classroom, teachers can get through to their students and build a community of learners who strive to do their best on their literacy assignments.

April Todd, an 11-year English and language arts teacher who was named Maryland Teacher of the Year in 2008, offers this advice: "Know your students. Reading can be an intimidating and challenging topic for many learners. You can't teach and the students can't learn without a mutual network of trust, respect, and communication."

Give Students Choices

Sullivan (2004) reminds us to give students "the chance to choose the type of reading materials they want and the level of difficulty they are comfortable with, and they won't regard reading as a chore and language as an enemy" (p. 39). The teachers interviewed for this chapter indicated three activities that are frequently used to make a place for student choice within their curriculums: literature circles, sustained silent reading, and a range of assessment tools.

Literature Circles

Literature circles are one way to bring students' choices about texts into the classroom, because choice is a primary component of literature circles (Daniels, 2001; Dutro, 2002). Generally, a teacher enacting literature circles presents a variety of texts that function as a text set to his or her class. If, for example, the theme to be studied is World War II, the text set may include copies of *Anne Frank: The Diary of a Young Girl*; *Night*, a memoir by Elie Wiesel that details the author's experiences as a Jewish man forced into several concentration camps; *Maus: A Survivor's Tale*, a memoir presented in the form of a graphic novel by Art Spiegelman; *The Summer of My German Soldier*, a young adult novel by Bette Greene that centers on a Jewish girl living in Arkansas and befriending a German prisoner; and *Number the Stars*, a Newbery Medal winner by Lois Lowry that tells the fictionalized story of 10-year-old Annemarie Johannesen, who helps her best friend, a Jewish girl named Ellen Rosen, escape with her family when the Jews are evacuated from Denmark. These texts together represent a variety of interests and reading levels.

Each student is allowed to choose the work that he or she would like to read. Students are then grouped into their circles according to their commonly selected texts. Students meet in circles on a regular, predictable schedule to discuss ideas that they generate about the novel, and they make notes to help them create more meaning from the work. Sometimes the members of literature circles are given specific roles to fulfill within their group, such as wordsmith, discussion director, illustrator, and summarizer. These roles, however, may be adapted or eliminated according to the needs of the particular students in the classroom. Laura Carlton, who has taught English for 15 years and has been named the 2008 Louisiana State Teacher of the Year, says,

> I let students pick their own books and use basic literature circle roles plus a 'connector'—someone who connects the book to something they like or have read before or talks about a current article in the news that connects to the book.

Sustained Silent Reading

Sustained silent reading has long been presented as one method of improving student reading. Different classrooms and schools currently enact this routine in varied ways. Some teachers devote the first 15 minutes of class time to sustained silent reading. Some schools as a whole have adopted Drop Everything and Read time, in which the entire school stops all other activities and everyone reads silently for a set amount of time (Cumming, 1997). Other classrooms, following a reading workshop approach similar to that advocated by Nancy Atwell (1998), set aside a certain number of days each week for sustained silent reading. In this case, students know, for example, that reading workshop will occur every Tuesday and Thursday, and on those days they are expected to read a self-selected book and complete a journal response about their reading.

Sustained silent reading is difficult to measure and justify in the current educational climate that is dominated by positivist research and objective test scores (Fisher, Flood, Lapp, & Frey, 2004); however, common sense and the expert teachers interviewed for this chapter maintain it is a worthwhile engagement of students' time. A central tenet of the practice is student choice, and at its best, sustained silent reading allows students the time and the opportunity to read a book that's written at their personal reading level and that is interesting to them. Any such program needs to ensure access to books; provide appealing books to students; ensure an environment conducive to silent reading; provide encouragement and staff development; create a sense of student-centered accountability in which traditional assessments are replaced by writing, discussion, and other alternative assessments; provide follow-up activities that encourage the students' excitement about their reading; and guarantee a definite, regular time to read (Pilgreen, 2000).

Teachers who regularly include sustained silent reading in their curriculums report a range of positive results. One of those positive results is the transformation of students' understandings of literacy. Earl DeMott, a 14-year teacher and recipient of the Human Rights Award for Ambassadors of Change: Uganda Project as well as a 2008 Teacher of the Year nominee, says the following about sustained silent reading as enacted at the Global Studies and World Languages Academy at Tallwood High School in Virginia Beach, Virginia: "What this gave, ultimately, was exposure to literature, as well as a very important visual aspect that everyone in the school (from the janitor to the principal) cared about literacy."

Assessments

Just as teachers can benefit students by offering them choices in reading materials, they also can better serve students' needs by relying on a variety of measures that assess student learning. Paul Cain, 2008 Texas State Teacher of the Year, reminds us, "Teachers have to recognize that students have different ways of learning, and we have to adjust our teaching and evaluation to the students' learning styles."

Although traditional testing may work well for some students, it certainly does not capture the full range of learning exhibited by all students, particularly students who have spent years struggling with literacy. Therefore, teachers need to consider alternative assessment measures in their classrooms. Beginning with the objectives in mind, teachers should consider the various ways that students might demonstrate their learning and then give students options regarding how they are assessed. Above all else, assessment should be authentic and interchangeable with good instruction (Shepard, 2000). For example, if the objective is to analyze how an author uses setting to advance characterization, a teacher could allow students to write a literary essay, perform a skit, create a piece of artwork, or design a PowerPoint presentation that explains the concept and provides illustrative examples from a variety of works with which the student is familiar.

Make Text Relevant

Researchers agree that reluctant readers need to find relevance in the work that they are asked to do (Lindfors, 1999; Newkirk, 2002; Smith & Wilhelm, 2002).

Relevance does not have a standard definition, however. It may involve incorporating humor and nontraditional genres in the classroom to build community (Newkirk, 2002). It may also include students engaging in authentic inquiry acts that involve "seeking new information, clarifying, confirming, rejecting, connecting, applying" (Lindfors, 1999, p. 9). Whatever the particular definition, relevance is what makes learning meaningful for the learner—either on a social level or an academic level.

Connecting Fictional Experiences to Students' Lives

With literature, teachers should help students find ways to connect their own life experiences to the characters, plot situations, and themes in the works that they study. Unfortunately, these connections may be more difficult for some students to find. Raymond Page, a 30-year teaching veteran at St. Anthony High School in Jersey City, New Jersey, and Princeton University Distinguished Secondary School Teacher Honoree, explains one aspect of this problem:

> I find that lack of motivation is often due to the fact that characters in books do not look like [the students], do not live in areas like the ones they live in, and do not encounter the same problems they do. Because of the realities in the books they have encountered in the past, they have come to believe that reading is an activity far removed from their lives.

An important way to help reluctant students find relevance in literature is to provide them with reading experiences that are reflective of their own lives. For this reason, multicultural literature needs to have a prominent place in English curriculum.

The teachers at Mr. Page's school create ways to incorporate literature that reflects the lives of their students into both their regular English curriculum and into an optional school book club. Multicultural literature can be especially powerful because of its ability to draw in students who may not see themselves and their experiences as represented in other, more traditional Western texts. Additionally, it has the power to help adolescent students transform their understandings of themselves and of people from other cultures, whom they are likely to encounter in their own lives (Banks, 1994; Bean, Valerio, Senior, & White, 1999; Dressel, 2005; Glazier & Seo, 2005; Ketter & Buter, 2004; Louie, 2005; Poole, 2005).

Inquiry Projects

Inquiry projects (Lindfors, 1999) can be another means of helping students find relevance in their work. Inquiry may take the form of information seeking or of wondering, but in either case it must come from the student rather than from the teacher or a predetermined curriculum. Students should be afforded the time and the opportunity to explore topics that are meaningful to them. This means that students need time to discuss their learning with their classmates as well as their teacher. They need to spend time reflecting on their learning, and they should be allowed to choose their own topics when conducting research, writing essays, and completing projects.

Laurie Jones, 2008 Washington State Teacher of the Year, reminds us of the importance of students saying, "I've got to solve this problem so I need to do research to find the answer." A student may be more willing to engage with reading if the reading serves as a practical means of answering a question the student has. In the classroom, inquiry projects can take many forms. If the purpose of a unit is to teach research skills, students could be allowed to choose any topic to research, rather than being required to write a paper or complete a project about an author or an historical figure. Instead of focusing on traditional academic topics, some students may choose to research how to fix a car or how to pursue a specific career. Students will read more and engage with their learning more when their assignments help them answer real questions that they have (Lindfors, 1999; Smith & Wilhelm, 2002).

Inquiry projects also have a place in the curriculum when a unit is content driven rather than skills driven. For example, if the purpose of a unit is for students to acquire more knowledge about African cultures, students could be asked what kind of information they would like to learn. They might be interested in topics as diverse as traditional music, wild animals, medical practices, modern religions, women's rights issues, the impact of AIDS, and genocide. Students should be given the time to delve deeper into the specific topics that interest them and to share what they learn with the class.

Front-Loading

Another way to help create relevance is front-loading information to create an instant interest for the students (Smith & Wilhelm, 2002). In other words, indicate the relevance at the start of the unit to compel students to want to learn. One lesson that helps front-load nonfiction is described by Donna Sharer, a national board-certified teacher who is also a Philadelphia Writing Project Scholar and a recipient of the James Madison Fellowship:

> I often use political cartoons to introduce a topic/issue, whether historical or current, to have students not only interpret the message but also reinforce literary elements and figurative language which is often in cartoons.... I've found some reluctant students more willing to read accompanying primary documents and secondary sources because it helped them interpret cartoons.

Sharer created a website for teachers to help them develop similar lessons, and it can be accessed at www.learningbycartooning.org.

Model Good Reading and Thinking Behaviors

Read-Alouds

Researchers have documented many benefits of teacher-conducted read-alouds, including increasing students' comprehension of texts (Beck & McKeown, 2001; Fisher, Frey, & Lapp, 2008; McGee & Schickendanz, 2007; Santoro, Chard, Howard, & Baker, 2008), students' understanding of text structures (Fisher et al., 2008; Santoro et al., 2008), students' vocabulary (Beck & McKeown, 2001; Fisher et al., 2008; McGee & Schickendanz, 2007; Santoro et al., 2008), and students' critical thinking skills (Pantaleo, 2004). Middle school students also report that teacher read-alouds are one of the top activities that they value in their language arts classrooms, and as such read-alouds can be used by teachers to scaffold students' understandings of other texts (Ivey & Broaddus, 2001). An additional benefit has been identified by Kathleen Mueller, recipient of Princeton University's Distinguished Secondary Teaching Prize: "Beyond [numerous academic benefits of reading aloud], it has proven to be a significant community building device, much as I imagine was the case when pre-literate people told stories as part of the oral tradition in literary history."

Fisher et al. (2004) observed expert teachers to identify the essential components for teacher read-alouds. Texts should be selected on the basis of students' interests and needs, and the books should be previewed and the read-alouds practiced by the teachers in advance. Teachers should model fluent oral reading, using animation and expression during the reading. Equally important, however, is the teacher's ability to establish and communicate a clear purpose for the read-aloud, making a connection to the students' independent reading and writing. For example, a particular text could be read to analyze the author's use of figurative language to create mood, and then students could be asked to practice a similar technique in their own writing. Finally, the text needs to be discussed before, during, and after the read-aloud. It needs to be appreciated and enjoyed as an art form as well as a hermeneutic that can help students strengthen a particular skill (Sipe, 2000).

Think-Alouds

Having students learn how to become more metacognitive is another way of helping them improve their own reading abilities. When students are able to recognize what they struggle with in reading and then access a range of cognitive strategies that might help them work through their problems, they are independent readers, and that is the goal of most reading instruction. Teachers can help their students develop these metacognitive skills by explicitly modeling them for their students. Kimberley K. Curran, 2007 Teacher of the Year at Sandalwood High School in Jacksonville, Florida, echoes many teachers' concerns when she says,

> I want [my students] to know what to do when they do not understand. I use embedded questions where I "interrupt" a reading with the questions most effective readers process

internally. This helps the struggling reader, and I find most of them during the course of the year start to automatically ask these questions themselves.

Coté and Goldman (1999) found when analyzing science students' think-alouds that "unless readers actively apply strategies to resolve problems they identify, they are likely to end up with fragmentary representations" (p. 189). Therefore, merely recognizing a problem is not enough; students need a skill set that helps them resolve problems when they are encountered. Here lies the appropriate instructional place of teacher think-alouds: By modeling strategies that can be used to solve reading problems, teachers can directly show students how to solve the problems that they encounter when reading.

Looking Ahead

One of the largest obstacles that teachers may face in trying to motivate reluctant adolescent readers stems from the testing culture that currently permeates most schools. Prescribed programs of study and mandated standardized tests can, contrary to their ostensible purpose of raising student achievement, actually stifle teachers' abilities to bring the most appropriate activities into their classrooms (Shannon, 2001). However, dedicated teachers continue to find ways to ensure that their students receive what they need. Teachers can help these adolescents achieve greater success by matching assignments to students' interests and needs; building relationships with students; giving students more choice and control over their learning by incorporating activities like literature circles, sustained silent reading, and alternative assessments in the curriculum; being more explicit in demonstrating the relevance of literacy tasks to students' own lives; and modeling what accomplished readers do through read-alouds and think-alouds. Successful teachers find ways to differentiate instruction even when rigidly defined curriculums are prescribed.

EXTEND YOUR THINKING

■ Reflecting on what you've learned in this chapter, describe three suggested actions that you think will have the most impact if you incorporate them with your own teaching repertoire. Why did you choose these?

■ Reflect upon a specific lesson that you have recently taught. How can you alter this particular lesson to increase motivation for struggling or reluctant readers?

■ Based on the information presented in this chapter, can you think of an additional action or activity that was not mentioned but that would have been consistent with the information presented? Explain why you chose this action or activity and how it would help motivate struggling or reluctant readers in your classroom.

REFERENCES

Atwell, N. (1998). *In the middle: New understanding about writing, reading, and learning.* Portsmouth, NH: Boynton/Cook.

Banks, J.A. (1994). Transforming the mainstream curriculum. *Educational Leadership, 51*(8), 4–8.

Bean, T.W., Valerio, P.C., Senior, H.M., & White, F. (1999). Secondary English students' engagement in reading and writing about a multicultural novel. *The Journal of Educational Research, 93*(1), 32–37.

Beck, I.L., & McKeown, M.G. (2001). Text talk: Capturing the benefits of read-aloud experiences for young children. *The Reading Teacher, 55*(1), 10–20.

Coté, N., & Goldman, S.R. (1999). Building representations of informational text: Evidence from children's think-aloud protocols. In H. Van Oostendorp & S.R. Goldman (Eds.), *The construction of mental representations during reading* (pp. 169–193). Mahwah, NJ: Erlbaum.

Cumming, P. (1997). Drop everything and read all over: Literacy and loving it. *The Horn Book Magazine, 73*(6), 714–718.

Daniels, H. (2001). *Literature circles: Voice and choice in book clubs and reading groups.* Portland, ME: Stenhouse.

Dressel, J.H. (2005). Personal response and social responsibility: Responses of middle school students to multicultural literature. *The Reading Teacher, 58*(8), 750–764. doi:10.1598/RT.58.8.5

Dutro, E. (2002). "Us boys like to read football and boy stuff": Reading masculinities, performing boyhood. *Journal of Literacy Research, 34*(4), 465–500. doi:10.1207/s15548430jlr3404_4

Fisher, D., Flood, J., Lapp, D., & Frey, N. (2004). Interactive read-alouds: Is there a common set of implementation practices? *The Reading Teacher, 58*(1), 8–17. doi:10.1598/RT.58.1.1

Fisher, D., Frey, N., & Lapp, D. (2008). Shared readings: Modeling comprehension, vocabulary, text structures, and text features for older readers. *The Reading Teacher, 61*(7), 548–556. doi:10.1598/RT.61.7.4

Glazier, J., & Seo, J.A. (2005). Multicultural literature and discussion as mirror and window? *Journal of Adolescent & Adult Literacy, 48*(8), 686–700. doi:10.1598/JAAL.48.8.6

Ivey, G., & Broaddus, K. (2001). "Just plain reading": A survey of what makes students want to read in middle school classrooms. *Reading Research Quarterly, 36*(4), 350–377. doi:10.1598/RRQ.36.4.2

Ketter, J., & Buter, D. (2004). Transcending spaces: Exploring identity in a rural American middle school. *English Journal, 93*(6), 47–53. doi:10.2307/4128893

Lindfors, J.W. (1999). *Children's inquiry: Using language to make sense of the world.* New York: Teachers College Press.

Louie, B. (2005). Development of empathetic responses with multicultural literature. *Journal of Adolescent & Adult Literacy, 48*(7), 566–578. doi:10.1598/JAAL.48.7.3

McGee, L.M., & Schickendanz, J.A. (2007). Repeated interactive read-alouds in preschool and kindergarten. *The Reading Teacher, 60*(8), 742–751. doi:10.1598/RT.60.8.4

National Council of Teachers of English. (2006). Resolution on increasing secondary school graduation rates. Retrieved July 29, 2008, from www.ncte.org/positions/statements/increasinggradrates

Newkirk, T. (2002). *Misreading masculinity: Boys, literacy, and popular culture.* Portsmouth, NH: Heinemann.

Pantaleo, S. (2004). Young children and radical change characteristics in picture books. *The Reading Teacher, 58*(2), 178–187. doi:10.1598/RT.58.2.6

Pilgreen, J.L. (2000). *The SSR handbook: How to organize and manage a sustained silent reading program.* Portsmouth, NH: Boynton/Cook.

Poole, J.A. (2005). Journey toward multiculturalism. *English Journal, 94*(3), 67–70.

Santoro, L.E., Chard, D.J., Howard, L., & Baker, S.K. (2008). Making the very most of classroom read-alouds to promote comprehension and vocabulary. *The Reading Teacher, 61*(5), 396–408. doi:10.1598/RT.61.5.4

Shannon, P. (2001). Every step you take. In P. Shannon (Ed.), *Becoming political, too: New readings and writings on the politics of literacy education* (pp. 175–179). Portsmouth, NH: Heinemann.

Shepard, L. (2000). The role of assessment in a learning culture. *Educational Researcher, 29*(7), 4–14.

Sipe, L.R. (2000). The construction of literary understanding by first and second graders in oral response to picture storybook read-alouds. *Reading Research Quarterly, 35*(2), 252–275. doi:10.1598/RRQ.35.2.4

Smith, M.W., & Wilhelm, J.D. (2002). *Reading don't fix no Chevys: Literacy in the lives of young men.* Portsmouth, NH: Heinemann.

Sullivan, M. (2004). Why Johnny won't read: Schools often dismiss what boys like. No wonder they're not wild about reading. *School Library Journal, 50*(8), 36–39.

Turner, J., & Paris, S.G. (1995). How literacy tasks influence children's motivation for literacy. *The Reading Teacher, 48*(8), 662–673.

CHAPTER 14

English-Language Learners in the Secondary Classroom

Carol Rothenberg

KEY POINTS AND STRATEGIES

Organizing Meaningful Collaborative Tasks

Providing Focused Small-Group Instruction

Teaching Language and Vocabulary

"I'm walking Dui to class. It's his first day. He's walking behind me as he's been taught to do in his country. As I watch him, I think, What must it be like? You're 14 years old. You left your home behind. You weigh maybe 120 lbs, and everywhere around you, you see these big kids talking and laughing on their way to class. You see no one who speaks your language. It couldn't be any lonelier."

—*Mike Askey, Head Counselor, Hoover High School, San Diego, California*

Language and literacy are more than words linked together to express thoughts and ideas. They are a representation of the people who use them. They are an expression, not just of words, but of a culture, its beliefs, values, and practices. In this chapter, as we explore the pedagogy of language and adolescent literacy, it is important that we do so with an understanding of who our students are, an awareness of the differences in cultures, and always through the lens of what it must feel like to be new and different in a new and different land.

A different culture and language are not the only differences English-language learners (ELLs) bring to our secondary schools. Even those students who, unlike Dui, have lived in this country for many years, do not always have the same

Adolescent Literacy, Field Tested: Effective Solutions for Every Classroom, edited by Sheri R. Parris, Douglas Fisher, and Kathy Headley. © 2009 by the International Reading Association.

instructional needs as native English speakers. The majority of ELLs in secondary schools, in fact, are not new to English (though it typically is not their first or primary language), or even new to the United States—an astonishing 57% of all ELLs were born in the United States (Batalova, Fix, & Murray, 2005). Those who are not proficient in English by the time they are in secondary school have generally reached a plateau at the intermediate, or even lower, level of proficiency. At first glance they exhibit the same behaviors as native English speakers who are struggling readers and writers. They have limited academic vocabulary, use everyday social language as they attempt to express sophisticated and complex academic concepts, and do not recognize or use the variations of language that are expected in varied genres and disciplines. Yet, when we take a closer look, we can see clear differences in their use of language, and thus in their ability to comprehend both written and oral language. Awareness of the differences in both the causes and the manifestation of below grade-level performance of ELLs and native English speakers can help us plan instruction that effectively develops language proficiency and knowledge of grade-level content. Table 14.1 highlights some of these differences.

Addressing these differences begins with knowledge—knowledge of the students, knowledge of language, and knowledge of pedagogy. Knowing your students means knowing their language proficiency levels, reading levels, prior schooling, cultural background, goals, and interests. Knowing about language means being able to analyze word parts, recognize word families, identify cognates (words that are similar and have similar meanings in two languages), and understand how language is used in your discipline (Wong-Fillmore & Snow 2000). Knowing about effective pedagogy for ELLs means consciously planning instruction that builds upon students' funds of knowledge (Moll, Amanti, & Neff, 1992; Moll & Arnot-Hopffer, 2005), explicitly teaches language and vocabulary, integrates language and content learning, provides multiple opportunities for students to interact with one another, and makes use of informal as well as formal assessments to plan instruction.

Our ELLs—and their teachers—are doing "double the work" (Short & Fitzsimmons, 2007) as they learn or teach a new language, and learn or teach the skills and concepts identified in the grade-level standards. ELLs who must learn a new language at the same time as they learn new content need additional and differentiated instruction to learn the vocabulary and develop the background knowledge that their native English speaking peers typically bring to their secondary school classrooms. In this chapter we will examine ways to use our knowledge of students, language, and pedagogy to develop language and literacy through collaborative practices, targeted small-group instruction, and a focus on explicit teaching of language.

TABLE 14.1
Factors That Influence Literacy Development

Factor	Native English Speaker: Struggling Reader/Writer	English-Language Learner
Background knowledge	• Has knowledge and understanding of common themes, character traits, plots, etc. in literature • Has been exposed to key concepts of core content areas	• Brings a different fund of knowledge of literature, history, and culture • May have little or no knowledge of key events in U.S. history or exposure to major concepts in other subjects
Prior schooling	• Has likely experienced repeated failure in school • May have learning disability	• May have experienced interrupted schooling • May have little or no native-language proficiency • May have advanced native-language literacy skills
Vocabulary	• Has knowledge of common English vocabulary • May be able to use context to determine meaning of polysemous words	• Has limited English vocabulary • May not know common words and signal words that are key to understanding • May not know • Can use knowledge of primary language to determine meaning (cognates) • May know only one meaning of common polysemous words
Oral proficiency in English	• Understands class discussions and teacher directions • Speaks fluently • Can express ideas he or she understands	• May not fully understand class discussions or teacher directions • May not be able to express ideas even when he or she understands them • Errors may not be developmental and may require explicit instruction
Written proficiency in English	• May write in a casual register • Makes many spelling errors • May organize writing in disjointed ways	• Makes many grammatical errors • May organize writing in ways unacceptable in the discipline
Motivation	• Has low motivation • Often has low self-esteem exhibited by disruptive behavior or lack of participation	• May have high motivation to learn and succeed • May have low motivation to learn English if planning to return to home country • May be fearful of participating because of lack of proficiency in English

Note. Copyright C. Rothenberg (2008). Used with permission.

Instructional Practices That Work

Among the best practices in teaching ELLs that the National Council of Teachers of English identified (2006), there is one overarching approach—teaching language through content. The goal of this approach is to develop language, literacy, and content knowledge simultaneously through listening, speaking, reading, and writing about grade-level content—English language arts, social studies, math, and science. There are three key practices that contribute to accelerating language and literacy development through the content: organizing meaningful collaborative tasks, providing focused small-group instruction, and explicitly teaching language and vocabulary. Although many of these practices have been discussed in previous chapters, in this chapter we will examine them from the point of view of students who are learning English at the same time as they are learning *in* English. We will highlight the unique considerations in planning and implementing effective instruction for this population.

Organize Meaningful Collaborative Tasks

There are two primary benefits of collaborative tasks in the classroom—development of oral language proficiency and a deeper understanding of the content. When the National Literacy Panel analyzed the research on achievement of language-minority children, they found that a key factor in the gap in reading and writing performance between native English speakers and ELLs was a lack of proficiency in oral language (August & Shanahan, 2006). This makes perfect sense when you think about the gap in oral language between these two groups of students as they enter school. When ELLs first enter school in this country with their limited vocabulary and limited understanding of English, they miss out on much of the instruction as they strive to make sense of the classroom discourse. It is easy to see how they can continue to fall behind from there.

We know that we must *use* language to *learn* language, yet, walk by a typical secondary classroom, and the language you are most likely to hear is coming from the teacher—reading to students, giving instructions or information, asking questions. This is particularly true in classrooms with many ELLs. Debbie Guan Eng Ho (2005) found that teachers often ask easier questions of ELLs, or even no questions at all, providing little or no opportunity for them to talk in the classroom. The students' primary modes of engagement then, are passive—listening or reading. I do not mean to suggest that these are unimportant functions, but rather that these receptive skills are disproportionately represented in most classrooms today, to the detriment of the productive skills—speaking and writing—those skills which play a critical role in constructing and clarifying understanding. It is through discussion and interaction that students develop understanding, and making meaning through collaborative analysis, synthesis, and evaluation. And when we organize instruction so that students work together, we gain the added benefit of being able to differentiate texts, tasks, and supports for students at different levels of language proficiency.

Effective collaborative tasks involve more than simply having students work together on a project. There are certain elements that must be in place to reach the dual goals of developing academic language and learning content.

Tasks Are Meaningful. Meaningful collaborative tasks are relevant to the curriculum, require critical thinking, stimulate interest, and, ideally, mirror real world functions as much as possible. Book discussions, surveys, investigations, brochures, advertisements, and problem-solving are tasks that have similar counterparts in the real world and require students to use the same skills they will need to apply in the future contexts of work, family, or personal goals.

If we want students to talk, we must give them something that makes them want to talk, something that strikes their interest, something that piques their curiosity. Asking them to work together to answer the questions or solve the odd-numbered problems at the end of the chapter is not likely to stimulate much conversation. Finding topics that are relevant and connect to their own lives, whether past, present, or future, can motivate even the most reticent of students to participate in the give and take of ideas.

Tasks Result in a Product. Effective collaborative tasks require students to create a product that reflects their understanding of the content. It is more than just a time for students to talk about the content. It is also a time for them to deconstruct the concept or text to construct a new way of representing the important ideas. Products can be oral but should also include a written component. Students might produce a skit or make an oral presentation. They might build a model and write a description of what it is and the process they used to design it.

Tasks Require and Facilitate Engagement for All. All students must have a role to play in producing the product. This does not mean assigning a timekeeper, a facilitator, a questioner, and a writer. All too often it is the ELL who is relegated to the role that does not require them to think critically or use language—timekeeper, illustrator, materials coordinator. The task should be organized in such a way that the group cannot complete it without information from each member of the group. Table 14.2 describes specific classroom application of some effective structures.

Tasks Include Clear Expectations. Setting expectations for the use of language as well as the demonstration of content knowledge helps to ensure that students will use the language of the discipline as they work together to create their product. Rubrics are perhaps the most effective way of making expectations clear to students. Criteria included in the rubric should describe expectations for language, content, presentation or organization, and process. The rubric should describe how we expect students to use academic language and vocabulary in the presentation of their product. We might give students a list that provides the specific vocabulary along with examples of the type of language they should be using. We might require them to use quotes from the text or summarize, compare, or explain. Rubrics should also include an opportunity for students to reflect on how well they

TABLE 14.2
Classroom Structures That Facilitate Collaboration

Structure	Description	Classroom Application
Jigsaw	Divide students into heterogeneous home base groups of four. Students number off 1 through 4 and form expert groups based on their number (all 1s together, all 2s, and so on). Assign each expert group a task. Each group has a different task, and each group's task relates to the final product and is necessary in order to complete the final product. Expert groups may be homogeneous as appropriate, and their tasks may be differentiated accordingly. After completing the expert group task, students return to their home groups to share their learning and create the final product.	Expert group: Analyze the theme in one genre. Home group final product: Compare and contrast a similar theme across genres. Describe how the choice of genre shapes the theme.
Barrier game	Two students work together to share information without being able to see the information the other has. They must impart their information only through oral description.	Student A has a diagram of a volcano. Student B has a similar diagram with one piece missing. Together they must describe their diagrams and determine how they are alike and how they are different. They can then write a description of a volcano.
Collaborative poster	Students create a poster reflecting their interpretation or their learning about a text or concept. Each student is required to contribute to both the writing and the drawing on the poster. Each uses a different color marker exclusively. Students are given a rubric that describes expectations. Expectations may include a direct quote from the text, an image that represents the concept, a summary statement, etc. Each student contributes their ideas for a quote, an image, and a summary statement. Then together students discuss their ideas and decide on one quote, one image, and one summary statement to best represent their understanding.	Students create a poster that represents the major ideas of a particular form of government. Include a quote from a leader of that form of government, an image that demonstrates how it functions, a chart that lists advantages and disadvantages, and a statement that describes an event that resulted from the way the government functions.

Note. Copyright C. Rothenberg (2008). Used with permission.

worked together as a group. Once students become familiar with the rubrics, they can coconstruct them for new projects, a process that helps them identify what sets a superior product apart from a mediocre one.

Tasks Include Opportunity for Self-Assessment. Reflection is often the process by which students develop independence as learners. As they reflect on both *what* they learned and *how* they learned it, they must review and summarize the main ideas of the content and analyze what facilitated or hindered their learning. As they evaluate what they learned, identify what they still need to learn, and reflect on their role in the learning process, they become acutely aware of the strategies that help them learn independently.

Provide Focused Small-Group Instruction

Knowing our students means that we recognize their diversity—diversity of language and cultural backgrounds, proficiency levels in English, background knowledge, comprehension of the content, use of comprehension strategies, interests, and so on. Recognizing this diversity leads us to the inevitable conclusion that one size does not fit all in education. Yet that is precisely what whole-class instruction tends to be. Although we may not be able to individualize our instruction for each and every student (nor do we necessarily want to), we can identify similar needs among groups of students and pull them together for a brief lesson targeted at their particular needs.

Small-group lessons may be devoted to a variety of purposes. Teachers may pull aside a small group of students for a 10- or 20-minute lesson that builds background knowledge and prepares students for an upcoming whole-class lesson. ELLs may benefit from a brief vocabulary lesson or practice with the language structures they will need to understand and talk or write about a particular topic or genre. A quick review can assure that students who didn't quite get everything from the whole-class lesson will understand the major concepts or skills.

Clearly, there are organizational considerations in addition to the content that drive planning for effective small-group instruction. The configuration of each group and the focus of each lesson will change depending on assessed need at any given point. One of the major concerns, of course, is what the other students are doing while the teacher works with a small group. There are a variety of ways to organize so that all students are working on challenging tasks with adequate supports. Teachers can work with one small group, or one expert group in a jigsaw collaborative structure, while the others are working on their own tasks. Alternatively, students may be reading, writing, or researching independently while the teacher meets with a group. The classroom may be organized so that there are learning centers with specific tasks. Small groups of students rotate through each center, with the teacher leading one of the centers.

Teach Language and Vocabulary

Proficiency in a language is a multidimensional construct that is central to academic literacy. Kern (2000) defines three dimensions of academic literacy— linguistic, cognitive, and sociocultural. Scarcella (2003) elaborates on this definition, describing the many components of language that make up each of these dimensions. In this framework, linguistic proficiency is defined by accurate and appropriate use of the sounds, vocabulary, grammar, and social norms appropriate for different audiences, disciplines, and situations. The cognitive element of academic language and literacy calls for relevant background knowledge, higher order thinking skills, strategic use of language, and metalinguistic awareness. The sociocultural component requires an understanding of the predominant values, beliefs, and customs of the culture. Table 14.3 provides details on the three dimensions.

One way to organize language instruction is to begin with the linguistic dimension and identify the cognitive functions required for the task. Dutro and Moran (2003) suggest that the functions that students must use to understand and communicate effectively in each situation or lesson determine the language we must teach. If we want students to describe a character, we might teach adjectives; if they will be conducting an interview, they will need to be able to formulate questions; when they compare two pieces of literature, two historical events, or two biological processes, they must be able to create complex sentence structures that use the language of similarities and differences. After determining the linguistic content of the language lesson, we design the structure of the lesson so that it addresses the cognitive and sociocultural aspects of language—including opportunities to access prior knowledge, build necessary background, think critically, and reflect on the use of language as well as the understanding of content.

Overcoming Challenges

Not only are ELL students doing "double the work" (Short & Fitzsimmons, 2007)—learning English and learning *in* English—but their teachers also face double the work, and often double the challenge, in planning lessons that teach English and content *in* English. Secondary ELLs bring varying levels of content area skills that must be addressed, as well as varying levels of proficiency in English. They may have wide gaps in the background knowledge needed to understand grade-level content. Compounding the challenges of filling in the gaps in knowledge and skill is a dearth of materials that are appropriate for teaching adolescent youth who are not proficient in English.

In order to meet these challenges, teachers must be able to differentiate their instruction. Small-group instruction, flexible grouping, and collaborative tasks that provide multiple entry points are effective methods of meeting the challenge of multiple levels of students. Teachers may vary the tasks, strategies, materials, and group configuration without varying the focus on grade-level content. Some students may need additional instructional time—after-school individual or small-group tutoring to accelerate learning.

We know that background knowledge is a major factor in reading comprehension (Bernhardt, 2005), yet many of our ELLs come to us with different funds of knowledge than students who have grown up in the United States. Teachers can use their knowledge of their students to help them make connections to what

TABLE 14.3
Dimensions of Academic Language Proficiency: What Students Need to Know

Dimension of Language	What Students Need to Know	Classroom Application
Linguistic	Pronunciation and stress patterns • Spelling, changes in stress according to part of speech e.g., *biólogy, biológical*	• Call students' attention to phonological features of new words. • Have students practice pronunciation and stress patterns through repetition of words, repeated oral reading, dialogues, skits, and partner/small-group discussions.
	Vocabulary • Technical and general • Collocations • Fixed expressions/idioms • Word parts	• Teach general academic vocabulary in addition to content-specific words. • Teach new words as part of common collocations—*decided to, indicator of.* • Teach fixed expressions—*salt and pepper.* • Teach new vocabulary in word families—*origin, originate, original.* • Teach roots and affixes.
	Grammatical structures • Syntax • Verb tenses, subject–verb agreement, phrasal verbs • Referential pronouns • Articles and plurals	• Use student text and writing to highlight examples and nonexamples of specific structures as a way of teaching grammar in context. • Call students' attention to everyday words that are important to meaning (mortar words)—*with, if, could have.*
	Sociolinguistics • Register • Language functions—describing, explaining, questioning, hypothesizing, etc.	• Teach students to vary their language appropriately for the audience, genre, purpose, and mode of communication (written and verbal). • Teach common vocabulary and expressions for the language functions needed in each discipline.
	Patterns of discourse	• Cohesion devices (e.g., transitions such as *although, in other words, similar to,* etc.) • Organizational patterns of genre • Preferred patterns of two-way discourse
Cognitive	Knowledge and skills • Background knowledge • Critical thinking • Strategic use of language • Metalinguistic awareness	• Be sure that students have adequate background knowledge about a topic in order to read, write, listen, and talk about it. • Be sure that questions and learning tasks require students to think critically. • Teach strategies to clarify meaning and enhance communication. • Provide opportunities to reflect on, edit, and revise language.
Sociocultural	Values, beliefs, cultural norms	• Include discussions about values and norms of mainstream American culture. • Provide opportunities to compare and contrast cultural practices and beliefs.

Note. Adapted from Scarcella, R. (2003). *Accelerating academic English: A focus on the English learner.* Irvine: University of California at Irvine.

they already know, thus building schema as they connect new knowledge to old. This strategy has the added benefit of raising motivation by demonstrating the application of learning in the real world.

Sadly, teachers cannot rely on adopted texts to guide them in building language proficiency and developing content literacy. Few materials adequately teach language or address secondary content standards in a manner accessible to ELL students. Teachers can overcome this challenge with a keen awareness of language as they plan, asking themselves: What language is key to understanding? What opportunities are there within the curriculum to develop that vocabulary and language? They can also collaborate with other teachers within and across content areas to create interdisciplinary units of study, lessons, and materials that develop language as well as content.

Looking Ahead

Approaches to language instruction have changed over the years, and still more changes are on the horizon, growing out of our evolving understanding about instruction and acknowledgment of the changing demographics of our schools. Three promising practices stand out at this point in time. First is a move to design assessments that give a clear picture of the strengths and areas of need of ELLs. Researchers and practitioners are exploring and developing benchmark assessments that can be used to inform instruction, accurately gauge progress, and help maintain the focus on grade-level standards and outcomes for all students.

A second promising practice has to do with the focus of instruction. As we analyze student assessments, we have come to realize that a balanced approach to language and literacy instruction is necessary to assure that students develop proficiency in language and content (Cummins, 2008). A focus only on language does not provide students with the authentic practice they need in order to be able to vary their language according to the situation. We cannot acquire language in a vacuum, so we must have content that provides something to read, write, and talk about. Similarly, a focus only on literacy does not build the language skills students need in order to become independent readers and writers. As we learn more about teaching ELLs, we are learning that developing proficiency requires opportunities to practice language in authentic contexts alongside explicit instruction about how language works.

And finally, as the wave of technological advances carries us along, we are finding innovative ways to use new technologies to advance learning. As new technologies develop, we can combine our knowledge about students, language, and pedagogy to use these new resources to promote language and literacy development. The Apple product iPod, for instance, can be used to help students develop fluency, learn content missed because of absences, or provide visual support for language.

The diversity of our country has always been part of our identity and our strength. If we are to maintain that strength, it is vital that we meet the diversity of our learners with instruction that builds upon their strengths and assures that they have the knowledge and skills demanded in this global society of the 21st century. To that end, we must use our knowledge of our students, of how language works, and of effective pedagogy as we design our instruction. We must provide opportunities for students to collaborate as they build and deepen understanding about grade-level content and about what it takes to be successful. We must differentiate instruction in small groups tailored to students' individual needs. And we must integrate a focus on academic language so that our students develop the proficiency they need to express the sophistication of their growing understanding. In short, our goal must be to provide both high challenge and high support for all students.

EXTEND YOUR THINKING

As you investigate the efficacy of the three practices described in this chapter, you may wish to conduct a case study of an ELL student. Select a student and analyze his or her participation, performance, and progress through the lens of the following questions:

- Collaboration—How do I know if carefully structured opportunities to interact with others around grade-level content make a difference for my ELLs? Plan a series of lessons that require students to listen, speak, read, and write as they interact with their classmates to create a product that demonstrates their understanding of the content.

- Small-group instruction—How can I organize my classroom so that I can work with small groups of students on particular areas of need? Use student progress assessment to form small groups with like areas of need. Plan a series of lessons that allow you to work with one small group for a brief period of time on a specific area of need identified by the assessment. Other students should be engaged in collaborative or independent tasks.

- Language and vocabulary—What is the language my students need to communicate successfully in my content area, and how can I integrate explicit teaching of that language and my lessons? Analyze class texts for language your students need in order to understand and talk about the content. Analyze student writing for use of that language. Analyze use of language structures and academic vocabulary.

REFERENCES

August, D., & Shanahan, T. (2006). *Developing literacy in second-language learners: Report of the National Literacy Panel on Language-Minority Children and Youth: Executive summary*. Mahwah, NJ: Erlbaum.

Batalova, J., Fix, M., & Murray, J. (2005). *English language learner adolescents: Demographics and literacy achievements. Report to the Center for Applied Linguistics.* Washington, DC: Migration Policy Institute.

Bernhardt, E. (2005). Progress and procrastination in second language reading. *Annual Review of Applied Linguistics, 25*(1), 133–150. doi:10.1017/S0267190505000073

Cummins, J. (2008). *Conceptualizing forms of language for learning and teaching.* Paper presented at the Teachers of English to Speakers of Other Languages annual convention, New York.

Dutro, S., & Moran, C. (2003). Rethinking English language instruction: An architectural approach. In G. Garcia (Ed.), *English learners: Reaching the highest level of English literacy* (pp. 227–258). Newark, DE: International Reading Association.

Ho, D.G.E. (2005). Why do teachers ask the questions they ask? *RELC Journal, 36*(3), 297–310. doi:10.1177/0033688205060052

Kern, R. (2000). Notions of literacy. In R. Kern (Ed.), *Literacy and language teaching* (pp. 13–41). New York: Oxford University Press.

Moll, L.C., Amanti, C., & Neff, D. (1992). Funds of knowledge for teaching: Using a qualitative approach to connect homes and classrooms. *Theory Into Practice, 31*(2), 132–141.

Moll, L.C., & Arnot-Hopffer, E. (2005). Socio-cultural competence in teacher education. *Journal of Teacher Education, 56*(3), 242–247. doi:10.1177/0022487105275919

National Council of Teachers of English. (2006). *NCTE position paper on the role of English teachers in educating English language Learners (ELLs).* Retrieved January 15, 2009, from www.ncte.org/positions/statements/teacherseducatingell

Scarcella, R. (2003). *Accelerating academic English: A focus on the English learner.* Irvine: University of California at Irvine.

Short, D., & Fitzsimmons, S. (2007). *Double the work: Challenges and solutions to acquiring language and academic literacy for adolescent English language learners. A report to Carnegie Corporation of New York.* Washington, DC: Alliance for Excellent Education.

Wong-Fillmore, L., & Snow, C.E. (2000). *What teachers need to know about language.* Washington, DC: Center for Applied Linguistics.

CHAPTER 15

Improving the Reading Skills of African American Secondary Students: What Teachers Can Do

Gail L. Thompson

> *"I have AP History, and I find myself doing better when I'm reading and writing about stuff that pertains to my culture. If they incorporated more of that, then maybe I could do better in that class."*
>
> —*Unnamed student (cited in Thompson, 2007, p. 48)*

The above statement by an African American male attending an underperforming high school in southern California speaks volumes, and it tells a story that is hidden by the current high-stakes test-score frenzy. In fact, each year U.S. national and state standardized test scores tell a familiar story about the reading skills of African American students: "They may be making progress, *but* they're *still* trailing their white counterparts." If you are a dedicated and hardworking teacher, this recurring message might cause you to lose hope. However, the test scores and statistics don't tell the *whole* story.

For example, the statistics don't reveal the measurement flaws (Popham, 2004) and biases in most commonly used standardized tests or how these biases harm low-income and certain minority students, including African Americans

Adolescent Literacy, Field Tested: Effective Solutions for Every Classroom, edited by Sheri R. Parris, Douglas Fisher, and Kathy Headley. © 2009 by the International Reading Association.

(Kohn, 2000; Popham, 2004). The statistics also don't reveal that the test scores don't necessarily reflect what students, especially African American students, really know and how well they can perform academically (Thompson, 2007). Moreover, the statistics fail to indicate that many African American students who like to read and who have good reading skills can become disillusioned about reading as a result of various school practices (Thompson, Madhuri, & Taylor, 2008). However, the most important thing that the statistics don't reveal is that when the common stumbling blocks to reading achievement are removed, most students—including African Americans—can become good readers. In this chapter, I describe seven strategies than can help you increase your efficacy with African American middle school and high school students.

Instructional Practices That Work

Eradicate Negative Beliefs

Our beliefs determine how we behave, and one of the most important ways that you can begin the process of becoming more effective with African American students is by dealing with your "mental roadblocks." By mental roadblocks, I'm referring to negative beliefs about African American students. If you believe that African American students aren't capable of excelling academically and that they don't want to learn, you are likely to create a self-fulfilling prophecy in your classroom. Your negative beliefs can actually create discipline problems and student apathy (Thompson, 2007, 2008).

Although teachers often claim to be "color blind" to racial differences, numerous researchers have found that the belief that African Americans are intellectually inferior to most other groups is widespread in the United States (Comer, 2002; Gould, 1996; Perry, 2003; West, 2002; Sue, 2003; Woods, 2001). Therefore it is imperative that you deal with any negative mindsets that you have about African American students. This will require extensive and ongoing self-reflection, honesty, and courage. One of the easiest ways for you to begin this process is to examine your core beliefs about African Americans through self-questioning (Thompson, 2004):

- Do I honestly believe that African American students are capable of academic excellence?
- What do I believe about African American females?
- What do I believe about African American males?
- What do I believe about my current African American students?
- What stereotypes do I have about African Americans?

Next, you should examine your responses to these questions and determine what they mean in terms of mindsets that you need to change. Then, you should begin to read educational research and other research-based literature about African Americans (see my list of recommended reading in *Through Ebony Eyes: What Teachers Need to Know but Are Afraid to Ask About African American Students*, Thompson, 2004). After identifying the recurring themes in the research, you should develop an action plan. This action plan should be based on a synthesis of what you learned from examining your mindsets about African Americans and from research to create a series of activities and steps to improve your instructional practices in the classroom. Finally, you will need to reexamine and modify your action plan on an ongoing basis. Staying abreast of research about African American students will be invaluable, and reading the works of literacy experts such as Tatum (2005), Hammond, Hoover, and McPhail (2005), Mahiri (1998, 2004), and others will be beneficial to you. The goal is not for you to try to become perfect, but for you to be willing to continue to work on your efficacy with African American students through continuous self-reflection. Ongoing self-reflection decreases the likelihood that negative mindsets will prevent you from working effectively with African American students (Thompson, 2007).

Make the Curriculum Comprehensible

Great teachers find ways to make the curriculum comprehensible to all students, including African Americans. When students don't understand what you're trying to teach, they can "tune out," become disillusioned, or even begin to misbehave (Thompson, 2004). Therefore, making the curriculum understandable to all students is a top priority.

In terms of helping struggling readers, McEwan (2007) stresses that through scaffolding, modeling, extensive practice, and frequent checks for understanding, teachers reduce the cognitive load, chunk information to prevent students from becoming overwhelmed, teach them how to monitor their comprehension, question what students read, make inferences, and summarize the main ideas. The classic Directed Reading Lesson (DRL; Roe, Stoodt, & Burns, 1998) is a great way to make the curriculum comprehensible. This guided reading model and similar versions include three types of activities: (1) into, (2) through, and (3) beyond exercises. *Into* exercises are done before students begin to read and consist of exposing students to important vocabulary words from the text that they will be reading and giving them exercises that help them link their prior knowledge to the text. *Through* exercises consist of guided reading activities: telling students what to look for in the text based on questions that they have been given beforehand; the actual reading of the text; related discussions; and asking students to support their answers to the questions with evidence from the text. *Beyond* activities include various types of assessments, writing assignments, and projects related to the text (Roe, Stoodt, & Burns, 1998).

Make the Curriculum Interesting and Relevant

Researchers have found that most elementary school students believe that what they learn in class is interesting, but as students get older, they are less likely to say this. Consequently, by middle school and high school, many students believe that the curriculum is boring and irrelevant. For example, in a study that I conducted at a low-performing high school, African American and Latino students were more likely than white students to say that the curriculum was boring, that it wasn't preparing them for the real world, and that they wanted to learn more about their cultures at school (Thompson, 2007). Obviously, making the curriculum interesting and relevant are two ways that you can improve African American students' reading skills.

Many researchers have emphasized the importance of a culturally relevant education, particularly for African Americans and Latinos (Bennett, 1999; Delpit, 1995; Duncan-Andrade, 2002/2003; Gay, 2000; Ladson-Billings, 1994). Not only does this enable students to feel connected to the text, but also it increases the likelihood that they will be intrinsically motivated, because the text will be more interesting and relevant to them. In fact, a very common criticism from African American high school students is that with the exception of books about slavery, they don't get many reading assignments that pertain to their culture (Thompson, 2007).

Therefore, one of the easiest ways to make the curriculum interesting and relevant to African American students is to make sure that students have access to a lot of reading materials about black history, black culture, noteworthy African Americans, and so on. Your classroom library can be stocked with a diverse array of multicultural literature, you can assign culturally relevant reading assignments on an ongoing basis (not just during Black History Month), and you can be cautious about assigning what can be culturally offensive literature, such as books containing the "N word" and stereotypes.

Two educators have actually taken the philosophy of culturally relevant teaching a step further. Jeffery Duncan-Andrade and Ernest Morrell, professors who also teach high school, use hip hop literature and rap literature to improve students' critical thinking skills and their reading skills. After learning what students were interested in, Duncan-Andrade (2002/2003) used texts from youth popular culture to create assignments that "increased student engagement" (¶7) and improved their academic skills.

Allow Ample Time for Class Discussions and Collaboration

A common problem in many schools is that teachers are more likely to view African Americans rather than other students as discipline problems. One of the main reasons why African American students often get into trouble with teachers is for excessive talking in class. However, you can prevent this problem from arising in your classroom by creating lessons that allow students ample time to interact with one another. Researchers have stressed that cooperative learning is an effective teaching strategy and several have emphasized its benefits to students of color (Delpit, 1995; Gay, 2000; Ladson-Billings, 1994). Giving students opportunities to discuss assigned texts during class discussions, with a partner, or in small groups are simple ways that you can do this. Class debates, mock trials, and presentations that link required texts to real-world situations and community issues are other options. When African American students know that they will have opportunities to exchange their viewpoints about the text with classmates instead of merely having to listen to a lecture for most of the class period, followed by, "Open your book and read," they will, undoubtedly, be more likely to comply during times for quiet, independent work (Thompson, 2004).

Use Multiple Types of Assessments

As I stated in the introduction, it's important during the current high-stakes testing era to remember that test scores don't tell the whole story. Many students who may not perform well on standardized tests as a result of anxiety or stereotypes about their ability may do extremely well on other types of assessments (Aronson, 2004; Steele, 2003). In fact, these other types of assessments may be even more beneficial to students, especially if they are given feedback in a timely manner and opportunities to improve their work (McEwan, 2007).

Allowing students to do projects, writing assignments, and presentations that are based on reading assignments are three simple nontraditional assessment strategies. These assessments not only will allow students to demonstrate what they learned from the texts but also will help them improve other skills and will allow their creativity to shine. For example, many students graduate from high school with weak writing skills (National Commission on Writing for America's Families, Schools, and Colleges, 2005). When you assess students' knowledge of reading assignments by requiring them to write related essays, stories, and research papers, students also gain writing practice and have the opportunity to improve their writing skills. In fact, according to McEwan (2007), "lasting learning" (p. 141) cannot occur unless students have to write about what they read. Having students answer questions about the text, infer outcomes, and summarize the main idea of the texts are just three of the writing assessments that you can use (McEwan, 2007).

Overcoming Challenges

Provide Extra In-Class Support for Struggling Readers

According to McEwan (2007), most struggling readers in grades 6–12 already know how to read, but they may read below grade level, read dysfluently, and lack knowledge about the academic vocabulary that is necessary for success in various content areas. If any of your students don't know how to decode words, ask the reading specialist to provide intensive remediation for those students. However, most middle and high school struggling readers don't fit into that category. Keep in mind that "struggling readers can master content as well as improve their reading and writing skills" (McEwan, 2007, p. xx), but they need explicit, intensive, and sometimes, individualized instruction from you.

There are several ways to provide in-class support for struggling readers. First, you must let students know that you are *willing* to provide extra help to *all* struggling students, and you must *mean* what you say. For African American students, knowing that you mean it is very important; many African American students infer that although their teachers *say* that they are willing to give extra help, they don't really mean it or they don't want to give this assistance to African American students (Thompson, 2007). When an African American student raises his or her hand and requests assistance and you are sincere about providing extra help to all students, you won't demean the student, accuse the student of not paying attention, or ignore the student. Moreover, you won't tell the struggling student to come after school, before school, or at lunch time to receive the requested assistance, because many secondary students have jobs that require them to report for work after school or have family responsibilities that prevent them from arriving at school early or staying late, and those who are eligible for the free or reduced-cost meal program may be unlikely to come during lunch time when school might be the only place where they have access to meals. Unfortunately, these problems often surface in classrooms when African American students request assistance.

In addition to the suggestions that I've made previously in this chapter, there are other well-known strategies that you can use to provide in-class assistance for struggling students. You can pair struggling students with stronger readers, frequently check for comprehension through questioning, front-load content by giving students repeated exposure to important vocabulary words, and preteach the content by providing overviews and graphic organizers before students actually read the text (McEwan, 2007). More than anything, you must be patient. By the time that they reach middle school or high school, struggling readers have had many frustrating, and possibly embarrassing, schooling experiences. It will behoove you to be as patient as possible when working with them (Thompson, 2003).

Educate Yourself About Dyslexia

According to Shaywitz (2005), a neuroscientist and reading expert, dyslexia affects a considerable number of K–12 students, but most dyslexic students aren't diagnosed until after third grade. Therefore, it is very likely that one or more students in your class might struggle with reading because their brain uses a different method of processing print. In other words, dyslexics differ from "ordinary" struggling readers. Knowing the characteristics of dyslexia and educating yourself about this type of reading problem will enable you to identify dyslexic students and help them become successful in your classroom.

One of the telltale signs of dyslexia is that the student tends to perform well in other areas but struggles with reading. Poor handwriting, poor spelling, test anxiety, slow reading, avoiding oral reading, and dysfluent reading are other signs that you need to watch for (Shaywitz, 2005). If you suspect that a student has dyslexia, ask the reading specialist to administer appropriate reading tests. Also, Shaywitz strongly advises teachers to give dyslexic students extra time to complete tests. Reading the literature on dyslexia, starting with Shaywitz's reader-friendly *Overcoming Dyslexia: A New and Complete Science-Based Program for Reading Problems at Any Level*, is one of the best ways for you to get a clear understanding of dyslexia, dispel myths about dyslexia, and more than anything, learn information and strategies that will help you to work successfully with this type of struggling reader.

Looking Ahead

Teaching young children to read isn't an easy task, and teaching older students to read may be even more challenging because they have experienced reading difficulties or struggled with reading for a longer period than younger students. By the time they arrive in your classroom, struggling readers may have formed a negative perspective of reading and may have developed a repertoire of tactics to avoid having to read. To compound matters, many African American secondary students may have become even more disillusioned about reading after being forced to read boring, irrelevant, and culturally offensive material for years. Therefore, as a middle school or high school teacher who seeks to improve the reading skills of African American struggling readers, you face a daunting task. However, the task isn't insurmountable, because with motivation, knowledge, patience, and an ongoing quest to leave no stone unturned to help *all* students become better readers, you can succeed. Periodically reviewing the strategies that I've recommended (see the list at the beginning of the chapter) and incorporating them with your pedagogy should help you to do this. Then, you will find that you have given your students an invaluable gift: the ability to read well, and thereby increase their chances of being academically successful for the rest of their school years. In other words, you can help to change the ending of the story that is written about the reading scores of African American students.

EXTEND YOUR THINKING

- Reflecting on what you've learned in this chapter, what changes can you make to your own teaching practices to improve literacy learning for African American students?

- Compare the information in this chapter with the information you have learned in the other chapters in this book (which are not designed to look at adolescent literacy from the viewpoint of African American students). Which instructional practices do you find that are also consistent with the recommendations in this chapter? Are any inconsistent? If so, how can you make adaptations so the instruction is more applicable to African American students?

■ Early in this chapter you were asked to examine your core beliefs about African American students through a series of self-reflection questions and then to compare your beliefs with research-based information. Answer these questions about your core beliefs now and note if your views changed during the reading of this chapter. Choose one of the texts suggested in this chapter to help you continue to examine your beliefs about African American students. As you read this second text, continue to reflect on your original answers to the self-reflection questions and note how your beliefs (and approach to teaching) continue to transform as you expand your knowledge base about African American students.

REFERENCES

Aronson, J. (2004). The threat of stereotype: To close the achievement gap, we must address negative stereotypes that suppress student achievement. *Educational Leadership, 62*(3), 14–19.

Bennett, C.I. (1999). *Comprehensive multicultural education: Theory and practice* (4th ed.). Boston: Allyn & Bacon.

Comer, J.P. (2002). My view. In S. Denbo & L. Beaulieu (Eds.), *Improving schools for African American students* (pp. 5–11). Springfield, IL: Charles C. Thomas.

Delpit, L. (1995). *Other people's children: Cultural conflict in the classroom.* New York: The New Press.

Duncan-Andrade, J. (2002/2003). Why must school be boring? Invigorating the curriculum with youth culture. *TCLA's School Report Card, 3*(1–7). Retrieved June 14, 2008, from tcla.gseis.ucla.edu/reportcard/features/3/andrade/youthculture.html

Gay, G. (2000). *Culturally responsive teaching: Theory, research, and practice.* New York: Teachers College Press.

Gould, S.J. (1996). *The mismeasure of man.* New York: Norton.

Hammond, B., Hoover, M.E.R., & McPhail, I.P. (Eds.). (2005). *Teaching African American learners to read: Perspectives and practices.* Newark, DE: International Reading Association.

Kohn, A. (2000, September 27). Standardized testing and its victims. *Education Week.* Retrieved February 17, 2005, from www.edweek.org/ew/articles/2000/09/27/04kohn.h20.html

Ladson-Billings, G. (1994). *The dreamkeepers: Successful teachers of African-American children.* San Francisco: Jossey-Bass.

Mahiri, J. (1998). *Shooting for excellence: African American and youth culture in new century schools.* New York: Teachers College Press.

Mahiri, J. (2004). *What they don't learn in school: Literacy in the lives of urban youth.* New York: Peter Lang.

McEwan, E. (2007). *40 ways to support struggling readers in content classrooms, grades 6–12.* Thousand Oaks, CA: Corwin.

National Commission on Writing for America's Families, Schools, and Colleges. (2005). *A powerful message from state government.* Retrieved July 5, 2005, from www.writingcommission.org/report.html

Perry, T. (2003). Achieving in post-civil rights America: The outline of a theory. In T. Perry, C. Steele, & A.G. Hilliard III (Eds.), *Young, gifted, and black: Promoting high achievement among African-American students* (pp. 87–108). Boston: Beacon.

Popham, W.J. (2004). A game without winners. *Educational Leadership, 62*(3), 46–50.

Roe, B.D., Stoodt, B.D., & Burns, P.C. (1998). *Secondary school literacy instruction: The content areas* (6th ed.). Boston: Houghton Mifflin.

Shaywitz, S. (2005). *Overcoming dyslexia: A new and complete science-based program for reading problems at any level*. New York: Vintage.

Steele, C. (2003). Stereotype threat and African-American student achievement. In T. Perry, C. Steele, & A.G. Hilliard III (Eds.), *Young, gifted, and black: Promoting high achievement among African-American students* (pp. 109–130). Boston: Beacon.

Sue, D.W. (2003). *Overcoming our racism: The journey to liberation*. San Francisco: Jossey-Bass.

Tatum, A.W. (2005). *Teaching reading to black adolescent males: Closing the achievement gap*. Portland, ME: Stenhouse.

Thompson, G.L. (2003). *What African American parents want educators to know*. Westport, CT: Praeger.

Thompson, G.L. (2004). *Through ebony eyes: What teachers need to know but are afraid to ask about African American students*. San Francisco: Jossey-Bass.

Thompson, G.L. (2007). *Up where we belong: Helping African American and Latino students rise in school and in life*. San Francisco: Jossey-Bass.

Thompson, G.L. (2008). Beneath the apathy: Black and Latino students in a low-performing high school identify the school factors that keep them from engaging in learning. *Educational Leadership, 65*(6), 50–54.

Thompson, G.L., Madhuri, M., & Taylor, D. (2008). How the Accelerated Reader Program can become counterproductive for high school students. *Journal of Adolescent & Adult Literacy, 51*(7), 550–560. doi:10.1598/JAAL.51.7.3

West, C. (2002). Foreword. In L. Jones (Ed.), *Making it on broken promises: African American male scholars confront the culture of higher education* (pp. xi–xii). Sterling, VA: Stylus.

Woods, R.L. (2001). Invisible women: The experiences of black female doctoral students at the University of Michigan. In R.O. Mabokela & A.L. Green (Eds.), *Sisters of the academy: Emergent black women scholars in higher education* (pp. 105–115). Sterling, VA: Stylus.

PART III

On the Front Line: Teachers, Classrooms, and Schools

A Diploma That Matters: Schoolwide Efforts to Improve High School Teaching and Learning

Douglas Fisher, Nancy Frey, Maria Grant

> *"You have to build confidence."*
>
> —*John Kline Jr., 2008 New Jersey State*
> *Teacher of the Year*

KEY POINTS AND STRATEGIES

Culture of Success

Gradual Release of Responsibility

   Focus Lessons

   Guided Instruction

   Collaborative Learning

   Independent Work

Common Formative Assessments

College-Going Culture

   Rigorous Curriculum

   Understanding the System

   Internships

   Dual Enrollment

There are many ways for high school teachers to ensure that students learn. This book is filled with cognitive strategies and instructional routines that develop students' thinking and understanding about content. This book also has a number of ideas about literacy development and how teachers can ensure that struggling readers become increasingly proficient. As such, it's an excellent resource for high school teachers and administrators who want to improve student achievement.

But our task in this chapter is not to focus on these aspects of high school teaching and learning. Instead, our task is to suggest ways that entire schools, not just individual classrooms, can become amazing places for learning and growth. We know that there are interventions that promise results, and many of them are able to deliver for individual students. The three of us work in a small learning community high school focused on health careers. Our students, over half of whom qualify for free or reduced-cost lunches, are a diverse mix from across the city who were selected as part of a public lottery for attendance. Because our high school is considered a "middle college," our students, grades 9–12, receive community college credits for some of their health classes. Our intervention efforts focus on the

Adolescent Literacy, Field Tested: Effective Solutions for Every Classroom, edited by Sheri R. Parris, Douglas Fisher, and Kathy Headley. © 2009 by the International Reading Association.

whole school and start with the idea that failure is not an option. Once we have that cultural shift in place, including the associated policies and procedures, we're ready to take on instructional innovations that increase achievement. But first, we have to show students that they can learn.

You're Not a Failure

Most high schools accept the fact that a certain percentage of their students will fail a course and then repeat it the next year. In a typical World History class in San Diego, for example, 5 of the 36 students are repeating the course. This "intervention" is expensive and increases class size. It also sends a powerful message to students—you're a failure. And when you tell students they are failures, that's exactly how they'll act.

Over the past several years, we've come to understand the impact that cumulative failure has on our students. Most teachers (people who have historically been successful in school and have decided to spend their life in school) do not appreciate the learned helplessness, lack of motivation, and vicious cycle that develop when students are told over and over, "you're not good enough" as they fail yet another course.

As a small learning community school focused on health careers whose motto is "first, do no harm" we knew that we had to exit this cycle of failure by reworking the grading policy while maintaining rigor. But we acknowledge that it is a complex cycle to break. In fact, it has taken us the first several years of our school's existence to begin to break the cycle. We started with the identification of course competencies. Without clearly communicated expectations, a change in the grading policy might be seen as watering down the expectations. For example, the mathematics department developed the following competency strands for Algebra I, historically the most commonly failed class in our school:

- Introduction to Algebra
- Solving Linear Equations
- Graphing Linear Functions and Solving Systems of Equations
- Introduction to Statistics
- Graphing Inequalities and Absolute Value
- Quadratic Functions
- Rational Expressions
- Polynomials and Factoring Polynomials

Each competency has an associated assessment, and students are allowed to take the competency assessments as many times as they want to earn the grade they want. As Zander and Zander (2000) remind us, "Grades say little about the work done" (p. 25). We wanted to change that. The grades we assign for a course represent students' content knowledge and not their behavior, time management, or acceptance of responsibility. We know that student behavior, work habits, and sense of responsibility will develop with feedback from and honest conversations with caring adults who take the time to develop relationships.

With the subject competencies in place, the grades students earn are the average of the competency scores, with two modifications that we will discuss shortly. Students do not have to do the homework to take the competency assessment for the first time, but retaking a competency requires that all of the homework (practice) related to that competency has been completed. Homework is graded so that students have feedback, but it is not part of the students' grades. There are two modifications to the grade earned on the competency assessments. First, we can add up to 10% (one full letter grade) for the various projects students do while in class. These include productive group-work tasks as well as individual assignments. And second, we can deduct up to 10% (one full letter grade) for lack of participation in the class. This also represents a philosophical shift. We no longer think of participation and interaction in the classroom as something that should be rewarded but rather as an expectation. As such, students do not earn points for doing what is expected but may be penalized for not engaging. This is essential to a learning community that runs on the interactions learners have with one another.

Although our approach to grading is a huge conceptual shift for an entire school to make, it's not enough to make us an example for other schools to consider. The competency-based grading system is much more transparent for students and teachers and probably ensures that more students are successful than ever before. But it's still entirely possible for students to experience failure under this system. So we—teachers and administrators—voted to eliminate any grade below C minus. Again, the concerns surfaced about rigor and academic standards. But the teachers held firm by saying that we would do what it takes to make sure that students have mastered, at least at the basic level, course content. It was important for all teachers to have a voice in policies related to course work and associated grades. We knew that for such policies to have merit, all those presenting and implementing them would have to be in agreement. We understood that we could differentiate the curriculum enough and develop academic recovery plans for students to make sure that they succeeded.

The school grading policy can be found in Figure 16.1. Essentially, it says that students can't earn anything below a C minus. If a student's grade is "incomplete" an academic recovery plan is developed. Figure 16.2 and Figure 16.3 show the forms we currently use for academic recovery. We were required to add some safeguards, such as length of time an incomplete can stand before credit is transferred, but the policy stands as an expression of our value: Failure is not an option.

Consistent with our mission and vision, as well as our middle college identity, students will receive the grade of "incomplete" when their performance does not meet the standard of quality established by the instructor and based on state standards. If a student's overall performance in any given nine-week term falls below the level of earning credit (C-), the student will earn an incomplete in the course. An incomplete in any course requires the development of an *academic recovery plan*, which must be approved by the teacher, parent, and Vice President for Academic Affairs. When the student completes the work outlined on the academic recovery plan, the student is assigned a grade for the course. However, if the student leaves the school, or one year elapses after the development of the contract, the course grade will be recorded as "F" and no units will be awarded.

Furthermore, our expectation is that each student's academic performance is of the highest quality. Students who believe their performance in any nine-week term does not represent their best capabilities and competence will be permitted to petition their teacher to negotiate a *work quality plan*. The proposal must be submitted within two weeks of the close of the grading period. If the plan is approved by the teacher, parent, and Vice President for Academic Affairs, the student will be assigned an incomplete for the course. When the student completes the work outlined on the work quality plan, the student is assigned a grade for the course. However, if the student leaves the school, or the contract expires, the course grade will be recorded as the grade the student would have been assigned at the completion of the term.

We think that Ibrahim, a 10th grader, said it best. As a student with numerous failures from a previous school, he told a visitor to the campus, "They don't let you fail here. They really do harass you, in a good way, so it's easier to just do your work and learn."

Making Learning Transparent and Transportable

Once we communicate to students that failure is not an option, we have to do a number of things differently to make sure we're right. Students in most high schools experience a significantly fractured day. They're asked to think about different content every 50 or so minutes. They're also asked to process that content in number of different ways. As a result, many students fail to develop habits for reading, writing, and thinking that they can take with them from class to class, and then to college and work.

In a discussion with Ibrahim, he told us about the different routines that were part of each class he took at his previous school. As he said, "It made it hard, you know what I mean? They like, make your notes different in every class. Not like here where it's the same. I know how to take notes now, and I'm getting good grades on my notebook checks. It makes sense this way. It makes it easier for me, too."

At our school, we've agreed on specific content literacy strategies that we all use, a list of which can be found in Figure 16.4. We chronicled the impact of

FIGURE 16.2
Academic Recovery for Incomplete Course Grade

STUDENT NAME: _____

DATE OF CONFERENCE: _____

COURSE(S):
☐ Algebra   ☐ Geometry   ☐ Algebra II   ☐ Calculus
☐ Geography   ☐ World History   ☐ US History   ☐ Govt/Econ
☐ English 9   ☐ English 10   ☐ English 11   ☐ English 12
☐ Earth Science   ☐ Biology   ☐ Physics   ☐ Chemistry
☐ Other (specify) _____

Concerns:

The Student Will:
☐ Enter assignments into agenda with a target completion date.
☐ Have a separate folder for incomplete work.
☐ Have a daily progress report signed.
☐ Have a weekly progress report signed.
☐ Print grades from Power School weekly and return to teacher with parent's signature.
☐ See an administrator (how often): _____
☐ Meet with teacher during lunch every **M T W Th F** at _____ (circle all that apply).

The Parent/Guardian Will:
☐ Provide a consistent and quiet place to do homework.
☐ Provide encouragement, motivation, and prompting.
☐ Provide reasonable time expectations.

The Teacher/School Will:
☐ Post homework on chalkboard and in class.
☐ Return corrected work to student mailbox in a timely fashion.
☐ Meet with the student to ensure he or she has the missing assignments.
☐ Initiate another student conference if progress is not seen.
☐ Initiate a family conference if progress is not seen.

_____   _____   _____
Student Signature   Parent Signature   Date

_____   _____   _____
Teacher Signature   Teacher Signature   Teacher Signature

FIGURE 16.3
Assignment Contract

I, _____, commit that on this _____ day of _____, 2008
I will fulfill my obligations to complete, or make significant progress on the following tasks. In the
likelihood that I do fulfill these obligations, I hereby acknowledge that the degree to which I am pestered,
nagged, and generally bothered by teachers will be significantly reduced. Failure to comply with said
obligations will result in a drastic increase in the intensity and regularity with which I will be nagged,
pestered, bothered, reminded, urged, and generally annoyed by teachers to finish my work.

ASSIGNMENT DESCRIPTION / PROGRESS	by	DATE

By signing below, I acknowledge that I have read and agree to the terms of this contract. It is clear to
me that the decision to complete or not complete these assignments is mine alone, and I am aware of
the outcomes of either choice. I understand there is a risk that failure to complete assignments will be
interpreted by teachers as a sign I actually enjoy being annoyed on a daily basis.

SIGNATURE _____   DATE _____

WITNESS _____   DATE _____

instructional consistency and documented the impact that schoolwide agreements
related to instructional routines can have on student achievement (e.g., Fisher &
Frey, 2007; Frey, 2006). The key is that teachers at the school negotiate the instructional routines that they'll use rather than simply adopting plans developed
elsewhere. As we have told many visitors, "We love our literacy plan because we

- *Building background*: Instructional routines such as bellwork, quick writes, anticipation guides, and K–W–L charts are designed to activate background knowledge and make connections between what students already know and what they are learning. These procedures also help students see the relevance of the curriculum.
- *Cornell note-taking*: Using split pages in which students take notes on the right side, identify key ideas on the left, and write a summary at the bottom, this strategy improves listening comprehension as well as provides students with a study tool.
- *Graphic organizers*: Any number of tools for displaying information in visual form are taught. Common graphic organizers include semantic webs, cause/effect charts, Venn diagrams, matrices, and flowcharts.
- *Read-alouds and shared readings*: On a daily basis, the teacher reads aloud material connected with the content standards being taught. This short, 3–5 minute reading provides students with a context for learning, builds their background knowledge, improves vocabulary, and provides them with a fluent reading model.
- *Reciprocal teaching*: In groups of four, students read a piece of text and engage in a structured conversation in which they summarize, clarify, question, and predict. In doing so, they learn to use strategies that good readers use while reading for information.
- *Vocabulary development*: In addition to the incidental vocabulary learning that is done through read-alouds and anticipatory activities, students are taught specialized and technical vocabulary words.
- *Writing to learn*: These brief writing prompts provide students with an opportunity to clarify their understanding of the content as well as provide the teacher a glimpse into students' thinking. As such, teachers know when reteaching or clarifications are necessary.

developed it. You'll need to develop your own." Our criteria for selecting school-wide instructional routines included the following:

- A strong evidence base for effectiveness
- Transportability so that students could use the routine in different content area classrooms
- Transparency, meaning that the routine could be transferred to students as a habit useful in thinking and learning
- Relevance to the world of college and work such that our students would be successful beyond their high school years

In addition to the instructional routines related to content literacy, we've worked hard to develop and refine our classroom teaching. Based on the gradual release of responsibility model (Pearson & Gallagher, 1983), our instructional model consists of four components: focus lessons, guided instruction, collaborative learning, and independent work (Fisher & Frey, 2008).

Focus Lessons

During this phase of instruction, the teacher establishes the purpose and models his or her own thinking. This is important because students are not always sure what to pay attention to. In a focus lesson, students are alerted to the big ideas for the day and are provided with an example of expert thinking.

Guided Instruction

Another phase of instruction requires that students think while their teacher provides prompts, cues, and questions. Guided instruction can occur with the whole class, in small groups, or individually. Ideally, guided instruction is based on misconceptions and errors that show up on formative assessments. In this way, the teacher can link instruction with student needs.

Collaborative Learning

While the teacher works with individuals or small groups, the other students work together productively. The idea here is to create situations in which students consolidate their understanding and negotiate meaning with peers. However, it's critical that each student is individually accountable for some aspect of the collaborative task.

Independent Work

The goal of instruction is for students to be able to apply what they have learned independently. In most schools, independent tasks are assigned prematurely. Our idea is that independent work should allow for spiral review of previously taught and learned content. Students should have a good sense of what is expected of them before engaging in independent work. When independent work is aligned with instruction, student learning is accelerated.

Of course, these four phases are not completed in the order we presented them above, lockstep hour after hour. Instead, teachers mix and match but make sure that they address each phase daily. For example, in her earth science class, Maria starts with an independent task with which students are familiar: writing journal entries. On one particular day, students are writing entries related to the rock cycle based on their observational notes from a video they watched the day before. They then move to collaborative learning by talking with a partner about their observational notes and journal entries. Maria next provides the purpose for the day and models her thinking. On one of the days, her purpose centers on identifying steps in the rock cycle, and on another day the purpose focuses on the role of metamorphic rock in the cycle. She models from a piece of text with excellent illustrations, demonstrating how the rock cycle works and how she herself remembers each phase of the cycle. She then meets with small groups of students to prompt and guide their thinking. Maria knows that she has some students who still need to learn about the various types of rocks and will meet with them as a group. As she's doing so, the other students in the class are working on their iMovie projects, which they'll present to the rest of the class at the end of the week.

Common Formative Assessments

This instructional model also assumes that assessment information is used to make instructional decisions. Common formative assessments are a powerful way to align course expectations and link instruction with assessment (Ainsworth & Viegut, 2006). We use them to check for understanding and plan next steps for instruction. We've agreed to give the same formative assessments to all students within each content area class, regardless of which teacher they have. Test items have been developed to assess achievement of specific course standards. Using an item analysis, we can determine which standards our students have mastered and which they have yet to learn.

In addition to individual student mastery, we use the item analysis to look for trends in learning and to plan instructional interventions. Sometimes the results of the common formative assessments suggest a need for reteaching the entire class, while at other times the results suggest the need for an after-school intervention for a smaller group. For example, in algebra, most of the students missed the question *Solve the proportion 2/7 = x/42.* Analyzing their work revealed a trend, namely that they multiplied across, not diagonally. In doing so, most of the students indicated that the answer was 147 rather than the correct answer of 12. The conversation the teachers had about this involved them all going back to review proportions and cross multiplying. They also decided to conduct a number of think-alouds focused on the reasonableness of an answer. This assessment item suggested that students didn't have a strong sense of numbers, given that the top number was smaller in the given (2/7) and thus should have been smaller than the denominator (e.g., less than 42).

A College-Going Culture

A colleague of ours regularly says that the best college prep course work is also vocational and that the best vocational course work is also college prep. In other words, we have to move past the idea that we are forced to choose between quality, rigorous schooling and preparing students for work. Some schools, like ours, have addressed this issue by creating a college-going culture, not a series of classes called "college prep." A college-going culture provides students with choices. Although most middle school students (about 88% according to a study by Haycock, Barth, Mitchell, & Wilkins, 1999) think that they're going to college, the reality is that very few of them do. A study of high school students who indicated that they planned to go to college suggests that only about 40% really do end up there. As depicted in Figure 16.5, the others end up lost along the way.

Rigorous Curriculum

As Kirst (2004) noted, "The best predictor of whether a student will go on to complete a bachelor's degree is the intensity and quality of that student's secondary

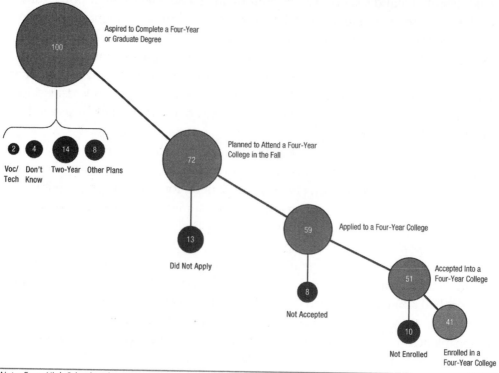

FIGURE 16.5
Tracking Students Through the Steps to College Enrollment

100 — Aspired to Complete a Four-Year or Graduate Degree

2 — Voc/Tech
4 — Don't Know
14 — Two-Year
8 — Other Plans

72 — Planned to Attend a Four-Year College in the Fall

13 — Did Not Apply

59 — Applied to a Four-Year College

8 — Not Accepted

51 — Accepted Into a Four-Year College

10 — Not Enrolled

41 — Enrolled in a Four-Year College

Note. From *High School to the Future: Potholes on the Road to College*, Consortium on Chicago School Research, 1313 East 60th Street, Chicago, Illinois 60637. Reprinted with permission.

school curriculum" (p. 52). That's why we've focused the majority of this chapter on curriculum. But we also know that simply making classes harder for students is not going to get more of them into college. As we have discussed, teachers have to change their practices and ensure that students are well supported while reaching for these high standards. The goal has to be that every learning experience for every student is challenging but not frustrating. The school system has to provide the necessary supports—do whatever it takes—to hold students to high expectations.

Understanding the System

Another aspect of the college-going culture is knowing what is expected by the college admissions system. High school students must know their current GPAs and what colleges expect GPAs to be. They also have to know which classes they are required to take and pass for entrance into college. Unfortunately, most students have no idea what classes they are required to complete to be college ready and instead rely on the school system to schedule them into classes (Kirst &

Venezia, 2004). At our school we didn't leave this to chance and instead provided students with clear guidelines for college entrance and a monitoring system for GPAs, required entrance exams, and the like. We do this early on, during the students' freshman year—a time when decisions about course work are most likely to affect the options that that students have during their senior year and beyond.

Internships

Most high school students have a sense of what they think they want to become later in life. We have had students who wanted to be professional football players, big-city rappers, and movie stars, and some of them just might do that. We also have students who want to go to college to become a nurse, teacher, doctor, lawyer, psychologist, and so on. We have one student who is sure he will be a neuroscientist and another who is sure she'll be a pediatrician. We have other students who want to own their own businesses, from Internet commerce to gardening.

At our school, students intern one day every other week in local hospitals and health care settings that we have agreements with. Half of the students attend each week for their entire high school experience. The students who remain on campus each week (50% of the grade level) attend seminars on health care and health issues and the teachers use that time for reteaching, recovery, and extension activities.

Internships are one way that we can introduce students into the world of work and careers. Some internships expand students' career options, while other internships confirm their existing choices. We use internships to show students that people go to college to enter the workforce. We also use internships as a way to increase the relevance of the curriculum. The impact that community members can have when they talk with high school students about the importance of school is amazing. We can't imagine a high-performing high school without an internship program in which students regularly apply their learning in an authentic work environment surrounded by community members engaged in their daily tasks.

Dual Enrollment

A college-going culture requires more than a visit to the local college. As Kirst (2004) recommends, schools should "expand successful dual or concurrent enrollment programs between high schools and colleges so they include all students, not just traditionally college-bound students" (p. 55). Our goal is that every one of our high school students enroll in college classes before graduation. We've had students take Spanish, calculus, philosophy, history, kayaking, and many other classes. But we can do more. Through our middle college partnership with Mesa Community College, every one of our 9th, 10th, 11th, and 12th graders take health related electives as part of their schooling experience. The classes include infection control, legal and ethical issues in health care, anatomy and physiology, patient care, records management, and health care systems. By the time they graduate, all of our students will have completed at least 18 units of college credit. These additional credits beyond their high school diplomas provide a jumpstart on earning the credits they will need for a college degree. Perhaps more important, these early credits instill a sense of confidence in their ability to do college-level work.

Looking Ahead

To be effective, high schools have to move beyond the factory model in which students travel from one class to the next collecting bits of information. Changing this model is not easy; it's easier to admire the problem, talk about the changing demographics, and lament about how students today are different from those of yesteryear. But that simply won't help. As high school educators and experts in our disciplines, we have to engage students in ways that ensure their learning. We have to show students that they can succeed and that we have developed the systems of support necessary for them to do so. And we have to establish a culture of achievement such that college is a real option for anyone who wants to attend.

EXTEND YOUR THINKING

▨ Investigate your school or district grading policy and compare and contrast it with ours. Identify strengths and weaknesses of each and determine how you might update yours.

▨ Consider each aspect of the gradual release of responsibility as we have presented them here. In which areas are you, or teachers at your school, really good? If you selected one aspect to focus instructional improvement on, which would it be?

▨ Interview several students about their college-going plans. Ask if they know their GPA and the course of study required to enter college. If they do not, develop a plan to create a college-going culture.

REFERENCES

Ainsworth, L., & Viegut, D. (2006). *Common formative assessments: How to connect standards-based instruction and assessment.* Thousand Oaks, CA: Corwin.

Consortium on Chicago School Research (2008, March). *From high school to the future: Potholes on the road to college.* Retrieved February 19, 2009, from ccsr.uchicago.edu/downloads/1835ccsr_potholes_summary.pdf

Fisher, D., & Frey, N. (2007). A tale of two middle schools: The differences in structure and instruction. *Journal of Adolescent & Adult Literacy, 51*(3), 204–211. doi:10.1598/JAAL.51.3.1

Fisher, D., & Frey, N. (2008). *Better learning through structured teaching: A framework for the gradual release of responsibility.* Alexandria, VA: Association for Supervision and Curriculum Development.

Frey, N. (2006). "We can't afford to rest on our laurels": Creating a district-wide content literacy instructional plan. *NASSP Bulletin, 90*(1), 37–48. doi:10.1177/0192636505283862

Haycock, A., Barth, P., Mitchell, R., & Wilkins, A. (Eds.). (1999). *Ticket to nowhere: The gap between leaving high school and entering college and high-performance jobs.* Washington, DC: Education Trust.

Kirst, M.W. (2004). The high school-college disconnect. *Educational Leadership, 62*(3), 51–55.

Kirst, M.W., & Venezia, A. (2004). *From high school to college: Improving opportunities for success in postsecondary education.* San Francisco: Jossey-Bass.

Pearson, P.D., & Gallagher, M.C. (1983). The instruction of reading comprehension. *Contemporary Educational Psychology, 8*(3), 317–344. doi:10.1016/0361-476X(83)90019-X

Zander, R.S., & Zander, B. (2000). *The art of possibility: Transforming professional and personal life.* New York: Penguin.

CHAPTER 17

Center of Excellence for Adolescent Literacy and Learning

Kathy Headley, Victoria Gillis

"It isn't something extra."

—*Dr. Mary Dillingham, biology teacher,*
Wren High School, South Carolina

"It isn't something extra." This simple statement from a high school biology teacher captures the essence of Clemson University's Center of Excellence for Adolescent Literacy and Learning (CEALL) and its mission to infuse literacy supports for content learning across the secondary curriculum. Based on similar projects at the local (Alvermann & Ridgeway, 1990) and international levels (Klooster, Steele, & Bloem, 2001), CEALL focuses on improving literacy and learning in middle and high schools by using a *train the trainer* model. Through a two-year program, teaching consultants in the four major content areas (science, mathematics, English language arts, and social studies) are trained to use research-based strategies that improve the efficiency and effectiveness of their instruction and that concurrently improve students' literacy. After their initial year of professional development, teaching consultants experience another level of training in strategies for working with adults and for planning their own series of workshops tailored to their schools and districts.

CEALL is funded through South Carolina's Commission on Higher Education. Goals and objectives that undergird our mission and outreach include the following:

- To train middle and high school content area teachers in the fields of English language arts, mathematics, science, and social science in the use of strategies that improve the efficiency and effectiveness of classroom instruction and improve students' literacy skills.

Adolescent Literacy, Field Tested: Effective Solutions for Every Classroom, edited by Sheri R. Parris, Douglas Fisher, and Kathy Headley. © 2009 by the International Reading Association.

- To build capacity in schools and districts across the state through the development of teaching consultants, who, after two years of training, will serve as resources for their middle and high school faculties and will provide continuing professional development for the school and district.
- To coordinate and disseminate research on adolescent literacy practices, both in-school and out-of-school, to teachers, parents, administrators, and other stakeholders across the state.
- To provide an opportunity for inservice teachers to support preservice teachers' development by providing exemplar lessons and assessments.
- To establish a virtual resource center for middle and high school teachers in the major content areas. The virtual resource center (www.clemson.edu/ceall) provides lesson plans, strategies, links to useful websites, and other supporting materials.

Now in its fourth year of funding, the first CEALL cohort included two English language arts teachers, two social studies teachers, five science teachers, and three mathematics teachers, averaging 17.7 years of teaching experience. Two middle school teachers taught two content areas, one in math/science and the other in language arts/social studies. Subsequent cohorts have been similar with respect to participants' experience and content areas. As Center directors, we have been colearners with the cohort members over the course of time. Each year, in concert with participant feedback, the Center directors implement changes and reinforce elements that motivate teacher change at the middle and high school levels.

Current Research

Secondary teachers have historically dealt with struggling adolescent readers by turning to lecture and opting out of requiring students to read text (Hall, 2005; Stewart & O'Brien, 1989). Students who can read but choose not to do so, collectively described as *aliterate*, are the disengaged students who are populating classrooms today (Alvermann, 2003). Because they do not read, either for school assignments or for pleasure, their reading skills remain stagnant or decline as they move through middle and high school. National data provide evidence that a crisis in adolescent literacy exists in the United States (National Assessment of Educational Progress [NEAP], 2007). Although NAEP scores from 2005 and 2007 increased in the percentage of fourth-grade and eighth-grade students scoring basic and above, they were not significant increases (NAEP, 2007). Furthermore, there was no change at the eighth grade level in the percentage of students scoring proficient and advanced from 2005 to 2007, and the percentage of students scoring proficient and advanced actually declined from fourth to eighth grade. This does not bode well for the economic health of this nation. Proficient and advanced levels of literacy will be entry levels of competence for most jobs in the 21st century. It is clear that teaching a child to read well by third grade does not ensure an end to adolescent literacy problems (Elkins & Luke, 1999; Landrum, 2002). The goal to improve high school students' achievement is one that researchers investigating adolescent literacy welcome. However, factors underlying reading achievement must be addressed so that meaningful change in adolescent reading achievement can be made.

One factor that impedes progress toward improving adolescent literacy is the context of academic instruction in middle and high schools. The culture of high school in particular, with its teacher-centered, transmission model of instruction, does not provide sufficient support for struggling, marginalized students (Alvermann & Moore, 1991; Moje, Young, Readence, & Moore, 2000; O'Brien, Stewart, & Moje, 1995). In part, the transition from largely student-centered instruction in elementary schools to the largely teacher-centered instruction found in secondary schools accounts for the decline in adolescent literacy (Oldfather, 1995). In the past, remediation has focused primarily on students rather than on changing teachers' classroom instruction and the culture of teaching (Alvermann, 2003). Perhaps it is time to view the problem of adolescent literacy from another perspective. Instead of focusing on "fixing students," perhaps a more fruitful focus might be on changing classroom contexts. It takes time and support to help inservice teachers transform their pedagogy from teacher-centered to more student-centered approaches and include activities that require critical thinking.

Another factor that impedes progress toward improved adolescent literacy is the lack of developmental literacy instruction for students above grade six or seven (Vacca, 1998). Secondary reading instruction tends to be remedial in nature. No one would suggest teaching Venus and Serena Williams tennis on an asphalt surface until they were 9 or 10 years old, and then assuming they could play tennis and needed no further instruction. Likewise, after years without instruction, no one would suggest they compete at Wimbledon at the age of 15 or 16 on a completely different court surface and under stressful conditions. Yet that is essentially what happens to students with respect to literacy. We teach students to read in the elementary grades using primarily narrative text. Once students become fluent readers, we assume they can read. At about this time in students' educational careers, reading demands change. As students move into middle and high school, narrative text is increasingly more scarce and expository or informational text becomes the norm (Vacca & Vacca, 2005). Literacy demands increase, both in the amount and difficulty of reading. At the same time, literacy instruction decreases or ceases to be a visible part of students' learning landscape. Reading instruction offered at middle and high school levels tends to be a separate course in the curriculum taught by teachers educated in reading, but not in any specific content area. Lack of transfer to subject matter contexts renders such literacy instruction less than effective (Johnston & Allington, 1991). In short, literacy instruction cannot be provided in isolation. It must be infused through all content area classes. Yet, secondary teachers are educated in specific content areas, not in reading, and are often resistant to content area reading strategies (O'Brien et al., 1995; Stewart & O'Brien, 1989).

A review of the research on teachers and content area reading (Hall, 2005) identified 19 studies published in peer-reviewed journals between 1970 and 2003 that investigated content teachers' attitudes and beliefs about content area reading. Studies involved both pre- and inservice content area teachers. Hall's review found that teachers either do not believe they are qualified to teach reading or they should not be responsible for doing so. Some preservice teachers believed reading would not be necessary for their future students to be successful. It appears that not much has changed in the over 30 years since Herber (1970) called for reading to be taught across the curriculum. After this much time, one wonders why change seems so elusive at the secondary level. In part, the lack of change is rooted in the pervasive culture of secondary schools (O'Brien et al., 1995). The link between the quality of instruction and student achievement suggests that professional development in literacy for content area teachers is critical to advancing levels of student literacy (Frey & Fisher, 2004).

Instructional Practices That Work

Current research on adolescent learning and teacher change provided the basis for our creation of CEALL. We frame the workshops for teachers around research on student learning (Bonwell & Eison, 1991; Gillis & MacDougall, 2007; Temple, Meredith, & Steele, 1997), adult learning (McLeish, cited in Penner, 1984; Worthman, 2008), and professional development (McKinney, 2003; Peck, 2002). In the following paragraphs, we discuss (a) the learning cycle framework that is used to organize lessons, (b) the importance of active engagement in learning as teachers experience strategies embedded in lessons appropriate for middle and high school students, (c) the two-year professional development cycle used in the CEALL program, and (d) the importance of reflection and conversation among the participants.

In the CEALL workshops, we present content-specific strategies embedded in a learning cycle (see Figure 17.1) using meaningful texts for optimum engagement and understanding. The learning cycle is an instructional framework used to support literacy and content knowledge development simultaneously. In the cycle, teachers plan instruction that prepares students to learn by activating prior knowledge and focusing students' attention on the relevant content. They guide student learning, helping students learn to differentiate between important and unimportant information, make connections within the content, and organize the information meaningfully. Finally, teachers help students reflect on their learning and the processes involved in learning, thus developing habits of mind unique to particular content areas. The specific content—math, science, English, or social studies—determines

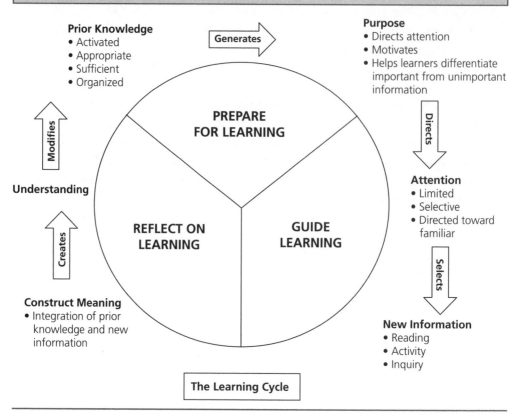

FIGURE 17.1
The Learning Cycle

Prior Knowledge
• Activated
• Appropriate
• Sufficient
• Organized

Generates

Purpose
• Directs attention
• Motivates
• Helps learners differentiate important from unimportant information

Modifies

PREPARE FOR LEARNING

Directs

Understanding

Attention
• Limited
• Selective
• Directed toward familiar

Creates

REFLECT ON LEARNING

GUIDE LEARNING

Selects

Construct Meaning
• Integration of prior knowledge and new information

New Information
• Reading
• Activity
• Inquiry

The Learning Cycle

the cognitive processes involved in learning the content, which in turn determines strategy selection (see Figure 17.2). Herber's (1970) long-ago mantra of content determines process serves as a guiding principle in CEALL.

An underlying principle of CEALL is active engagement in learning. As part of their training, participating teachers experience strategies embedded in lessons, which enables them to see the strategies from their students' viewpoint. Unpacking the lesson and exploring the underlying research and theory helps teachers envision strategy adaptations for their own classrooms. Having teachers adapt and use the strategies with their own students, then reflect on the experience and share their results helps teachers build confidence in using new pedagogies and promotes a sense of community among the participants.

Key to our philosophy is the belief that teachers teaching teachers supports the greatest chance for change. On this premise, we developed a two-year professional development cycle. In year one, teachers learn, plan, and reflect on lessons, then share their experiences about content instruction and student learning. During year two, these same teachers return to refine their knowledge and practices by

FIGURE 17.2
The Learning Cycle: Teaching Models

Content Areas / Cognitive Process	Prepare for Learning — Connecting	Guide the Learning — Processing new information	Reflect on Learning — Transforming and personalizing information	Lesson
Math	Anticipation guide	Inquiry activity with Anticipation Guide	Application problem	Order of operations
Science	Brainstorming	Interactive lecture	Create graphic organizer	The genetic code
English	Paired free write and share	Dual-entry journal	5-minute write	Poem: "As Best She Could"
Social Studies	Paired structured brainstorming	Structured three-column note making	Forced choice (discussion) Cinquain (writing)	Columbus and the New World

mentoring the next group of new teachers. In this way, the teacher-learning cycle revolves in two parallel manners: teachers in their first year of CEALL participation learn about their own teaching and their students' learning while teachers in their second year of CEALL reinforce their learning by mentoring the new participating teachers and designing/delivering professional development sessions for the new teachers. Hence, the teachers in their first year of CEALL benefit from the professional development provided by the previous year's participants, while these second-year teachers, now "teaching" what they had experienced in their own first year, experience the role of teaching consultant within a supportive, reflective environment.

Conversations with and communications from teachers who "get it" are precious gems in the professional development realm. CEALL has been fortunate to attract and nurture teachers who truly want to provide the best instruction for their students and who want to develop their expertise in a shared learning environment. Just this year, Victoria received an enthusiastic e-mail from one of our CEALL teaching consultants, LaTonya Capers, an algebra teacher at Orangeburg-Wilkinson High School in South Carolina's Orangeburg Consolidated School District Five (see Figure 17.3). The brief message is powerful. LaTonya, aware that she has stepped

From: LaTonya Capers
Date: Oct. 30, 2007
Subject: I'm Excited!!!
To: Victoria Ridgeway Gillis

Dr. Gillis,

I volunteered to take an extra class, because there was a vacancy. This is a Geometry class and totally out of my comfort zone. I started the class with a biopoem ... to get to know students. We then did the anticipation guide I developed for a lesson on Conditional Statements ... IT WORKED!!!!

Even though the students didn't know any of the information before reading ... the guide focused their reading.... I am excited!!!! I attached the guide ... and I am working on the Frayer [Model] I am going to try on tomorrow.

Looking forward to your feedback.

LaTonya

---

outside her comfort zone, possesses the courage and confidence to take knowledgeable risks with her own learning and that of her students. Ever reflective, she assesses her own teaching in tandem with her students' learning. LaTonya's teacher-constructed anticipation guide, which she designed for her geometry class, is shown in Figure 17.4. Take notice that the guide combines a quick Think-Write as well.

LaTonya, along with the other teachers participating in CEALL, is engaged in intensive, long-term professional development that connects her own learning with that of her students. To accomplish this connection, CEALL's focus is on active learning and reflection. This focus is initiated throughout CEALL's model of professional development and is based on the premise that teacher-as-learner engagement is critical to instructional changes (Gillis, Headley, & Dunston, 2006). Through ongoing, relevant assessment of students' learning, teachers effectively design instruction that actively engages students in all stages of the learning cycle (see Figure 17.1 on p. 208).

CEALL's professional development framework has evolved over the past three years. Each year, we assess our own learning as Center directors and reflect upon changes for the upcoming offerings. The planning matrix in Table 17.1 gives an overall perspective of our teacher–learner curriculum.

As we reflect upon the workshops that we've designed across the four years, it seems that in the beginning, we delivered a lot of traditional "show and tell" professional development. As CEALL has evolved, we have revisioned, redesigned,

FIGURE 17.4
LaTonya Capers's Strategy Lesson

Anticipation Guide
Geometry Section 2.1: Conditional Statements

Directions *before* **reading the assigned text:** Read the statements below. If you <u>agree</u> with the statement, place a check on the line in front of the statement under the column labeled *Me*. If you <u>disagree</u> with the statement, leave the line blank.

Directions *after* **reading the assigned text:** Review the statements below. If the text <u>supports</u> the statement, place a check on the line in front of the statement under the column labeled *Textbook*. If the text <u>does not support</u> the statement, leave the line blank.

Me   Textbook

_____   _____   A conditional statement consists of 2 parts—the hypothesis and the conclusion.

_____   _____   A conditional statement is written as an "if–then" statement.

_____   _____   The "if" part of a conditional statement is called the **conclusion**.

_____   _____   A **negation** makes the parts of a conditional statement negative.

_____   _____   The **converse** of a conditional statement is formed by switching the order of the hypothesis and the conclusion.

_____   _____   The **inverse** of a conditional statement is formed by negating the hypothesis and the conclusion.

_____   _____   The **contrapositive** is the negation of the inverse.

Think-Write

This section is easy because…

This section is hard because…

TABLE 17.1
CEALL: Curricular Framework Years 1–4

	YEAR I	YEAR II	YEAR III	YEAR IV
Workshop I / INSTITUTE—Day 1	Bionic Trees (text) • Anticipation guide • Structured note making • Discussion web • RAFT² How do humans learn? Interactive session to connect theory to practice: schema, cognitive flexibility, Vygotsky's social learning, reader response	Bionic Trees (text) • Anticipation guide • Structured note making • Discussion web • RAFT² Assessment *for* learning—affective • What's easy/what's hard • All-about-me letters • Interest inventory • AMRP	Data collection Get-to-know-you activities How do humans learn? Interactive session to connect theory to practice: schema, cognitive flexibility, Vygotsky's social learning, reader response	Active learning experiments Interactive session to connect theory to practice: schema, cognitive flexibility, Vygotsky's social learning, reader response Columbus (text) • Paired brainstorming • Structured note making • Forced-choice discussion • Cinquain
Workshop II / INSTITUTE—Day 2	Study strategies jigsaw—Participants teach each other how to take different kinds of notes • 2-column notes • Chapter mapping • INSERT	Assessment *for* learning—content • CLOZE • Think-writes Study strategies jigsaw with same text, then discuss methods • 2-column notes • Chapter mapping • INSERT	Manatee (text) • Anticipation guide • Chapter mapping • Biopoem—posted for • Gallery walk El Cazador (text) • Video to augment prior knowledge • Student generated questions based on artifact • INSERT • Partners create graphic organizer from INSERT chart	Bionic Trees (text) • Anticipation guide • Structured note making • Discussion web • RAFT² Math Lesson—demonstration by teacher consultant

		INSTITUTE—Day 3		Leadership Team (LT)
Workshop III	Bird Flu (text)—vocabulary • VSS strategy + preteaching vocabulary • Guiding learning with four-square, Frayer model, concept of definition map Interactive vocabulary lecture—reinforcement/interpretive activities: word sorts/categories/ SFA/concept circles	Cloning (text)—vocabulary • VSS strategy + preteaching vocabulary • Guiding learning with four-square, Frayer model, concept of definition map Interactive vocabulary lecture—reinforcement/interpretive activities: word sorts/categories/ SFA/concept circles	Assessment *for* learning • What's easy/what's hard • Interest Inventory • CLOZE • Think-write Assessment *of* learning • Think-writes evaluated • Authentic assessment • Creating criteria Assessment *as* learning • Student self-assessment • Peer evaluation	Assessment *of* learning—LT • Authentic assessment Assessment *as* learning—LT • Peer assessment—lab reports • Create criteria with students • Teacher self-assessment Assessment *for* learning • Think-writes • Interest inventories • What's easy/what's hard • SCLA
		INSTITUTE—Day 4		
Workshop IV	Columbus: Part I (text) • Paired brainstorming • Structured note making • Forced-choice discussion • Cinquain Writing to learn interactive lecture • Reflective [personal]—think-writes • Informal [guided writing procedure; response heuristic] • Creative W2L [cinquain, biopoem]	Columbus Part I (text) • Paired brainstorming • Structured note making • Forced-choice discussion • Cinquain Columbus Part II (text) • Think-write + partner discussion—create criteria for hero • INSERT • Discussion of notes • Cubing • Discussion web	Sea of Life (text)—vocabulary • VSS strategy • Four-square • Cinquain Interactive lecture on vocabulary • Morphology • Context clues • Semantic maps • Frayer model • Word sorts • Categories	Photosynthesis (text) • Latin roots: create your own vocabulary • Read and complete: Four-squares • Cinquain to reflect • Frayer model • Concept of definition map • Categories and analogies Vocabulary reinforcement—Interns share their success stories

(continued)

TABLE 17.1
CEALL: Curricular Framework Years 1–4 (continued)

YEAR I	YEAR II	YEAR III	YEAR IV
Math—Hands-on manipulative lesson creating data table, reading for patterns, translating data into mathematics "sentence" [expression] reinforce how literacy supports hands-on/manipulative learning • Problem to solve • Collect data using T-chart • Use data to describe pattern • Translate English to math expression	A Warming Earth (text) • Political cartoon as advance organizer • Paired reading or Questioning the Author during reading + structured note making • RAFT[2]—letter to editor Alternative energy sources [jigsaw w/ different text] • Brainstorming • INSERT + Inquiry chart • Jigsaw teaching • Whip Around—address Congress with ideas on alternative energy sources Intern-led lessons by content area	Assessment follow-up • Analysis of think-writes—modeled process Middle East Crisis—[jigsaw w/ text] • Brainstorming • Expert groups read + take notes in Inquiry Chart • Student-generated graphic organizer Math: Measures of Central Tendency • Data collection • Read text—complete structured notes • Problem solving • Cubing • RAFT[2]	Ordeal by Cheque (text) • Use nonfiction text to augment prior knowledge • Brainstorm with timeline • Dual-entry diary as read story • Discussion: collective story • Literary report card • Character map • Polar opposites Intern share: Capacity Matrix Intern share: Faculty Newsletters Apprentice share: Thinking aloud while modeling comprehension of nonfiction text

Workshop V

Follow-up Workshop 1

	Column 1	Column 2	Column 3
Workshop VI	Demo lesson—Paired reading w/ new text [silent; summarizer and questioner] Save the Last Word for Me—discussion strategy Ordeal By Cheque (text) • Using nonfiction text to augment prior knowledge for brainstorming with a graphic organizer • Dual-entry diary as read story • Discussion of story • RAFT²	Ordeal by Cheque (text) • Use nonfiction text to augment prior knowledge • Brainstorm with timeline [GO] • Dual-entry diary as read story • Discussion: collective story • Literary report card • Character map • Polar opposites Math lesson: hands-on w/ manipulatives • Problem solving • Collect data using T-chart • Use data to describe pattern • Translate English to math expression	
Follow-up Workshop 2		Road Less Traveled (text) • Anticipation Guide • Response heuristic • Cinquain Global Warming (text) • Cartoon as advance organizer • K–W–L to prepare for and guide reading • Discussion web • RAFT²: Write letter to editor of local paper in response to problem and information from reading	Disciplinary Literacy lesson • Paired silent reading w/ text—roles to include summarizer and connector • Save the Last Word for Me discussion strategy • Create a graphic organizer to summarize text Intern Share: math lesson Intern Share: English lesson
Follow-up Workshop 3		Train the trainer workshop w/ interns • Working w/ adults • Elements of successful professional development • Structure of workshops Apprentices work in content-specific groups—develop presentations for CEALL conference; present practice presentation	RETREAT • Interns—create and share introductory workshop • Apprentices—create strategy description for CEALL newsletter

and reenergized our efforts to support our belief that teachers who engage in their own learning will and can engage their students in meaningful learning, too. We incorporate content-learning strategies into lessons in such a way that with very few exceptions, CEALL participants are learning about their teaching through participating in lessons and reflecting with other CEALL teachers about adolescent literacy and learning in their English, math, science, and social studies classrooms.

Looking Ahead

To increase student learning, teachers need to increase their own learning. Professional development can be and should be an avenue of learning for teachers. For this to happen, professional development must engage teachers in exploring content area learning as both student and teacher. Our challenge is motivating and supporting teachers to engage in this type of learning opportunity. Relatedly, we have to motivate and inform administrators that teachers who are supported to learn will return that support through enriched student learning and sharing with colleagues. To accomplish both of these challenges, teachers need connections with other teachers, their students, and their administrators; in other words, ongoing professional development is about relationships, communication, and growth. No small task, progress develops through engagement, inquiry, and communication.

Professional development, such as that provided by CEALL, is particularly relevant today and in times ahead. Requiring subject area teachers to take a content area reading course, either in preservice education courses or in content area reading inservice programs, is not adequate to effect change in secondary classroom instruction and student learning (O'Brien et al., 1995). Literacy coaches, originally employed in the elementary schools to help elementary teachers teach reading, are now being assigned to middle and high schools. The new Standards for Literacy Coaches (International Reading Association, 2006) provide evidence of this trend. But literacy coaches, like their predecessors, reading resource specialists and reading teachers, cannot be expected to do the job alone. What is needed is widespread change in teacher beliefs and attitudes, teachers' content area instruction, and teacher efficacy with respect to literacy across the curriculum. Effective professional development seeks to change the culture of middle and high schools by creating content area teacher specialists—what CEALL calls teaching consultants—who, unlike literacy coaches, remain in their classrooms while providing both formal and informal professional development to their colleagues.

EXTEND YOUR THINKING

▨ What aspects of your own professional development experiences have been instrumental in changing your pedagogy?

■ What motivates (or would motivate) you and your colleagues to include more content literacy strategies in your teaching repertoire?

■ Have you integrated content literacy strategies into your own instruction? If so, did your use of content literacy strategies result in better student learning? If not, why have you not used content literacy strategies?

REFERENCES

Alvermann, D.E. (2003). *Seeing themselves as capable and engaged readers: Adolescents and re/mediated instruction*. Naperville, IL: Learning Point Associates. Retrieved January 7, 2009, from www.learningpt.org/pdfs/literacy/readers.pdf

Alvermann, D.E., & Moore, D.W. (1991). Secondary school reading. In R. Barr, M.L. Kamil, P. Mosenthal, & P.D. Pearson (Eds.), *Handbook of reading research* (Vol. 2, pp. 951–983). White Plains, NY: Longman.

Alvermann, D.E., & Ridgeway, V.G. (1990). Implementing content area reading with limited finances. In G.G. Duffy (Ed.), *Reading in the middle school* (2nd ed., pp. 200–208). Newark, DE: International Reading Association.

Bonwell, C.C., & Eison, J.A. (1991). *Active learning: Creating excitement in the classroom* (ASHE-ERIC Higher Education Reports). Washington, DC: School of Education and Human Development, George Washington University.

Elkins, J., & Luke, A. (1999). Redefining adolescent literacies. *Journal of Adolescent & Adult Literacy, 43*(3), 212–215.

Frey, N., & Fisher, D. (2004). Teachers matter and what they do matters most: Using literacy strategies, grouping, and texts to promote learning. In D. Fisher & N. Frey (Eds.), *Improving adolescent literacy: Strategies at work* (pp. 1–14). Upper Saddle River, NJ: Pearson Education.

Gillis, V.R., & Headley, K.N. (2007, November). *"It isn't something extra": Motivating teacher change across the curriculum*. Roundtable session presented at the 57th National Reading Conference, Austin, TX.

Gillis, V.R., Headley, K.N., & Dunston, P.J. (2006, December). *Changing teachers/changing cultures: Year one South Carolina Center of Excellence for Adolescent Literacy and Learning*. Roundtable session presented at the 56th National Reading Conference, Los Angeles, CA.

Gillis, V.R., & MacDougall, G. (2007). Reading to learn science as an active process. *The Science Teacher, 74*(5), 45–50.

Hall, L.A. (2005). Teachers and content area reading: Attitudes, beliefs and change. *Teaching and Teacher Education, 21*(4), 403–414. doi:10.1016/j.tate.2005.01.009

Herber, H.L. (1970). *Teaching reading in content areas*. Englewood Cliffs, NJ: Prentice Hall.

International Reading Association. (2006). *Standards for middle and high school literacy coaches*. Newark, DE: Author.

Johnston, P., & Allington, R. (1991). Remediation. In R. Barr, M.L. Kamil, P. Mosenthal, & P.D. Pearson (Eds.), *Handbook of reading research* (Vol. 2, pp. 984–1012). New York: Longman.

Klooster, D.J., Steele, J.L., & Bloem P.L. (Eds.). (2001). *Ideas without boundaries: International education reform through reading and writing for critical thinking*. Newark, DE: International Reading Association.

Landrum, C. (2002, January 28). Reading plan faulted for ignoring older kids. *The Greenville News*, pp. B1, B3.

McKinney, M. (2003). Learning communities: An exploration of theoretical conceptualizations. In C.M. Fairbanks, J. Worthy, B. Maloch, J.V. Hoffman, & D.L. Schallert (Eds.), *52nd yearbook of the National Reading Conference* (pp. 295–307). Oak Creek, WI: National Reading Conference.

Moje, E.B., Young, J.P., Readence, J.E., & Moore, D.W. (2000). Reinventing adolescent literacy for new times: Perennial and millennial issues. *Journal of Adolescent & Adult Literacy, 43*(5), 400–410.

National Assessment of Educational Progress. (2007). *The nation's report card: Reading 2007*. Washington DC: National Center for Education Statistics. Retrieved May 2, 2008, from nationsreportcard.gov/reading_2007/r0001.asp

O'Brien, D.G., Stewart, R.A., & Moje, E.B. (1995). Why content literacy is difficult to infuse into the secondary school: Complexities of curriculum, pedagogy, and school culture. *Reading Research Quarterly, 30*(3), 442–463. doi:10.2307/747625

Oldfather, P. (1995). Commentary: What's needed to maintain and extend motivation for literacy in the middle grades. *Journal of Reading, 38*(6), 420–422.

Peck, S.M. (2002). "I do have this right. You can't strip that from me": Valuing teacher's knowledge during literacy instructional change. In D.L. Schallert, C.M. Fairbanks, J. Worthy, B. Maloch, & J.V. Hoffman (Eds.), *51st yearbook of the National Reading Conference* (pp. 344–356). Oak Creek, WI: National Reading Conference.

Penner, J.H. (1984). *Why many college teachers cannot lecture: How to avoid communication breakdown in the classroom.* Springfield, IL: Charles C. Thomas.

Stewart, R.A., & O'Brien, D.G. (1989). Resistance to content area reading: A focus on preservice teachers. *Journal of Reading, 32*(5), 396–401.

Temple, C., Meredith, K., & Steele, J.L. (1997). *How children learn: A statement of first principles.* Geneva, NY: Reading & Writing for Critical Thinking Project.

Vacca, R.T. (1998). Let's not marginalize adolescent literacy. *Journal of Adolescent & Adult Literacy, 41*(8), 604–609. doi:10.1598/JAAL.41.8.1

Vacca, R.T., & Vacca, J.L. (2005). *Content area reading: Literacy and learning across the curriculum* (8th ed.). Boston: Pearson/Allyn & Bacon.

Worthman, C. (2008). The positioning of adult learners: Appropriating learner experience on the continuum of empowerment to emancipation. *International Journal of Lifelong Education, 27*(4), 443–462. doi:10.1080/02601370802051355

CHAPTER 18

Successful Secondary Teachers Share Their Most Effective Teaching Practices

Sheri R. Parris, Cheryl Taliaferro

KEY POINTS AND STRATEGIES
Chunking
Creating Student Buy-In and Choice for Lessons
Providing a Safe and Supportive Classroom Environment
Developing Lessons for Different Learning Styles
Encouraging Higher Level Thinking Skills
Building Relationships With Students

"When you are teaching adolescents, never forget what that age was like for you."

—*Ruth Meissen, 2008 Illinois State Teacher of the Year*

This chapter gives voice to award-winning secondary teachers to share the insights and practices that are important to their teaching success. The teachers interviewed for this chapter come from a variety of content areas and even electives, but they all have one thing in common. They each use instructional practices that support literacy learning in their classrooms and believe this to be an important part of a successful teaching routine. Upon analyzing the interviews from this group of teachers, common instructional themes emerged, including chunking, creating student buy-in and student choice for lessons, providing a safe and supportive classroom environment, developing lessons for different learning styles, encouraging higher level thinking skills, and building relationships with students. We will listen to what they have to say about each of these important aspects of successful teaching, and then we will wrap up with final thoughts from these successful teachers.

Instructional Practices That Work

Chunking

When talking to teachers who have won state or national recognition for their teaching, we learned that many seem to follow the wisdom of one the greatest

Adolescent Literacy, Field Tested: Effective Solutions for Every Classroom, edited by Sheri R. Parris, Douglas Fisher, and Kathy Headley. © 2009 by the International Reading Association.

minds of all time, Albert Einstein. He said, "Everything should be made as simple as possible, but not simpler." These teachers have developed their teaching methods to break down content into logical learning "chunks" that students can grasp and be successful at accomplishing. All of these teachers give their students a chance to experience success.

For instance, Josh Anderson, 2007 Kansas Teacher of the Year, uses a method he calls the "meat and potatoes" approach to finding critical parts of a sentence in his high school English language arts classroom. Using this approach, he takes lengthy sentences from literature and upper level textbooks (often between 30 and 50 words per sentence) and then has students look for the meat (the main subject and main verb) in the sentence. Once they have located these, they learn that everything else in the sentence can be considered the "side items." This helps students to create a simple, graspable mental framework for lengthy sentences, and once this concept is achieved, they can build to more complex grammatical applications.

Andy Mogle, 2008 Iowa Teacher of the Year, is a big proponent of having students teach the material to one another, because, he insightfully states, "Students will remember 90% of what they teach, but only 10% of what they hear." In his high school's family consumer science classes, he maintains that one of the most effective ways of doing this is through the jigsaw method (also described in Chapter 14). By using a jigsaw grouping strategy, Andy breaks content material into smaller chunks, with each group member responsible for learning a different piece of the material and teaching it to the other group members. In this way, each student becomes an expert on his or her chunk of the material and is responsible to share it with and teach it to the other group members. When using this approach, he ensures that each group and group member is assigned a chunk of content according to a difficulty level that matches their ability, ensuring that all groups are able to complete the task on time.

Laurie Jones, vocational education teacher and winner of the 2008 Washington Teacher of the Year, states, "If you break a chapter into mini chunks, the students will see it as doable. Pull an article from a magazine for lower level readers and a different one on the same topic to suit higher level readers." Laurie has also found vocabulary to be an important part of learning content. She has developed an effective way to tackle content vocabulary through teamwork. For example, before a unit, she gives teams of students 5 to 10 new vocabulary words. (If there are a lot of words to learn, she gives each team a different list of words). Everyone on the team must predict the meaning of each word, whether right or not—this has them make connections to prior knowledge. Laurie then provides the appropriate definitions and facilitates a class discussion of the words. Next, students create an illustration (after the teacher provides an example) to represent each word in its various contexts. For example, the word *trend* can be used in different contexts (e.g., economics, fashion, weather, a sequence of numbers for a pattern). Laurie uses butcher paper for this activity and gives each student a different colored marker so that as she walks around the room, she can see that everyone is participating. Afterwards, the illustrations are posted up around the room.

Marcie Belgard, high school literature teacher and winner of the 2007 Washington State Literacy Award, describes strategies for teaching reading that engage students:

> When I find a really good book for the class, I do many prereading strategies to get students ready to read the book, and I play vocabulary games to prepare students to read the book. During the reading, we do prediction games and summaries, and one of the best endings for a book is Alpha Boxes. The Alpha Boxes strategy [Hoyt, 1999] is a postreading strategy that can be used to help learners summarize key ideas from assigned readings by identifying concepts, connections, and examples that correspond to each letter of the alphabet. After my students have filled in the boxes, they know that they must present their reasons for picking certain words for a certain box. It is done orally, and my reluctant readers adore it. Also, find the right book! Read aloud to students. Play games and dramatize. In other words, make reading fun and interactive. Have students reflect about what they have learned on a weekly basis.

Create Student Buy-In and Choice for Lessons

Another common theme among our award-winning teachers is the importance of creating student buy-in for each lesson. In other words, students must see the importance of lessons to their own lives and take a personal interest in learning the material. This includes incorporating an element of student choice, which increases student motivation and ownership of these lessons.

Ken Russell, a high school history teacher with 27 years experience who was also the Professional Association of Georgia Educators State President, 2005–2006, describes the payoff when students get on board:

> It's important to be an expert in your content, but you have to be flexible enough to adapt your lessons and plans when your students need it. It takes patience and the drive to be persistent even when your students balk. It's important for your students to have both confidence and challenge. It takes a decent mix of the two, but they can and will come through. It's a real motivation when a teacher knows a student is engaged because they want to be. It's rewarding when students take charge of their learning and strive to succeed in their own right.

Steve Gardiner is the 2008 Montana Teacher of the Year. He has found that vocabulary acquisition, as well as independent reading, are critical aspects of literacy instruction:

> During the 30 years that I have taught high school English, I have tried numerous techniques to motivate readers. Some have lasted a year or two, some have lasted several years, but only one technique has stayed with me for all 30 years—Sustained Silent Reading (SSR). This is clearly the most effective way to help struggling and reluctant teen readers and it is effective with students at all reading levels and all socioeconomic levels.

My program is based on 15 minutes of silent reading at the beginning of every class period. Students choose their own books, and this point is extremely important. I do not give them reading lists but will help with recommendations if a student requests help. The English Department makes many choices for students with the core novels, stories, and poems we select for classroom lessons. Giving students a chance to make some decisions about their own education is very important.

SSR is the most efficient way to teach students vocabulary, spelling, sentence fluency, reading comprehension, and most important, reading enjoyment. If students do not enjoy reading, teachers can give them thousands of worksheets and make no difference in student learning. It will not transfer to their reading unless they want to make the connections. SSR gives students the chance to practice reading in a safe environment. It allows them to explore many kinds of reading, and it opens the door for a student to find the "Home Run Book," the book that changes their attitudes toward reading and often toward school in general. I have watched hundreds of students' lives transformed by the simple means of daily independent reading.

Gardiner continues,

Nagy and Anderson estimate that there are 88,000 words in the English language. They found that most vocabulary programs successfully teach about 200 to 400 words during a school year, yet most students learn some 3,000 words per year. Those additional words, the bulk of the yearly progress, come from interaction with the language rather than specific instruction, and SSR gives students access to books and time to work with the language.

When I meet former students, they seldom talk about the novels or stories we read as a group and then very rarely reference writing assignments we did in class. They do, however, frequently and passionately, remember the independent reading time and the effect it had on their high school and college studies. I have received hundreds of notes, letters, phone calls, and e-mails thanking me for giving students the huge benefits that come from SSR. It is the most effective teaching technique I have used over the past 30 years and I will never teach without it.

Gardiner feels so passionately about the positive effects of SSR that he has published articles and a book about it (see *Building Student Literacy Through Sustained Silent Reading*, Gardiner, 2005a, and his articles in *Educational Leadership*, Gardiner, 2001, 2005b).

Provide a Safe and Supportive Classroom Environment

Ruth Meissen, middle school art teacher and 2008 Illinois Teacher of the Year, uses a talk show format as a safe and fun way to do oral reports in her middle school art classroom:

I have my students do research papers and oral presentations on portraiture artists. A "talk show" style is less threatening and more laid back. I play the part of Oprah (which is also an acronym for Outstanding People Researching Art History). For research, students can use books from the classroom or library, or use approved websites (the Biography Channel website is particularly good for this type of research). I also have a large collection of art books in my room so students don't have to leave the room to do research—and I will sometimes take them to the library where they can use bigger tables and spread out.

The students (guest speakers) are scheduled ahead of time so they know when and at what time they are on OPRAH. Students are interviewed as experts on their topic. Students must be ready to go when it's their turn to go. One student is appointed to be in charge of the projector to display the art that students are using in their presentation.

As part of the project, students must create a timeline of the artist's life to put his work in perspective. They must also learn who or what events had a major influence on this artist, and other interesting facts that the students discover on their own.

As a guest on OPRAH, each student sits down and answers questions about information that is supposed to be in their research paper. Meanwhile, the rest of the class sits in a semicircle as the audience. Students get extra credit if they come in costume as the artist, or artist's significant other, because this makes the presentation more entertaining and engaging for the class. Because we have many English-language learners in our school, I also have "Español OPRAH." For Español OPRAH, one student is selected to translate in Spanish (or other native language) so that the nonnative speakers can participate equally in the talk show sessions. Extra credit is given to the translator.

Ruth uses the OPRAH format anytime students need to discuss, explain, or justify their work. This format allows "guest speakers" to sit down and look at the teacher while expressing their knowledge, creating a safer environment for students because they don't have to look directly at their peers if this makes them uncomfortable. For her part as the talk show host, Ruth uses a list of 10 questions to ask each student during the interview. At the end of each interview there is also time for audience questions and answers.

The class rule for OPRAH interviews is that everyone must applaud when each guest is announced and also when they return to their seat. The applause must be equal for everyone, so each student leaves the interview on a positive note. You can set the stage with furniture such as a sofa and coffee table from the teacher's lounge or more simply by using chairs from the classroom and a box for a coffee table. The OPRAH method also works well for students working in groups of two, with pairs being interviewed together.

Develop Lessons for Different Learning Styles

Michael Geissen, 2008 National Teacher of the Year, tries to appeal to many types of learners through incorporating the idea of multiple intelligences and different learning styles into his classroom. As a middle school science teacher, Michael incorporates music, movement, technology, and creativity into classroom assignments. For instance, when teaching his students about the concept of gravity, he instructs his students to imagine they are particles of space dust and to move about the classroom to show how the particles are attracted to each other in space.

Michael also has his students demonstrate what they've learned in a variety of ways. Often they are allowed to build, draw, write, or otherwise find a way to show what they know. Having a choice in how to express learning appeals to many types of learning styles and multiple intelligences. He notes that letting students be creative when expressing learning is especially effective for reluctant learners. Music is also a staple in his instructional arsenal. He uses music often, even making up his own songs when necessary. He uses songs for everything from "cleaning up" to learning about science concepts. He has found that songs make learning enjoyable and help students better retain information. Michael also incorporates technology—two common ways he does this is by accessing content online and by using animations to demonstrate science concepts to students.

George Goodfellow, a high school chemistry teacher and 2008 Rhode Island Teacher of the Year, describes the importance of using multiple intelligences to make curriculum relevant for students:

> All students are motivated in the same manner. Make the content relevant and *useful* to his personal environment and he will become motivated. Content rigor occurs after content inspiration. We use Gardner's [1993] theory of multiple intelligence to "celebrate student strengths and to develop student weaknesses." We connect chemistry (or whatever subject material) to the *real world* in every class. This real world is the real world of the student whether this is a present, past, or future world. Also, if you believe that *all* students are intelligent in some way, then they will believe it as well.

Encourage Higher Level Thinking Skills

The successful teachers we interviewed used various approaches to developing students' higher level thinking skills. Eric Kincaid, high school biology teacher and 2008 West Virginia Teacher of the Year, describes the challenge and reward of asking students to interpret their own visual notes:

> I encourage students to draw what they read. I find that students enjoy drawing and art projects, so I incorporate them into many assignments. I then ask that they go back and label/describe what they have drawn on their work. This requires students to look back into the text or other resources for the information. Struggling readers find this aspect difficult but sometimes just a few words put down is rewarding.

Steve Gardiner reminds us that Albert Einstein once wrote, "Setting an example is not the main means of influencing another, it is the only means." Steve goes on to explain how he models higher level thinking for his students by revealing his thinking processes to them. Students get a better grasp of higher level thinking when teachers share their own thinking patterns with their students:

> Teachers are models in the classroom and the things they say and do have a large impact on students. With that in mind, I model the behaviors and attitudes I want to elicit from my students. For example, every day during silent reading, I read with my students. Most of them do not see an adult read, so I want them to see me involved with my own books. I want them to hear me discuss what I like or dislike about my books. I want them to see that I enjoy reading and sharing the ideas I find while reading. When we are working on writing assignments, I bring in articles and essays I have published so they can see how I solved problems similar to the ones they face in their own writing. They know I

understand the writing process, and they are comfortable asking me to help because they know I understand the struggle it takes to produce a good piece of writing.

It is much the same with the cross-country team I coach. Both my assistant coach and I run every workout we assign to the team. As coaches, we are three times as old as any runner on the team, but by being with them during the runs, they know we love running, appreciate the efforts they are putting into the sport, and appreciate them as athletes and persons. I talk with them about running and have run both the Boston Marathon and New York City Marathon to show them that running is a lifetime sport and fitness activity. The actions and attitudes teachers model in the classroom are critical to building foundations in students' educations.

Build Relationships With Students

Successful secondary teachers acknowledge the importance of having good relationships with students. Josh Anderson notes,

> It's all about the relationships between the teachers and the students, because when you have a good relationship with your students then they will be willing to work for you.

Laurie Jones states that by getting to know students, she also learns what they are interested in and can adapt lessons to her students' interests. She says this also helps her get past students' mental roadblocks to reading, because she can use what she knows about them to help them read what they are interested in.

Kathy Day, high school teacher of 28 years, DAR Texas History Teacher of the Year 2008, and Outstanding Teacher of Humanities in Texas 2008, describes the ways she builds relationships with her students:

> Often reluctant readers are young men who are more drawn to the action-packed violence found in computer games and movies. Finding selections from history that appeal to these young men also encourages reading. Offering a variety in lengths and difficulty in reading is another skill to encourage reading. If a student will read one line under a political cartoon, that is a start. Then, offering song lyrics, although much longer, is an appealing way to "trick" students into reading. Before long, that expectation is established, and they are reading longer, more difficult passages with minimum complaining. I strongly believe much of the motivation comes from the relationship between the teacher and the class. If the students believe that the teacher really cares for their learning and their lives—they will rise to the expectations set by the teacher. Take time to talk to the students and learn about them as people. Attend their extracurricular activities—many have parents that don't go—so you then become the surrogate parent. Explain to them why it's so important to read…. Don't give up on them or expect any less.

Looking Ahead

George Goodfellow reminds us that

> teaching begins with a relationship and knowledge of who the teacher and student are, inside. It continues with constant hard work, inspirational successes, and culminates with a feeling of gratification and pride for the growth that has occurred. *All* learning occurs at 'the moment of wonder.

Goodfellow goes on to state,

> I have very few *formal* lessons in literacy or reading, however the strategy is always the same: Work hard at the skill while encouraging the student where his strengths lie. We assess the *growth* of each individual student toward expressed examples of excellence. Students need three mindsets to learn: (1) They need to be humble enough to see the value of the gained knowledge, (2) they need to be inspired for the value of their time on learning, and (3) they need to believe that they are capable of succeeding in the task. Developing these three beliefs in a student is the description of teaching.

Ron Canos, 2008 Guam State Teacher of the Year, reminds us that teaching is a profession of the heart:

> We are not in the business of "telling" people what to do, but rather helping them develop the skills to make decisions that will enrich or improve their lives. Especially at the secondary level, there is such a struggle between student independence and traditional teacher classroom management. The trick is finding the balance between students finding themselves and coming into their own, and guiding that need for the structure of learning in the classroom. In my experience, motivation comes from focusing on the classroom practices with which students can identify most closely with regards to their independence. These things include

> - Humor: Laughter in the classroom helps level the playing field between students and teachers. It is a shared emotion that closes generation gaps and builds bonds of understanding.

> - Shared decision making and self-direction: Students must be actively involved in their learning. By doing so, students will self-direct their learning and in turn build confidence. An example of shared decision making may include giving students options as to the types of approaches they can take to complete an assignment or helping develop the criteria for evaluation of projects.

> - Technology: In this day and age, more and more students identify with the use of technology than the general paper-and-pencil approach. Students today are more educated in the use of technology, and teachers who incorporate these tools will benefit greatly from the resource of knowledge that students can provide in this area.

> - Recognition: In my opinion, one of the greatest motivation practices is recognizing student work, especially for students who may not receive such recognition on a normal basis.

Ron Canos mentioned the four traits he has found to be at the center of his teaching success. This chapter also discusses the practices of other award-winning teachers, such as chunking, creating student buy-in and student choice, providing a safe and supportive classroom environment, developing lessons for different learning styles, encouraging higher level thinking skills, and building relationships with students. The teachers we interviewed have provided a glimpse into their teaching lives and how they have come to master their craft. It is apparent that these teachers view their profession with a creative, thoughtful, and optimistic spirit. They believe in themselves and their students, and they believe in sharing their own hard-won wisdom with other teachers. They remind us that the best teaching resource is often other teachers who have struggled with situations much like our own and who have found a way to emerge triumphantly from the trenches to continue daily to enrich the lives and intellect of their students.

EXTEND YOUR THINKING

▨ Review and reflect on the ideas presented in this chapter. Name two main themes that you feel embody the essence of what these teachers have shared? How did you come to this conclusion?

▨ What three specific teaching practices from this chapter would you most like to implement in your classroom? Why do you feel these practices would work well for you and your students?

▨ Prepare a detailed lesson plan for one of your own courses using one of the specific practices you previously selected. How do you think you will need to modify, limit, or extend this particular practice to meet the needs of your students and classroom?

REFERENCES

Gardiner, S. (2001). Ten minutes a day for silent reading. *Educational Leadership, 59*(2), 32–35.

Gardiner, S. (2005a). *Building student literacy through sustained silent reading.* Alexandria, VA: Association for Supervision and Curriculum Development.

Gardiner, S. (2005b). A skill for life. *Educational Leadership, 63*(2), 67–70.

Gardner, H. (1993). *Frames of mind: The theory of multiple intelligences* (2nd ed.). New York: Basic.

Hoyt, L. (1999). *Revisit, reflect, retell: Strategies for improving reading comprehension.* Portsmouth, NH: Heinemann.

CHAPTER 19

Mentoring Literacy Practices in Academic Disciplines

Doug Buehl

"Many middle and high school teachers question the relevance of literacy inservices, especially when strategies are not directly related to their content areas. As a music teacher, I know that inservice presentations will rarely focus on my discipline. I enter the room with the expectation that I will have to sift, sort, and synthesize the ideas, to shape them to fit my curriculum. When teachers do not seek to transfer new ideas to their classroom realities, how can they expect to respond to their students who ask, 'What does this lesson have to do with my life?'"

—*Wendy Buehl, Orchestra Teacher, Oregon Middle School, Oregon, Wisconsin*

A common frustration voiced by middle and high school teachers is that literacy practices emphasized at inservices and workshops frequently do not mesh comfortably with their curriculum. Although many teachers may accept the concept of integrating literacy practices with their instruction in the abstract, it is the specifics that make this goal a challenge. Teachers may encounter strategies that seem to work quite well with language arts materials or general nonfiction, but they do not see how to extend the same ideas to the actual texts they use in their curriculum. "Will this workshop help me perceive more effective ways of teaching math?" math teachers might ask. "Or will it present things

Adolescent Literacy, Field Tested: Effective Solutions for Every Classroom, edited by Sheri R. Parris, Douglas Fisher, and Kathy Headley. © 2009 by the International Reading Association.

I am supposed to do *in addition* to teaching math?" Often, teachers leave professional development sessions with the second notion in mind—that the literacy practices they have witnessed are an add-on to classroom routines rather than a foundation for their instruction.

Since 2004, a series of significant policy reports focusing on adolescent literacy have been released by influential organizations in the United States as widespread as the American College Testing program, the National Governors Association, and the National Association of Secondary School Principals. A consistent theme across these documents is the need to support teachers through professional growth initiatives that build their capacity to meet the literacy needs of their students. *Reading Next*, published by the Alliance for Excellent Education, a highly respected educational policy consortium, identified the following as one of the 15 Key Elements of Effective Adolescent Literacy Programs: "Ongoing, long-term professional development, which is more likely to promote lasting, positive changes in teacher knowledge and practice" (Biancarosa & Snow, 2004, p. 21). But as Wendy Buehl articulated in the opening quote, literacy workshops can often be problematic for teachers.

This chapter presents a perspective on adolescent literacy that will help teachers maximize the utility of professional growth opportunities. The concept of "disciplinary literacy," or teaching students to think like content area "insiders," is outlined, and extensions of a specific literacy strategy—self-questioning—are modeled. The chapter concludes with a discussion of some of the issues facing content area teachers as they strive to integrate literacy practices with instruction of their subject area.

Teaching Students to Think Like "Insiders"

Typically, teachers experience generic literacy strategies during workshop presentations. A generic strategy—for example, graphic organizers—may have application across disciplines, but how graphic organizers might be used and what form they may take could vary markedly from one academic discipline to another. Graphic organizers should be viewed as tools for comprehension that help learners engage in the thinking characteristic of a particular academic discipline, rather than as ends in themselves. Instead, many teachers get the message that "we need to use more graphic organizers with our students," rather than that they need to explore more deeply how visual representations of information might facilitate learning of subject matter.

In their excellent treatise *Literacy Instruction in the Content Areas*, Heller and Greenleaf (2007) acknowledge that generic literacy strategies are beneficial but are not sufficient to develop adolescent readers and writers. They argue that discipline-specific literacy practices are the necessary extension teachers need to make:

> All content area teachers should know what is distinct about the reading, writing, and reasoning processes that go on in their discipline; they should give students frequent opportunities to read, write, and think in these ways; and they should explain how those

conventions, formats, styles, and modes of communication differ from those that students might encounter elsewhere in school. (p. 27)

In other words, middle and high school teachers need to aggressively examine how generic literacy strategies can be customized to fit the unique demands of their curriculum.

Shanahan and Shanahan (2008) argue that literacy instruction can be envisioned as progressing in three phases. The initial phase, *basic literacy*, represents instruction during primary grades that builds the foundation for reading and writing. Students learn to decode words, recognize high-frequency words, and attend to meaning, and they begin to understand conventions of print. The middle phase, *intermediate literacy*, receives attention during upper elementary grades, as student develop reading fluency, expand their vocabularies, and encounter increasingly more sophisticated texts. Comprehension strategies become increasingly important as students are exposed to more complex text structures. It is the third phase, *disciplinary literacy*, that is most neglected in our instruction. As Shanahan and Shanahan concluded, "Although most students manage to master basic and even intermediate literacy skills, many never gain proficiency with the more advanced skills that would enable them to read challenging texts in science, history, literature, mathematics, or technology" (p. 45).

What are these "more advanced skills" that compose disciplinary literacy? The answer is, "It depends." As students transition to reading an array of texts from disparate and increasingly distinct academic disciplines, they are expected to fine-tune generic comprehension strategies to accommodate the demands of each of these different subject areas. To illustrate, consider what it would mean to successfully read a short story, and then contrast that experience with reading a chapter in a geometry textbook. We would agree that although both tasks assume basic and intermediate literacy skills, qualitatively different approaches must be taken for understanding to occur. Literacy practices that might be an excellent fit for helping students crack meaning in a short story might be inadequate or even wrongly conceived for handling a geometry chapter. For example, students who are taught to be sensitive to an author's use of symbols in a short story cannot be expected to generalize this instruction in any meaningful way to another author's use of symbols in a mathematics textbook. These are different worlds: different purposes, different writing styles, different organizations, different language, different modes of communication, different visual layouts, different expectations of relevant background and experiences, and different uses of knowledge.

In effect, disciplinary literacy instruction mentors students to begin to read, write, and think like "insiders," persons with deep professional knowledge and experience in a field. Students learn to "talk the talk" of an academic discipline; they can access communications in particular subject areas through reading and listening, and equally important, they develop the facility through writing and speaking to communicate in the ways insiders such as historians, mathematicians, physicists, or musicians do. Disciplinary literacy necessitates, as Gee (2000) explained, "that we see reading (and writing and speaking) as not one thing, but many: many different socioculturally situated reading (writing, speaking) practices" (p. 204). As a result, a student might be quite comfortable reading fictional works in a literature class, be less proficient reading biological texts, and feel helpless understanding the algebra textbook.

Middle and high school teachers tend to assume that if students have had adequate basic and intermediate literacy instruction, then they will automatically and on their own develop disciplinary literacy skills at that time when reading branches out into dramatically dissimilar texts during the learning of content subjects. As Shanahan and Shanahan (2008) observe, students are expected to master texts dealing with complex concepts—and that are more abstract, ambiguous, and subtle—by applying sophisticated literacy skills that "are rarely taught" (p. 45).

Disciplinary literacy instruction mandates that teachers ask "What does this literacy practice look like in my curriculum?" as an ongoing dynamic during professional development sessions. Teachers should view the literacy techniques frequently modeled at workshops as prototypes—instructional examples of embedding comprehension strategies into classroom practice. Such prototypes are unlikely to be sufficiently generalizable so that "one size fits all." As Wendy stated in our opening quote, she recognizes that as a middle school orchestra teacher she will need to probe how a generic literacy strategy might manifest itself in a music performance classroom. Her application of a strategy, in the context of her academic discipline, will take students deeper into thinking like a musician, and the variation of the strategy in a music context will likely look substantially different from how that literacy strategy is reformulated to guide students across the hall into thinking, let's say, like a mathematician.

The rest of this chapter contrasts two examples of disciplinary literacy practices that represent extending a generic strategy to guide student reading, writing, and thinking in two different academic disciplines: English language arts and biological science.

Exploring Student Questioning Strategies in Disciplinary Contexts

One powerful generic comprehension strategy is student self-questioning. An extensive body of research confirms that teaching students to generate their own questions about texts can significantly improve their comprehension (e.g., Duke & Pearson, 2002; National Institute of Child Health and Human Development, 2000). Instructional prototypes for student self-questioning include Reciprocal Teaching

(Palincsar & Brown, 1984), Question–Answer Relationships (Raphael, 1982, 1986), and Questioning the Author (QtA; Beck, McKeown, Hamilton, & Kucan, 1997).

QtA is an especially promising strategy for middle and high school learners. QtA is predicated on teacher modeling of queries directed to an author at various key junctures in a text. The strategy consciously reinforces that reading is in many respects a dialogue between a reader and an author. Students are prompted to pose QtA queries such as What is the author telling you? What does the author assume you already know? Why is the author telling you this? What is the point of the author's message? What does the author apparently think is most important? How does this connect with what the author told you before? Did the author explain this clearly? What could the author have done to help you better understand this?

These QtA queries reflect questions that all readers, as a habit of mind, should ask of any text within any academic discipline. QtA is a generic strategy that provides a solid foundation for student generated questioning. Rather than encouraging references to "what the book said" or "what the article stated," the QtA strategy encourages students to view reading as an act of communication with another person. Their QtA queries stimulate an inquiring mind-set as they think about what an author is telling them and expects readers to understand.

Table 19.1 displays an extension of the QtA strategy, which prompts a deeper level of self-questioning using the revised Bloom's Taxonomy (Anderson & Krathwohl, 2001) as a guide. This self-questioning taxonomy (Buehl, 2007a) cues thinking on all six cognitive levels—remembering, understanding, applying, analyzing, evaluating, and creating—through author-directed queries. The strategy

TABLE 19.1
Self-Questioning Taxonomy

Level of Thinking	Comprehension Self-Assessment	Focusing Questions
Creating	I have created new knowledge.	How has this author changed what I understand?
Evaluating	I can critically examine this author's message.	How has the author's perspective influenced what he or she tells me?
Analyzing	I can take my understanding to a deeper level.	How is this similar to (or different from) other material I've read?
Applying	I can use my understanding in some meaningful way.	How can I connect what this author is telling me to understand something better?
Understanding	I can understand what the author is telling me.	What does this author want me to understand?
Remembering	I can recall specific details, information, and ideas from this text.	What do I need to remember to make sense of this text?

Note. From Buehl, D. (2007a). *Modeling self-questioning on Bloom's taxonomy.* Madison, WI: Wisconsin Education Association Council.

exhibits a strong metacognitive component, as students are in effect using these questions to monitor their comprehension. The strategy prompts students to "check in" at all six levels with any text they are reading, using standard questions such as "How can I connect what this author is telling me to understand something better?" "How has the author's perspective influenced what he or she tells me?" and "How has this author changed what I understand?" The taxonomy questions are designed to facilitate students in assuming responsibility for expanding their thinking more deeply into comprehension of an author's message.

The self-questioning taxonomy is an instructional prototype that provides a vehicle for combining two critical comprehension processes: self-questioning and deeper questioning of classroom texts. But these questions, while valuable models, are generic and do not necessarily reflect the extent of deeper questioning that insiders within an academic discipline would pose about the texts they read. What are discipline-specific variations of these questions that historians ask about historical texts? Or that mathematicians ask as they read texts within their field? Accountants, chemists, or computer scientists? The charge for teachers in academic subjects is to tailor their own set of questions from the generic strategy prototype to mentor their students as readers in their content areas.

Table 19.2 represents one variation of the self-questioning taxonomy that can be used by English language arts teachers to teach student questioning of literary fiction—short stories and novels (Buehl, 2007b). The questions for each level of the taxonomy are discipline-specific questions, customized for thinking about how authors communicate through fictional literature. The generic comprehension self-assessment for *remembering*—"I can recall specific details, information, and ideas from this text"—is refined to reflect the basic components of story structure—"I can follow what happens in this story"—which leads the reader to pose a series of questions appropriate for reading story structure. Likewise, at the *creating* level, the generic statement "I have created new knowledge" is translated to "I have developed an interpretation of what this story means," resulting in questions that invite grappling with an author's possible message as well as articulating what a story means to an individual reader. At the *analyzing* level, students prompt themselves to be sensitive to author's craft—the use of literary devices such as figurative language, symbolism, or unreliable narrator, for example—as they construct their understandings.

The questions throughout this version of a self-questioning taxonomy are geared toward developing readers of literary fiction. Fictional works can be regarded as indirect forms of communication; fiction challenges readers to develop their own interpretations of what an author might want them to understand. Biography, a related nonfiction genre that shares some of the attributes of story form, tends to feature direct statements of author conclusions and viewpoints. Thus, although biographies also usually follow a storyline, a different set of questions would be necessary to guide thinking of this genre of literature. History teachers would need

TABLE 19.2
Self-Questioning Taxonomy for Literary Fiction

Level of Thinking	Comprehension Self-Assessment	Focusing Questions
Creating	I have developed an interpretation of what this story means.	• Why is the author telling me this story? • What theme or idea might the author be exploring in this story? • What does this story to mean to me?
Evaluating	I can critically examine this author's story.	• Who is the author and how has the author's perspective influenced the telling of this story? • What does the author's choice of words indicate about what the author might be thinking? • What emotions is the author eliciting? • Does the author have an attitude, and if so, about what?
Analyzing	I can take my understanding to a deeper level.	• What literary devices does the author use? • What seems to be the purpose for using these literary devices?
Applying	I can use my understanding in some meaningful way.	• How can I connect this story to my life and experiences? • Why might the author have the characters say or do this? • What point might the author be making about the characters' actions? • Why might the author place the story in this setting?
Understanding	I can understand what the author is telling me.	• How does the author have the characters interact with each other? • How do the characters feel about each other? • How do character feelings and interactions change? • How does the author use conflict in this story? • How does the author resolve this conflict?
Remembering	I can follow what happens in this story.	• Who are the characters? • Where does the story take place? • What are the major events of the story? • What is the sequence of these events? • What event initiates the action of the story?

Note. From Buehl, D. (2007b). *Questioning literary fiction.* Madison, WI: Wisconsin Education Association Council.

to adapt this self-questioning taxonomy for literary fiction to reflect those questions most appropriate for reading biographies or autobiographies.

In contrast, Table 19.3 reformulates the self-questioning taxonomy to mentor students studying the biological sciences to think like a biologist (Buehl, 2008). Discipline-specific questions appropriate for reading biological texts represent a dramatically different direction for student self-assessment of comprehension. Although both taxonomies reflect student self-questioning that encompasses all six levels of thinking, there are few similarities between the two question sets. As a result, students who have mastered self-questioning for literary fiction in an English

TABLE 19.3
Self-Questioning Taxonomy for Biological Texts

Level of Thinking	Comprehension Self-Assessment	Focusing Questions
Creating	I have created new knowledge about the biological world.	• How has this author changed what I understand? • How has this author corrected previous misunderstandings?
Evaluating	I can critically examine this author's conclusions/theories/explanations.	• What conclusions/theories/explanations does the author provide? • How do we know? What is the evidence? • What other conclusions/theories/explanations could be justified by the evidence?
Analyzing	I can understand why.	• What happened? Why did it happen? How did it happen? • How does this [biological concept] "work"? • Why does this [biological concept] "work" the way it does? • What are the defining characteristics? • How is this similar to (or different from) other related biological concepts?
Applying	I can use my understanding to better understand the biological world.	• How can I connect my experiences to what this author is telling me? • How can I use what this author is telling me to better understand living things? • How is what the author is telling me different from what I previously understood?
Understanding	I can understand what the author is telling me about the biological world.	• What does this author want me to understand about living things? • What do I currently understand about what the author is telling me?
Remembering	I can recall specific information and ideas from this text.	• What biological concepts do I need to remember for future understandings? • What biological vocabulary do I need to become comfortable using?

Note. From Buehl, D. (2008). *Questioning biological texts.* Madison, WI: Wisconsin Education Association Council.

language arts class would need extensive parallel instruction by a science expert during science class to internalize appropriate thinking for biology texts.

A biological science teacher would model questions at the *remembering* level that focus on key concepts and vocabulary. A central concern in science learning is the tenacity of student misconceptions, so questions at the *understanding* level ask students to inventory their current understandings of specific biological phenomena, while questions at the *creating* level prompt students to verbalize how a text has transformed previous misunderstandings. In effect, students are prompted to remind themselves that people often hold naïve, incomplete, or erroneous ideas about the scientific world, and that as learners we need to constantly monitor the need to adjust or replace our current understandings. Questions at the *analyzing* level emphasize cause–effect relationships and revolve around explaining "why" and "how," as well as establishing the defining characteristics that identify a biological concept.

A major distinction between the literary fiction and biological science self-questioning taxonomies exists at the *evaluating* level. Readers of literary fiction need to be conscious of the "voice behind the keyboard" and tune into perspectives, beliefs, and attitudes that an author may be weaving into the telling of the story; readers of fiction need to be especially aware of emotional content that is displayed or elicited by an author. Readers of biological science texts are more concerned with how an author communicates a conclusion, theory, or explanation, and what evidence is presented to justify these interpretations of biological life.

Both taxonomies are presented to illustrate how a research-based generic literacy practice—QtA—provides the foundation for more discipline-specific questioning practices that are grounded in the thinking inherent in different academic subjects. If students are to ask the kinds of questions that insiders ask, they need to be mentored by insiders—their content teachers—as they learn across the curriculum.

Looking Ahead

A significant challenge for middle and high school teachers is to uncover the literacy practices that underlie the thinking in their disciplines. Insiders who have gradually become accomplished readers, writers, and thinkers in an academic discipline may take for granted the processes that have become second nature to them. Initially, all teachers need to carefully examine what it is that they, and professionals in their field, do when they engage in literacy behaviors in their subject area.

One reason that teachers will find this process challenging is that disciplinary literacy has generally proceeded under the radar in our classrooms. As Shanahan and Shanahan (2008) have noted, such practices have rarely been overt facets of instruction in middle and high school classrooms and have not been the tradition in university teacher preparatory programs—not in subject area methods courses or in supplementary literacy methods classes, which usually introduce generic strategies. As a result, teachers have not experienced many discipline-specific models of appropriate literacy practices for their subject area.

An important first step for middle and high school teachers is to recognize that many of the literacy practices they will experience in workshops will be generic strategies and instructional prototypes, perhaps modeled in a different subject area. Although this can be a frustrating dynamic, it is evident that many of these generic literacy practices are not yet common knowledge to many teachers, and generic strategies do provide the foundation for deeper exploration into the reading and writing demands of a specific curriculum. Ideally, as adolescent literacy receives increased attention from educators and policymakers, workshops will eventually feature more discipline-specific models like the two examples presented in this chapter.

Disciplinary literacy instruction mandates that middle and high school teachers adopt a "translator" orientation to literacy professional development—an expectation that they will regularly need to translate generic literacy practices into more discipline-specific variations that approximate what insiders do as readers and writers in their discipline. A recurring question for teachers will be, How can instruction of the literacy practices inherent in my discipline be organically integrated into daily classroom routines to guide student learning of the curriculum? In particular, teachers need to be accorded collaboration time with their colleagues to investigate how to explicitly teach discipline-specific literacy practices in their content area.

Finally, the process of mentoring students needs continued exploration. Mentoring assumes an expert–novice relationship between teacher and students—teachers model the thinking they engage in as insiders in an academic discipline through explicit instruction, think-alouds, and frequent opportunities for students themselves to begin to test-drive this thinking as readers and writers. Currently, students are often expected to make the jump to independent learning before they have experienced sufficient instruction and adequate guided practice. Mentoring includes ongoing interaction and dialogue with the expert—the teacher—who provides continual feedback, and collaborations with their peers as students strive to approximate the literacy practices of insiders. In addition, metacognitive conversations that occur at regular intervals during classroom activities are necessary to ensure that literacy practices are openly discussed and deconstructed. Teachers need to condition students to expect these debriefing sessions—in which student confusions, frustrations, and successes are shared and commented upon—as an ongoing classroom dynamic. As a result, disciplinary literacy instruction will mentor students to perceive the adjustments they need to make from one academic environment to another each time the bell rings and they make the transition into learning in a different subject area.

EXTEND YOUR THINKING

- What does "thinking like an insider" entail in your subject area? What are the literacy practices that experts follow as readers of texts in your subject area?

- What would a self-questioning taxonomy look like in your subject area? What are the questions insiders pose as readers?

- How can you mentor your students to begin to think like insiders as a regular facet of your instruction? How would you teach a self-questioning taxonomy for your academic discipline?

REFERENCES

Anderson, L.W., & Krathwohl, D.R. (Eds.). (2001). *A taxonomy for learning, teaching, and assessing: A revision of Bloom's taxonomy of educational objectives.* New York: Longman.

Beck, I.L., McKeown, M.G., Hamilton, R.L., & Kucan, L. (1997). *Questioning the Author: An approach for enhancing student engagement with text.* Newark, DE: International Reading Association.

Biancarosa, G., & Snow, C.E. (2004). *Reading next: A vision for action and research in middle and high school literacy.* Washington, DC: Alliance for Excellent Education.

Buehl, D. (2007a, September). *Modeling self-questioning on Bloom's taxonomy.* Retrieved January 8, 2009, from www.weac.org/News/2007-08/sept07/readingroom.htm

Buehl, D. (2007b, November). *Questioning literary fiction.* Retrieved January 8, 2009, from www.weac.org/News/2007-08/nov07/readingroom.htm

Buehl, D. (2008, May). *Questioning biological texts.* Retrieved January 8, 2009, from www.weac.org/News/2007-08/may08/readingroom.htm

Duke, N.K., & Pearson, P.D. (2002). Effective practices for developing reading comprehension. In A.E. Farstrup & S.J. Samuels (Eds.), *What research has to say about reading instruction* (3rd ed., pp. 205–242). Newark, DE: International Reading Association.

Gee, J.P. (2000). Discourse and sociocultural studies in reading. In M.L. Kamil, P.B. Mosenthal, P.D. Pearson, & R. Barr (Eds.), *Handbook of reading research* (Vol. 3, pp. 195–207). Mahwah, NJ: Erlbaum.

Heller, R., & Greenleaf, C. (2007). *Literacy instruction in the content areas: Getting to the core of middle and high school improvement.* Washington, DC: Alliance for Excellent Education.

National Institute of Child Health and Human Development. (2000). *Report of the National Reading Panel. Teaching children to read: An evidence-based assessment of the scientific research literature on reading and its implications for reading instruction* (NIH Publication No. 00-4769). Washington, DC: U.S. Government Printing Office.

Palincsar, A.S., & Brown, A.L. (1984). Reciprocal teaching of comprehension-fostering and comprehension-monitoring activities. *Cognition and Instruction, 1*(2), 117–175. doi:10.1207/s1532690 xci0102_1

Raphael, T.E. (1982). Question-answering strategies for children. *The Reading Teacher, 36*(2), 186–190.

Raphael, T.E. (1986). Teaching question answer relationships, revisited. *The Reading Teacher, 39*(6), 516–522.

Shanahan, T., & Shanahan, C. (2008). Teaching disciplinary literacy to adolescents: Rethinking content-area literacy. *Harvard Educational Review, 78*(1), 40–59.

AUTHOR INDEX

SUBJECT INDEX

Note. Page numbers followed by *f* or *t* indicate figures or tables, respectively.

BLOGGING: asking students to blog, 87–88; critical analysis of blogs, 85–86; literacy skills required for, 92t; modeling content-specific blogs, 86–87; overview of, 84–85; websites for exploring, 84t

BOOK PASS, 152–153

BOOK TALK, 153

BOOKLIST MAGAZINE, 150

BRAINSTORMING, 22–23, 24–25f

BRIDGING STRATEGY, 136

BUEHL, WENDY, 228, 229

BUY-IN FOR LESSONS, 221–222

C

CAIN, PAUL, 161

CANOS, RON, 226

CAPERS, LATONYA, 209–210, 210f, 211f

CARLTON, LAURA, 160

CENSORSHIP ISSUES, 154

CENTER OF EXCELLENCE FOR ADOLESCENT LITERACY AND LEARNING (CEALL): active engagement principle, 208; evolution of, 210, 216; goals and objectives, 204–205; learning cycle framework, 207–208, 208f, 209f; professional development cycle, 208–209, 210, 212–215t; reflection and conversation, 209–210, 210f; train the trainer model, 204

CHARNEY, DENNIS, 150

CHINESE CINDERELLA (MAH), 151

CHOICE, AND MOTIVATION, 159–161, 221–222

CHUNKING, 219–221

CLASS SIZES, AND WRITING INSTRUCTION, 31–32

CLASSROOM MANAGEMENT, AND FUSION READING, 136

COLLABORATION: allowing time for, 183–184, 198; classroom structures that facilitate, 173t; classroom tasks

for, 171–174; between content area teachers and literacy specialists, 113–115; in writing, 27–29, 76–78. *See also* group work

COLLEGE ENROLLMENT, STEPS TO, 200f

COLLEGE-GOING CULTURE, 199–202

COMPREHENSION: background knowledge and, 175, 177; factors undermining, 48; learning and, 34; theories and tools for, 48–49; vocabulary and, 59

COMPREHENSION DEVELOPMENT: Adolescent Literacy Support Project, 51–52; appropriate reading materials and, 43, 45; for ASRs, 134–135; beginning with clear purposes, 39; challenges to, 41–44; checking multiple perspectives, 41; classroom instruction for, 35–38; IDEAS model, 50–51; Literacy Navigator, 52–53, 54; making thinking visible, 40–41; matching reader to text, 39–40; navigating texts, 40; program comparison, 53–54; reciprocal teaching and, 75; reconstructing materials for, 55–56; self-questioning strategy, 231–236, 232t, 234t, 235t; team approach to, 42

CONTENT, ATTENTION TO, 49–50

CONTENT AREA LITERACY. *See* content literacy; disciplinary literacy

CONTENT AREA MASTERY, 54–55

CONTENT ENHANCEMENT PROGRAM, 135

CONTENT LEARNING: adolescent literacy and, 9–14; cooperative learning and, 72; inquiry activities in writing for, 29–31

CONTENT LITERACY: attitudes and beliefs about, 207; challenges of promoting, 16; definition of, 9; in mathematics and science classrooms, 105–107; role of reading and writing in, 14–16. *See also* disciplinary literacy

Kuropatwa, Darren, 86
K-W-L chart, 62, 63f
K-W-L strategy, 15, 35–36

L

Lambert, Joe, 88
Language arts classrooms: definitions and practices for, 95–96; improving links between in-school and out-of-school literacy in, 96–99; new literacies in, 100–102; overview of, 94–95; self-questioning taxonomy for, 233–234, 234t; teaching and evaluating literacy in English and, 99–100
Language instruction, for ELLs, 174–175, 176t, 177
Language proficiency, dimensions of, 176t
Language structures, attention to, 49
Learning: cooperative, 72; mindsets for, 226; problem-based, 78–79; social interaction and, 59–60, 70; styles of, 223–224; true or deep, 50. See also content learning
Learning cycle framework, 207–208, 208f, 209f
Learning goals, content-based, 10
Learningbycartooning.org website, 163
Lee, Carol, 49
Literacy: academic, dimensions of, 174–175, 176t; definition of, 9, 95–96; factors influencing development of, 170t; intermediate, 230; visual, 44. See also content literacy; in-school literacy; out-of-school literacy
Literacy coaches, 216
Literacy Navigator, 52–53, 54
Literacy specialists, in science or mathematics classrooms, 109–110, 113–115
Literature, reasons for teaching and studying, 145f

Literature circles, 159–160
Lowry, Lois, 160

M

Matching reader to text, 39–40
Materials for reading, appropriateness of, 43, 45, 158. See also young adult texts
Mathematics classrooms: addressing all texts, 110–111; challenges in, 113; content area literacy in, 105–107; engaging students in inquiry and problem solving, 107–108; forming collaborations, 113–114; norms, establishing, 113; promoting sense making, 108–110; supporting explanation and justification, 111–112
Maus: A Survivor's Tale (Spiegelman), 160
McBride, Mekeel, 29
McLaughlin, Tim, 28
Meissen, Ruth, 219, 222–223
Mental model, constructing, 49–50
Mentoring students, 237
Metacognitive skill development, 164–165, 237
Mindsets for learning, 226
Miya, Sharon, 105
Modeling reading and thinking behaviors, and motivation, 164–165
Models of writing, study of, 27
Mogle, Andy, 220
Moodle course management system, 77
Motivation: choice and, 159–161, 221–222; Fusion Reading and, 135–136; modeling reading and thinking behaviors and, 164–165; overview of, 157–158; to read, 144–145; relevance and, 161–163, 183, 226; selection of texts and, 158; student-teacher relationships and, 158–159; testing culture and, 165

setting, and making time to read, 146, 147*f*, 148*f*; motivation to read and, 144–145; parental involvement and, 146, 149*f*; texts for, finding and choosing, 146–148, 150–152

STUDENT-TEACHER RELATIONSHIPS, 158–159, 225

STYLES OF LEARNING, 223–224

SUMMARIZATION STRATEGY, 137

SUPPORT, PROVIDING IN CLASSROOM, 184–185, 222–223

SUSTAINED SILENT READING, 146, 160–161, 222

T

TATUM, ALFRED, 43

TEACHER DEVELOPMENT. *See* professional development

TEACHING FOR UNDERSTANDING, STEPS OF, 10–11, 10*f*

TEACHING LANGUAGE THROUGH CONTENT APPROACH, AND ELLs: collaborative tasks, 171–174; language instruction, 174–175, 176*t*; overview of, 170–171; small-group instruction, 174

TEAM APPROACH TO COMPREHENSION DEVELOPMENT, 42

TECHNOLOGY: access to, 91; adolescent expertise with, 96; ELLs and, 177; incorporating, 226

TEST PREPARATION: education as, 21, 31, 32; in effective schools, 98; motivation and, 165

TEXT, BROADENED DEFINITION OF, 110–111

TEXTBASE, BUILDING, 49

THINKING: critical, development of, 44; encouraging higher level skills in, 224–225; like "insiders," 229–231; making visible, 40–41

THINKING ALOUD STRATEGY: example of, 224–225; motivation and, 164–165; vocabulary instruction and, 61

THINKING READING, 136–137

TIERED INSTRUCTIONAL CONTINUUMS, 132–133

TIERNEY, ROBERT, 29

TITLE I, 8

TODD, APRIL, 159

TOUCHING SPIRIT BEAR (MIKAELSEN), 151

TRACKING YOUR READING PROGRESS FORM, 148*f*

U

UNDERSTANDING: sense making and, 108–109; teaching for, steps of, 10–11, 10*f*

V

VIDEOTAPING CLASSROOM INSTRUCTION, 35

VISUAL LITERACY, 44

VISUAL MAPS, CREATING, 41

VISUAL TECHNIQUES FOR VOCABULARY INSTRUCTION, 61, 62*f*

VOCABULARY INSTRUCTION: for ASRs, 134; creativity and, 61–64, 63*f*, 64*f*; direct instruction rationale, 59–60; engagement and, 65–66, 66*f*, 67*f*; flexibility and, 60–61, 62*f*; overview of, 58; schoolwide focus on, 66–67; through teamwork, 220–221

VOCABULARY STRATEGY, 137

VOICES FROM THE MIDDLE, 147

VOICES OF YOUTH ADVOCATES, 150

W

WEB 2.0, 83

WHAT DADDY DID (SHUSTERMAN), 151

WIESEL, ELIE, 87, 160

WIKIPEDIA, 76

WORD LEARNING. *See* vocabulary instruction

WORD WEALTH PROGRAM, 63

WORD-LEVEL INTERVENTIONS, 134

WRITE WITH ME STRATEGY, 22–23, 24–25*f*

WRITING: finding time for, 31–32; lesson plans for, 32; role of, in developing

content literacy, 14–16. *See also* writing strategies
WRITING NEXT (REPORT), 21–22, 27, 29, 31
WRITING STRATEGIES: brainstorming, 22–23, 24–25*f;* collaborative, 27–29; digital collaborative, 76–78; overview of, 22; persuasive essay writing, 23, 25–26; process approach, 31; specific product goals and, 26–27; study of models, 27

Y

YOUNG ADULT TEXTS: finding, 146–148, 150; importance of, 150–152

Z

ZONE OF PROXIMAL DEVELOPMENT, 70
ZOOMING IN AND ZOOMING OUT ORGANIZER, 63, 63*f,* 64*f*